DIET PILLS AND THE INTERNET

EATING DISORDERS IN THE 21ST CENTURY

Additional books in this series can be found on Nova's website
under the Series tab.

Additional E-books in this series can be found on Nova's website
under the E-books tab.

INTERNET POLICIES AND ISSUES

Additional books in this series can be found on Nova's website
under the Series tab.

Additional E-books in this series can be found on Nova's website
under the E-books tab.

DIET PILLS AND THE INTERNET

TERENCE M. DOVEY

Nova Science Publishers, Inc.
New York

1713937

NOTICE TO THE READER

The Publisher has taken reasonable care in the preparation of this book, but makes no expressed or implied warranty of any kind and assumes no responsibility for any errors or omissions. No liability is assumed for incidental or consequential damages in connection with or arising out of information contained in this book. The Publisher shall not be liable for any special, consequential, or exemplary damages resulting, in whole or in part, from the readers' use of, or reliance upon, this material. Any parts of this book based on government reports are so indicated and copyright is claimed for those parts to the extent applicable to compilations of such works.

Independent verification should be sought for any data, advice or recommendations contained in this book. In addition, no responsibility is assumed by the publisher for any injury and/or damage to persons or property arising from any methods, products, instructions, ideas or otherwise contained in this publication.

This publication is designed to provide accurate and authoritative information with regard to the subject matter covered herein. It is sold with the clear understanding that the Publisher is not engaged in rendering legal or any other professional services. If legal or any other expert assistance is required, the services of a competent person should be sought. FROM A DECLARATION OF PARTICIPANTS JOINTLY ADOPTED BY A COMMITTEE OF THE AMERICAN BAR ASSOCIATION AND A COMMITTEE OF PUBLISHERS.

Additional color graphics may be available in the e-book version of this book.

LIBRARY OF CONGRESS CATALOGING-IN-PUBLICATION DATA

ISBN: 978-1-62081-420-8
Library of Congress Control Number: 2012935167

Published by Nova Science Publishers, Inc. † New York

CONTENTS

Preface – Of Motivations   vii

Introduction – Of Definitions and Assumptions   xi

Chapter 1   Of Why People Diet   1

Chapter 2   Of Law   21

Chapter 3   Of Internet versus Bricks and Mortar   33

Chapter 4   Of Pharmacological Targets: Hitting the Bull's-Eye   47

Chapter 5   Of the Fall of a Dynasty   65

Chapter 6   Of Credible Candidates?   75

Chapter 7   Of the Pretenders to the Throne: Selling Dreams?   89

Chapter 8   Of Success and Failure   113

Chapter 9   Of the Future and Final Thoughts   127

References   137

Notes   151

Index   153

PREFACE – OF MOTIVATIONS

On the 8th of July in 2010, a newsbeat story appeared on the radio in the UK. This story was about three sentences long and basically referred to the fact that there is an increase in drug abuse for the purposes of dieting and invariably weight loss. This in itself is not a particularly new story. It has long been known that some people, usually those with eating disorders, or on their way to having one, abuse drugs that are specifically designed for, or have a side effect that leads to, weight loss.

The reasons why these people do this are complex and derive from a variety of potential explanations. The drug type of choice for those with eating disorders is often the laxative. They will take these drugs for their obvious effect of speeding up peristalsis (i.e. the muscular contractions of the intestine that pushes food through the system), which, in turn, limits their ability to absorb nutrients from the little amount of food that manages to make it in to their system.

However, it is not this group that I believe the article was referring to and not why I started writing this book. It appears that there is an increased prevalence for people to take pharmacological treatments to aid weight loss or maintenance. These people are not like our previous sample as they have no form of psychopathology. What was once thought to be the remit of the eating disordered individual and a sign of serious psychological dysfunction has become the playground of the norm [1]. It is this surprising report that has galvanised my motivation to write this book. I want you to know why people are taking them (it is not just to lose weight) and how they work. Moreover, I want to arm people with the knowledge that will defend you from the diet drug vendors who are now pervasive across the Internet and thus our society.

The diet drug vendors and indeed the multitude of 'professionals' that claim to have information to save our social soul means that the first piece of advice I have to impart is *trust no one*. I am a professional who has written for many peer-reviewed journals on various components of eating behaviour from a biological, pharmacological and psychological perspective. I study this subject material every day and I do not have all the answers. Ironically, my opinion is one of those used to peddle weight loss drugs. The very day I provide information for dissemination in the media, you will find my name associated with a weight loss product. Sometimes this is done directly, others surreptitiously through reporting a 'news story' that eventually leads you to a place where they can sell you various dieting drugs.

Let me take this opportunity to say that I do not endorse any drugs, of any kind, for weight loss, and certainly not for weight maintenance, purposes. I am not suggesting that specific ones do or do not work, just that I do not endorse any. The desperation for the vendors to link their products to the specific experts, especially those who appear in the media, seems to know no bounds. Trust in the information given to the public is a commodity best reserved for primary sources and direct one-to-one or one-to-many conversations with credible experts. Never trust the secondary source on face value, especially if they are trying to sell you something. This is a somewhat obvious statement; however, it is the most common strategy used on the internet and appears to still work.

It is essential that every one of us questions every piece of information given to us. Personally, I am of the opinion that all answers for eating behaviour and weight loss are heavily tied up with individual differences and, as such, require an individualised multi-disciplinary response. Of course there are themes that can explain a proportion of why people gain weight, but these are not comprehensive enough to explain why an individual is, or thinks they are, overweight. This view conflicts with those people who are trying to sell the 'dream.' They want to tell the world that weight-loss is easy, that they have the answers and that anyone can do it – for a nominal fee. Within the pages of this book I want to take the time to explain specifically about dieting drugs. Against the traditional drug dealers we have a solid defence, it is called the police. Against the diet drug vendors we have only our minds and the knowledge it contains.

Irrespective of what I think should be or could be it is unlikely that the vendors or those who peddle misinformation will disappear. The traditional sciences have held the self proclaimed alternative therapists with disdain for generations now and yet they are still here. They always will be. The drawing of the line between what are credible strategies for interventions into biological and/or social problems lay with the individual. Some people will draw the 'credibility line' between the medical and, for want of better word, the credible new comers to the weight loss industry. Many people will claim that only pharmacological or surgical treatments will aid successful long-term weight-loss and that everything 'left of this line' is 'alterative.' Other people will shift this 'line' to include the psychologists and allied health professionals, distinguishing between these and the 'alternative' therapies. Finally, most people will suggest a 'horses for courses' route and will consider anything if it works. The majority of people I have met fall into the last category. Some in this final group are more critical by considering the evidence for scientific merit and rigour, while others will not. Those that do not run the risk of accepting everything they read at face value and are thus are open to manipulation. It really does not matter which of the three groups an individual falls into as long as they consider my second piece of advice – *question the evidence offered*. Even simple questions will unravel the overly convoluted pseudo-scientific explanations of how a substance is supposed to work.

World-wide consensus will never be reached for what is and is not a creditable strategy for any health problem; especially an emotive subject such as necessary weight loss. It is easy to forget from our Western seats that the majority of the world is reliant on what our medical profession would consider 'alternative' traditional therapies. Pharmacological and surgical treatments are very much in the minority if we look down on our planet from orbit. Therefore, consensus will never be reached as there is always a place for any therapy to hide from critical investigations into efficacy. This leads to my third piece of advice – *question the advocate's motivation*. Those individuals that hunt the fringes of any health problem are those who are after money. Of course, in any capitalist society everyone needs to make money; however, if the motivation is simply to be a 'middle man' then they are in the system unnecessarily. To do this they will say anything the buyer wishes to hear, just as long as they part with their money. If it does not work and a refund is requested they are likely to say it was the buyers fault and that their 'tried and tested' technique has worked for millions of people. You will see in the pages of this book that this is likely to be untrue. Whether they are purposefully lying or just do not understand what they are doing I will leave it to the reader to decide.

The pages of this book are comprised of my opinion, as an expert in this field, based on the evidence that is available in the published domain. Not all of these sources are publically accessible, as they are only found in scientific literature. To gain access to this it requires either subscription to the material or upfront payment for it. Where possible, information that is free-to-access will be used to reinforce the points made throughout this book. This should help anyone wishing to derive the value and content of the opinions offered in these pages in their entirety. The reason for offering opinions based on the same information that is either used to convince people to buy a particular weight-loss product or the evidence on which they have based their claims is essential. People buying these products are reliant on what they are told on the Internet by the seller. The Internet is, after all, the primary source of information for the vast majority of people. However, the information within it is not always reliable, as there are direct or indirect attempts to convince the reader to buy a particular product. It is essential that people understand that the 'truth' is not a democratic endeavour. Just because the majority believe in one thing does not make them correct. Furthermore, the scientific literature is neither accessible in terms of language nor accessible in terms of monetary funds. Therefore, the opinions offered in this book will offer an expert opinion about the efficacy of diet drugs in the most accessible manner possible in an attempt to counter popular opinion on the Internet and the misinformation that circulates throughout the wider, publically accessible, literature.

Defending my opinion on this matter is relatively straight-forward. The contents and evidence within this book will not be over-interpreted or played down based on an ulterior motive. At the end of this book there will not be, by happenstance, a link for you to buy any of the products talked about within. You will not be told what to or not to buy in order to lose weight. You will simply get the evidence with my interpretation on it. If you do not like the interpretation then that is fine. It is, after all, your mind, your life and your money to spend as you wish. In a world where the only opinion freely available and offered are those based on attempts to sell the product in question, it does not make for a well-rounded or necessarily helpful altruistic perspective.

The next comment that will inevitably follow by those people who do not want you to hear my opinion is that I am an agent of the pharmaceutical industry. Therefore, let me state now that I have never worked for a pharmaceutical company. I am truly independent to those wanting to sell the products. I am of course bound somewhat by the teachings of my predecessors to show me how to think, but I have not been indoctrinated into holding a specific opinion. Neither do I have a motivation to ensure that you hold a particular view. In summary, my motivations are relatively straight-forward. People may be becoming dependent, even if only psychologically, on diet drugs for the purposes of weight-loss or maintenance. Critical thinking is the key to both progression towards better understanding and defence against being manipulated into buying any particular dieting product prior to dependency. A well thought out decision irrespective of its resolution is crucial to ensure people are not manipulated. Helping people to avoid being manipulated is the remit of the field specific expert and effectively outlines and underpins my motivations to write this book. That is both the start and the end of my motivation.

All of this however does not offer insight into your motivations. Without being too presumptuous and arrogant to assume why people picked up this book, I will go ahead and state that you are either a doubter of medical interventions, you are attempting to lose weight and want to know about diet drugs, you are an affiliate attempting to write about diet drugs or you are a dissenter of the 'alternative' therapies. All of you will find what you are after in this book. Little will be left to interpretation of my opinions in the arguments for and against the various substances that are advocated for the purposes of weight-loss.

To ensure full appreciation for the conclusions that will be drawn about diet drugs, it is important that a little wider knowledge is offered. For this you will be taken on a whistle stop tour within this book of: why people diet and what the Internet diet drug vendors say to hook into this desire; the legality of diet drugs and what is and is not allowed to be said; how Internet vendors differ from your friendly local pharmacist; what the diet drugs are supposed to target in the body and what the various terms used by writers on the Internet; then we will get to the different drugs and how, and if, they work.

Before you get into the subject matter proper we must first discuss what all good scientists need to do before attempting to write about any topic. This is the assumptions that formulate the basis of interpretations, insights and investigations. These assumptions are not necessarily specific to any individual. They are specific to the subject matter of introducing any substance into the body for the purposes of weight-loss. They are the assumptions that anyone involved in the diet drug industry are supposed to hold.

Introduction – Of Definitions and Assumptions

Dieting is an extremely complex behaviour. Unlike in other behaviours where there is some linearity to the process where beliefs lead to intention that, in turn, leads to an assessment of the individual's perceived ability, which finally leads to the observable behaviour. Dieting is more-or-less a paradoxical behaviour. There are subtle influences on the beliefs about weight-loss and its success or failure. In effect, engaging in dieting can fail prior to it even being attempted. Indeed, dieting actually predicts long- to medium-term weight gain not loss [2].

This paradox is often quite difficult to understand for the non-psychologist, as it is counter-intuitive to popular beliefs, intention, short-term observation of the behaviour (i.e. getting thinner) and what popular media tells everyone. The message that dieting is easy and specific weight loss from a specific place in a specific time frame is pervasive throughout society. For example, you will find statements such as "lose 20 pounds of fat from your stomach in two weeks on our diet plan" everywhere on the Internet. In that simple sentence there are no fewer than four separate untrue statements (to call them 'lies' would suggest intention to mislead; here we will take the perspective that it is a misunderstanding by those who make such statements). Untrue in the context of this book will be defined as making claims that have no credible basis in the current evidence.

In the pages of this book, I will not reiterate what others have already written about evidence; this can be found elsewhere [3]. As much as it pains me to say, it is a better explanation than be provided here in the space available. Therefore, evidence in this context will include scientific experimentation to back a claim fortified by the legal criteria[1] that the claim should adhere to, to advertise as a weight-loss drug.

---

[1] The legal criteria in this book will be under British Law. A law had to be chosen and British law was chosen as it is widely used across the globe as a bench mark for national, usually ex-colonial, laws. It is understood that by taking one legal perspective that some of the legal statements do not hold up in all countries. I would argue that this in itself is a significant problem. If international consensus could be reached about acceptable and unacceptable marketing and sales strategies then many of the problems that buyers face when purchasing diet pills on the internet could be eradicated overnight. Despite the laws not being identical across the world, the general definitions of the terms are shared as they derive from the scientific literature. Therefore, interested parties can refer to their local laws and find similar legal criteria and definitions.

DEFINING DRUG

The term drug in this book will be presented in two forms. The term will be loosely defined as any substance that is put into the body with the express intention of losing weight. Usually the term is reserved for pharmaceutical grade substances that have either a medicinal effect or is an illicit substance; however, in the course of the subject material of this book, it is not possible to reserve the term to these two domains. Too many of the products sold on the Internet and wider forums do not meet this criterion and yet are expressly sold under the term drug. Where the public sector has failed to provide appropriate resources, the private sector in all its forms has tried to offer their own interventions. Some of these are credible and helpful, while others are far from it.

During the course of this book, the term drug will be separated out into drug and 'drug'. The inverted commas on the term will refer to any substance that is sold for weight-loss purposes, but either is not a registered medicinal product or has little or no evidence to support it. This will be a legal differentiation based on the Medicines Act (1968) rather than solely based on efficacy purposes.

Products that are registered as weight-loss products and therefore have a 'proven' efficacy will receive the collective term drug. Those that do not will be referred to as 'drug'. It is accepted that the collective term 'drug' is not advocated by proponents of the substances that fall under this term. However, many sources available on the Internet do refer to them as such. Attempts to criticise the opinions in this book based on such rudimentary terms is inevitable, because what you are going to learn are the things that the 'complementary' industry do not want people to know. It is not the pharmaceuticals that are the only ones that keep their data private – many of the alternative 'drugs' have not even attempted to show efficacy or have been shown to be ineffective. The most damning evidence as there could ever be.

The term 'drug' within this book could equally refer to pill or supplement. However, I will present you with some evidence that the use of the word drug, or pill, is an attempt to associate the product with medical interventions. It is a 'piggy back' approach to ensure that the consumer infers efficacy through association. The more accurate name for all of these terms would be supplements and those people that use this term have a lot more creditability than others that do not. The simple use of this term means that they both understand what they are selling and also are not attempting to link their product to medicinal interventions. Unfortunately, these people are in the minority.

With the definition of the simple term drug concluded, comes the need to extend our definition into the remit of assumption. Assumptions define the context of the weight-loss intervention and are the anchors that provide legitimacy to either the opinion or the mode of action of the drug. The assumptions that will be offered in the rest of this chapter are those derived from the psychopharmacological perspective. However, these are also the assumptions that everyone must adhere to, without exception, if they are attempting to alter behaviour through introducing a foreign substance into another person's body. To deny these assumptions effectively denies that the substance offered works to aid weight-loss.

WHAT MUST BE ASSUMED?

In the pages of this book, the perspective we will take is that of psychopharmacology. The principle behind this subfield of research is that pharmacological interventions can affect behaviour. This 'affect' can come in many forms. It may reinforce dieting behaviour through removing or increasing subjective feelings associated with hunger or it may simply prohibit the absorption of food in the gut. Therefore, one of the perspectives acts purely in the psychological domain, albeit through a pharmacological target, and the other operates in a purely biological domain. This leads directly to the assumptions held at the start of this book that are taken as true. The first assumption is:

1. Behaviour Can be Predicted

This is a difficult assumption to hold. The derivatives of behaviour itself are highly debated. Historically, we have cycled through three overarching theoretical viewpoints, as well as many smaller ones too. These are principally psychodynamic, behaviourism, and cognitive. Each school of thought holds very different assumptions to explain human behaviour. Currently, the cognitive school holds prominence; although it could be argued that this school has also fallen to be replaced with a cognitive-affective approach. 'Affective' in this approach refers to emotional processing. However, to suggest that one group has fallen away entirely would not be true. There are many proponents for each school still practicing today.

Predicting behaviour is difficult. To understand whether a particular drug will be successful it must accurately predict how it will work, when it will work and on whom it will work. Difficulties arise for this assumption when considering these components to a diet drug. In short, the creator of a drug must accurately predict the behaviours that lead to weight gain, find an appropriate pharmacological target that is responsible for that particular behaviour, and then develop a drug that specifically targets the identified biochemical. Thus, to actively predict behaviour, the creator of a drug must, as a starting point, choose a theoretical basis of behaviour to adhere to.

Before we continue through the discourse of diet drugs, we should spend some time discussing and defining the behavioural assumptions we will hold against a potential candidate. It is important to understand that we could spend the whole book, indeed three whole books, on each of these behavioural schools of thought. The average undergraduate psychologist will have to buy several books on each of these topics during their course. Therefore, we will consider only the base assumptions of the schools. Taking psychodynamic first, there are seven base assumptions underlining this perspective. These are:

(i)   Behaviour is genetically [pre]determined, thus it is the same for everyone.
(ii) An individual's personality determines their behaviour.
(iii) Personality is controlled by the mind, which has three separate components – Id, Ego and Superego.
(iv) That behaviour is both consciously and unconsciously determined.
(v)   Unconscious behaviour has two components to it – personal and collective.

(vi) Personality forms early in life through interactions with parents and significant others.

(vii) Adults go through psychosocial development which derives from psychosocial conflict.

For people interested in these base assumptions, they derive from the work of Sigmund Freud (1856-1939), Carl Jung (1875-1961), and Erik Erikson (1902-1994). Much of the work stems from studying psychopathology – when behaviour goes wrong or deviant to the 'normality'. Although these could be argued to be a somewhat simplistic representation of the field, they would be considered its basic immutable assumptions. Any proponent to this school of thought must adhere to them. Some of these are difficult to defend. In particular, the concept of unconscious awareness means that it is inherently immeasurable, indefinable and open to instant criticism. The criticism often stems from the positivistic psychologists who have an intellectual necessity for any theory to be testable and rely on experimentation to provide evidence. This, in turn, leads to a conflict in the quantitative/qualitative divide.

Quantitative psychology is based on positivism and adherence to the more traditional sciences. Within this approach, the psychologist makes a hypothesis, designs an experiment complete with variables, manipulates one of the independent variables and measures the outcome on a predefined dependent variable. Independent variables are those that are deemed to not matter on the outcome of the experiment. More often they are descriptive variables such as sex of the participant, which obviously will not change throughout the course of the experiment. The dependent variable is one that is deemed to change. So, for example, we could hypothesize that a person's salary is determined by their sex. Therefore, we would hypothesize that either males or females get paid more. Then we go out and ask a selection of people their salaries and statistically compare the two groups (males versus females) on their take home salaries.

Qualitative psychology is difficult to describe as a single approach to studying a phenomenon. Instead, it should be viewed as an umbrella term for the analysis of data based on linguistic interpretation of what the participants offer as an explanation for their behaviour. The psychodynamic school has its roots in the more qualitative end of the research perspective while both behaviourism and cognitive schools, which we will consider next, have theirs in the quantitative approach. To say that both have remained in these research methodologies would be false. Modern proponents to any school rarely adhere to a single base methodology. For example, the psychodynamic approach has led to the birth of individual difference research, often wrongly termed personality psychology, which has a rich history in both quantitative and qualitative doctrines.

Behaviourism was for a long time the antithesis to psychodynamic school of thought. For every base assumption that the psychodynamic advocates offered, theorists from the behaviourist perspective denied its existence. The largest conflict was over the theory of the mind. Behaviourists rejected the notion of mind through its inherent inability to measure it. Instead they adhered dogmatically to the scientific positivistic approach and its reductionist tendencies. Reductionism in this instance refers to reducing behaviour to its physical outcomes. Measuring what actually happens during the behaviour. Finding its component parts and predicting what happens to elicit specific behaviour. The base assumptions of behaviourism are:

(i) Behaviour is predictable if its component parts can be identified.

(ii) Behaviour is determined by the interaction between the individual and the environment not predetermined by the individual. It is reactive to positive and negative reinforcers (i.e. stimulus equals response)

(iii) Any human attribute is simply the extension of their behavioural dispositions. (I.e. Terry is happy changes to Terry is behaving as if he is happy). This is sometimes referred to as logical behaviourism and is this school's attempt to reinterpret the psychodynamic predispositions.

(iv) Empiricism, positivism, replicability, objectivity are the cornerstones of predicting behaviour.

(v) There is an evolutionary continuity between animals and man, thus there are similarities in their behaviours.

The behaviourism school derives from the work of two principle authors – John Watson (1878-1958) and Burrhus Skinner (1904-1990). It does not take a large leap of understanding to see that the 'rules' of behaviourism are closer to the traditional sciences (physics, biology, chemistry) and thus are easily adopted by proponents of pharmacology – a subfield of biochemistry. For example, the behaviourist approach allows for animal models to be used in experimentation; something that pharmacologists adhere to as part of the drug trial process. This could not be defended under the psychodynamic perspective. Moreover, this school of thought deconstructs the complexity of the human behaviour model to a series of measurable sub-components. Alterations in these behavioural measures then define the success or failure of an intervention. This also readily adheres to the traditional scientific approach and allows the pharmacologist to make specific claims about the drug as defined by the legal regulations. For example, under the behaviourist perspective, eating behaviour would be defined by hunger and fullness, therefore any drug that causes changes in fullness and hunger in the appropriate direction leading to observable changes in weight status would be marketable as a weight-loss drug. Rather worryingly, adherents to this school can legitimately claim that changes observed in an animal model can translate directly to changes that should be observed in humans. This perspective is common within the pharmacological literature which contains various animal models of weight-loss. For those who really adhere to this perspective, there is even a model of eating disorders based on this perspective. Many adherents to this perspective believe that they have a model of binge-eating/bulimia nervosa in rats. They then use this model to try and alter the 'bulimic' status of the rat. It is not suggested that this is an accurate model just that it can be, and frequently is, used to defend animal models for interventions. Critiques of this school suggest that this approach disregards the obvious complex mental process of decision-making and the plethora of information that is used by a human to decide to perform a specific behaviour. Proponents of this criticism started what we have now come to know as the cognitive revolution.

Even though it is possible to directly associated animal behaviour to human behaviour under the behaviourist perspective, in reality, few researchers would do this. Instead, uncovering human behaviour is reliant on similar basic principles of the behaviourist school but bring back the psychodynamic concept of the mind from a subtly different perspective. Cognitive psychology builds from similar doctrines of empiricism, positivism and experimentation of the behaviourists, but offers a little more specificity to humans. It does this by 'borrowing' one of the founding principles of the psychodynamic perspective – studying pathology.

The rise of cognitive psychology stems from the combined works of Noam Chomsky (1928-), George Miller (1920-) and many others. In its most condensed form, this approach refers to explaining how information is processed within the brain of a human. Many writers on this subject refer to this as explaining the miracle or the black box mysteries to how a person processed the stimuli and then why they expressed the specific behaviour. Compared to other theoretical approaches, the basic assumptions of this field are harder to define and conceptualise. This is because the field in itself has several facets to it that are difficult to propose as having a single conceptual base. Instead, the theoretical assumptions of this approach are better defined as have three separate strands, whereby each strand has specific assumptions associated with it.

Not all proponents of this school of thought adhere to each others' assumptions and may actively attack the basis of other subfields of cognition. The three strands are: cognitive science, cognitive psychology and cognitive neuropsychology. In the crudest form, the three groups differentiate themselves by what they use to examine the human brain to create valid experimental paradigms. For ease of explanation, these three groups will be treated separately, but in reality they should be considered as a continuum whereby the individual cognitive scientist finds their own settling point.

Cognitive scientists take the simile between the human brain and the internal working of the computer literally. They attempt to make a computer act like a human by software or hardware solutions (i.e. they actually create new processor components or new programmes to emulate human behaviour). It is a regression of the human brain to a computational model. Cognitive psychologists experiment with people in an attempt to link behaviour to underlying processes going on within the human brain. They literally measure human behaviour and in the strictest sense do not link this to any biological variables. The final group are the cognitive neuropsychologists who attempt to link behaviour to anatomical structures within the brain. As a discipline they favour brain imaging techniques to view functional (or, in terms of pathological individuals, anatomical) changes within the brain as a result of a stimuli that expresses a specific behaviour.

Each pseudo sub-group within the cognitive sciences has viable experimental models and rationales for their approach; however, for the purposes of psychopharmacological research into dieting, they do not necessarily have the same importance. As part of this first assumption – that behaviour is predictable –, so we can define viable targets for pharmacological interventions for dieting, it is integral that we observe the interaction between the drug and the behaviour in the human. This means that for our purposes, the computational approach to predicting behaviour is of less importance to experimental manipulations of behaviour in an actual human participant. In light of this, the assumptions mentioned below are those that are more important to cognitive psychologists and neuropsychologists.

(i)   The mind is not an indefinable or unconscious quantity. It is a processor of external information and created by the brain (i.e. the mind and the physical brain are interchangeable [isomorphism]).

(ii)   The brain has evolved as a general purpose organ to deal with our social and physical environment.

(iii) The brain is made up of two distinct hemispheres that are autonomous to each other but reliant on each other to process the world (parallel processing).

(iv) Each hemisphere has distinct anatomical component parts that can also operate independent of one another but are reliant on each other to fully process information (i.e. information is processed in serial in each half of the brain).

(v) Each anatomical part is responsible for processing one type of information (specialisation).

(vi) The brain has a limited capacity and will use strategies to save on computational resources.

(vii) To save cognitive resources, information processing organisation is eventually conserved through experience (cognitive scripts) creating predictable responses to formulate patterns of behaviour.

(viii) Information processing is made by interpretation of symbols stored as memory engrams.

This last list is the primary basis of the assumption that behaviour is predictable, as it is the only one that would explicitly dictate that biological manipulation would lead to altered behaviour. It is easy to see from the list of assumptions that the field of psychopharmacology, which is responsible for creating the drugs that manipulate behaviour, has a strong association with the cognitive neuropsychological school of thought. This is because they must make a strong association to some biological underlying structure and the expression of behaviour. To provide a pharmacological solution to an inherently behavioural problem means that they must inextricably link biology with behaviour. This leads directly to our next assumption.

2. Behaviour Has Distinct Neuroanatomical and Neurochemical Roots

The prediction of behaviour is exceptionally important to the psychopharmacologist otherwise they will not be able to measure how effective their proposed drug will be in manipulating it. However, it is not enough for a psychopharmacologist to suggest that behaviour is controlled by the brain like those proposed by the cognitive school. They have to take this assumption further. Arguably, it is more important that the psychopharmacologists make statements about the interaction between biology and behaviour, beyond the simple neuroanatomical responsibility or regional specificity of processing in the brain, to predict potential psychological outcomes. In short, they have to literally adhere to the assumption that behaviour is completely controlled by biology.

To meet this assumption, it must follow that behaviour is controlled by very specific brain cells. Moreover, as the psychopharmacologists employ chemistry solutions to their interventions, it is not the brain cells themselves that are necessarily important to behaviour; rather it is a specific chemical messenger(s) they employ to communicate with other brain cells around them. According to the adherents of the psychopharmacological perspective, it is the brain cells functioning in unison sending and receiving chemical messengers that is the basis of behaviour. Thus, manipulating this interaction manipulates behaviour. Although this may add strength in the argument as the psychopharmacologists are suggesting similar principles to the cognitive scientists (e.g. chemical communication between regions is important [psychopharmacologist] vs all regions needed to process information [cognitive scientist]), it has a very significant weakness. This assumption follows that behaviour in those who are healthy is simply alterations in the release of a specific chemical in the brain. If the assumption goes that a specific biochemical is responsible for specific behaviour then logically there must be different chemical messengers for different behaviours. Without going into too much detail at this early stage, there are very few chemical pathways that extend throughout the brain. Therefore, we have our first problem. The logical assumptions followed so far has been that: behaviour is predictable; distinct anatomical parts of the brain are responsible for processing component parts of the information; the whole brain is required to process all of the information; chemical messengers pass between the various regions of the brain; the processing of information leads to behaviour. Thus, changes in chemical messengers are related to changes in behaviour, but we do not have enough messengers to account for the behaviours.

To overcome this logical problem, we must switch from the chemical messengers to the chemical receivers. Instead of basing our logic on alterations in the concentrations of specific brain chemicals, which we do not have enough of to suggest specificity to behaviour, we have to switch emphasis back to the cells in the different regions of the brain and how they respond to the message. To explain this, I will wonder a little from our diet drug path. Although neurochemistry is an extremely complex system, it is possible to simplify it enough for non-specialist audiences.

Consider that the brain is a series of locked rooms, where to get to all the rooms we have to go through each room in turn. If each room contains two locked doors one leading back to the first region and the second leading eventually to the last room, then this would be the *pathway*. To fully complete the analogy, each room must contain two people where the language they are speaking is different to all the other rooms. One person in the room is the *cell* and the other is the *chemical messenger*. The cell can speak two languages – the language of the messenger coming from the previous room and the language of their own messenger. The messengers can only speak one language. As the doors are locked, each messenger in each room has the key to the next room in the pathway, but only that key. The first *chemical messenger* comes into the first room to pass on the message to the *cell*. The first cell then passes the message to their *chemical messenger*. This messenger then opens the door and passes the message on to the *cell* person in the next room etc...

This set up means we can have a more complex system with many different chemicals (if necessary) or complex communication between 'rooms'. In this analogy we can even have the same language to pass on the message, but as long as we have different 'locks on the door' means that we can have different behaviours with different biology despite having the exact same chemical message. These 'door locks' in neuroanatomy would be referred to as *receptors*. Receptors are proteins on the surface of the cell that cause changes within the cell once they receive the chemical message.

In fact we can make the pathway really complex with multiple rooms with varied and/or multiple doors and multiple messengers (all the messengers in each room would have to speak the same language), as long as the locks remain varied then we can have relatively few chemical pathways responsible for a lot of behaviours. These varied locks are known as receptor sub-types, but we will save these for later. At this stage, all you need to understand is that the assumption from psychopharmacological perspective is that you target the lock not the key. The drug effectively breaks into the pathway through flooding it with people who have skeleton keys who open all the doors letting communication flow 'better'. This is not the whole story, as the lock part is actually very complex and more can be done with it other than simply unlock and lock the door; however, it is enough to get through this assumption.

So the logic statements about the assumptions now follow that: behaviour is predictable; distinct anatomical parts of the brain are responsible for processing component parts of the information; the whole brain is required to process all of the information; chemical messengers pass between the various regions of the brain; the processing of information leads to behaviour; the chemical messengers can be copied and their effect emulated through their receptors on the cell; we can hijack these receptors to elicit (unlock the door) or block (lock the door) expression of behaviour.

There is another sort of sub-assumption within this argument that should be considered here. It is not an assumption on its own, but it is part of the neurochemical assumption of behaviour. This is that changing the concentration of the chemical messenger in the target brain area will increase or decrease the expression of the behaviour. This then follows that for the problem behaviour, which, in this case, led to perceived weight gain and the desire to take a weight-loss drug, is a result of faulty neurochemistry. In essence they must assume that something has 'broken' leading to the inability to naturally create the necessary chemical messengers.

The scientific pursuit to identify 'broken' biology in obese individuals has met with extremely limited success. These attempts have included genetic, hormonal and neurochemical explanations. All of these fail to explain the one damning criticism of this field – what has biologically changed amongst the human race in the last thirty to forty years to explain why rates of obesity have increased? The answer is nothing.

Therefore, arguments put forward by those who research the biological components to the development of weight gain are limited to identifying biological predispositions to weight gain. These predispositions come with the caveat that they may not, but they are more likely to, lead to obesity. Most of those identified are limited to predicting very small amounts of weight gain. This has inevitably led the biologist to argue that the explanation lies with having the total combination of all of the biological risk factors, however, this argument still does not answer why obesity has developed into pandemic proportions. It will only ever provide an answer to those who were 'destined' to be overweight. These are a very small amount of people within the population.

Furthermore, to not assume something is 'broken' then advocates of this theory must assume that the normal system is not suitable. Millions of years of evolution would disagree with that statement. If the assumption is that something is not biologically broken, which I adhere to in the case of weight gain and obesity, means that the psychopharmacologist is attempting to interfere with a highly evolved system that is functioning as it should. In medicine, it is always easier to replace a biochemical that is missing then it is to stop something from working (e.g. the efficacy of Insulin injections for treating diabetes compared to the efficacy of any weight loss drugs). However, we will save that for later chapters too.

If the pharmacologists who have picked up this book have not thrown it across the room yet and then carried on with their lives without reading on then it would be a surprise. Let me explain to the rest of you, who did not throw the book, why they did so, as well as what they said why they did it. Those that threw the book probably said "these aren't true; we do not have to target the brain at all".

This is completely true they do not have to target the brain at all. The first two assumptions thus far discussed are only appropriate to those drugs that target the brain and claim to alter behaviour. There are of course other pharmacological targets in the system that requires no *psycho-* suffix to them. One in particular, Orlistat, is very popular diet drug and is available over-the-counter. This drug does not purport to affect behaviour directly. It is a lipase inhibitor and stops a percentage of the fat consumed from crossing the intestinal wall and entering the body. Due to this mode of action, these first two assumptions are not pertinent to this particular drug. Drugs that act on the targets in the body rather than targets in the brain are very much in the minority. Although the first two assumptions may not be important to drugs that target the peripheral organs, the next two are still integral to drugs attempting to aid in weight loss. If a drug is reliant on behaviour being nothing more than the combination of biological changes then there must be little to no variation in how the biology functions between individuals.

3. People Are All Structurally and Functionally the Same Both in Biological and Psychological Terms

It stands to reason that in order for a drug to be marketable to the general population it must work for the general population. Therefore, the chemical structure of the drug must fit together with a receptor protein in the body no matter which particular individual takes it. Thus, to fulfill this need, the biology of each individual must be identical. Very minor inter-individual variations in receptor structure will mean that the diet drug will not work. This is because the process of binding between chemical messenger and receptor is quite precise. Because of this practicality, it is imperative that the structure of a receptor remains the same between people and ideally between species. Many drugs are first trialed on animal models and therefore, no matter how the drug works it has to be both structurally similar to the animal's chemical messenger and their receptor. For the model to then work in a human, the structure of the same target receptor must be very similar and have the same function.

Based on the previous two assumptions, if the drug is suggested to directly affect behaviour then it stands to reason that how the organism (animal or human) uses their biology must also be the same. This extends the need for the organism to have similar structural biology into the domain where they have very similar functional biology. For example, if the assumption goes that a specific biological target is the root cause of 'X' behaviour then it must be the same for all people. Thus there is no flexibility in the system for the animal to use the same biological material differently to another of the same species. Although this is a rather short and somewhat obvious assumption to explain, it will have large ramifications on the practicality of a specific drug. If there are any variations in either how the receptor is structured or how it is used between people then the drug is doomed to fail.

4. The Drug Must Specifically and Selectively Target the Theorised Anatomical Component in a Living Human

To say that a drug must act on a specific site sounds obvious to the lay person. In reality of the complex biological being this is not as straight-forward as first thought. Furthermore, the creation of a specific drug is not the end of the process. Just because a specific structure looks the same as the chemical found in the body does not mean that it will actually get to the site of the receptor intact. The overwhelmingly preferred strategy for drug delivery is through oral administration delivered in a tablet or capsule form. If the drug is designed to target a specific receptor in the brain then it has to contend with a lot of barriers that will do everything to stop it from reaching its destination. For example, it has to travel through the stomach (a highly acidic environment), the upper intestinal tract (a structure designed to break everything down), cross the intestinal wall (designed to only let through the smallest possible chemicals), travel through the blood (filled with immune cells designed to destroy anything deemed 'foreign' to the body), cross the blood brain barrier (designed to stop nearly everything from crossing it) and reach its destination in the brain avoiding being diverted into a non-target structure. As you can imagine, simply dumping a lot of a chosen chemical into the living body, which is comparatively massive compared to the chemical in question, as well as a highly complex environment complete with moving parts and barriers does not guarantee success. In fact, such procedures are likely to result in large and unpleasant side-effects.

Many of the less credible drugs or compounds offered on the Internet simply choose to ignore this assumption. They believe that if the compound works in a Petri dish on a single cell then the same thing will happen in the body. It will not. Your body is designed to take complex nutrients from the environment and break them down into their base elements. It is pretty good at doing it. Through this latent talent, giving a drug that requires administration through the digestive system is likely to be broken down into its composite nutrients and therefore made inert (chemically non-functioning). It becomes pharmacologically useless as a drug.

Within the sub-parts of this assumption, we see that a drug must be both specific and selective to its target. Many people many assume that this means the same thing; however, they are very different and both are very important. Any potential diet drug must be specific to its target. What is meant here is that the active part of the drug must specifically bind to the active part of the receptor. Both the chemical and the receptor will have something called an active site. This is the specific chemical area on both structures where the two will interact to have the desired effect in the cell itself. Simply binding to a receptor is not enough to elicit a reaction in the cell. Depending on the desired effect (to block or activate the receptor) the pharmacologist must consider how they want their drug to work.

Once the active site (the area of the receptor that causes the chain reaction in the cell) has been indentified then there are several options available to the pharmacologist. They can block the active site by creating a chemical agent that stops the endogenous (chemical that is created naturally in your body) chemical from binding with the receptor anymore. This stops the ability to produce the behaviour. Alternatively they could mimic the endogenous chemical by creating a drug that sits perfectly in the active site of the receptor artificially causing the chain reaction in the cell. Such a drug would elicit the desired behaviour. This is a rather simplistic representation of what is potentially available to the pharmacologist; however, it would constitute the basics of direct drug action.

One interesting biological phenomenon with our bodies is that they are lazy. It would appear that if our bodies can get away with it, they will use very similar biological structures with only minor alterations to do very different jobs. Therefore, any superfluous material bound to the drug beyond that required to bind with the active site of the receptor has the potential for binding with something else that it was not intended for. Any drug that binds with something it should not is considered to have problems with its selectivity. There are two words here that are important to understanding selectivity – *homology* and *affinity*. Homology refers to how similar two chemicals are. To say that something shares 'x'% homology simply means that they are 'x'% identical (i.e. made up of the same amino acid chains in exactly the same order). Affinity refers to how selectivity is measured in a given system. Usually it is reported as a chemical has an 'x'-fold affinity for receptor y over receptor z. This means that if placed side by side, the chemical will bind with receptor y 'x' times more frequently than receptor z. Both homology and affinity are very important for a drug. If they have poorly defined or unknown homology with a known endogenous chemical then simply put we do not know how it works. Poor affinity means that we know how it works, but it is just not very good at it.

Specificity and selectivity are therefore differentiated through whether the drug works where it should (specificity) or where it should not (selectivity). It is perfectly acceptable to have a drug that is very specific but not very selective. If the drug is not specific then it is pointless, if it is not selective then it is not desirable. Sometimes it is better to be specific and undesirable if the potential outcome is death. For example, the treatment for many cancers is chemotherapy. This effectively inhibits cell growth. This is great for stopping mutated cancer cells from developing, but also stops all cells from developing. The inevitable outcome of cancer is death. Therefore, people are willing to put up with the poor selectivity if it saves their life. People are less happy with poor selectivity if the result is not so urgent. Weight loss would be considered as a comparatively non-urgent problem by most people. Therefore, for dieting drugs, the problem of selectivity is of paramount importance. If you want people to keep buying the drugs then side-effects brought on by poor selectivity are not tolerated by the consumer. On the internet this concept is either ignored or very poorly explained and understood. The closest that the majority of sites come to touching on this are statements like "this drug works like…" This is obviously not enough information to formulate anything meaningful about the selectivity and specificity of a given drug and therefore leaves the buyer with little understanding of the likelihood and severity of the potential side-effects. Despite this poor understanding and/or explanation about selectivity and specificity it is an essential assumption concerning the function of any diet drug.

AND A FEW MORE THINGS BEYOND ASSUMPTIONS

Like all good scientists, we have defined the assumptions we are making prior to evaluating the evidence before us. In order to defend any claim made about a weight loss drug, we must first explore whether they are claiming that it is working through altering behaviour or prohibiting nutrients entering the body. In these scenarios, we will hold to the above four assumptions. Bad scientists will of course suggest that because there is no evidence then that is a defense for their theory of how something works. This is just that, bad science. We are not such people and will not proceed through the information known to us with such approaches. Science is made up of two hypotheses. One is experimental and the other is the null. The experimental is the one that requires defending. It must be rationalised based on previous literature and evidence for its derivation offered. This evidence must be defended in the light of its limitations and appropriate conclusions drawn. If I think that a particular theory is true then I have to defend it. Your average eleven year-old should be able to tell you this. It is simple basic protocol in science. In contrast, the null hypothesis need not be defended. It is the default position. All good scientists irrespective of their station, status, field, approach, thoughts, feelings, intuitions and any other driving force should hold to the principle of untrue until overwhelming evidence to the contrary. Good science never has to defend the statement of untrue. Good science never has to defend the null hypothesis. Basing statements or claims on no evidence does not mean "perhaps true" or "could be true" it always means "currently untrue".

Deriving a viable model or mode of action for a potential diet drug is always based on assumptions. These assumptions are not those that have no experimental evidence. They are assumptions derived from combined evidence for the best explanation of the world as we know it. In short, the base assumption about a drug is not supposition, it too must have evidence.

All is not equal in the world. Anyone can make up the assumptions as they go along if no one is there to stop them. Most will be stopped by their own conscience. They will consider "am I doing harm through the statements I am making?" Many will not be stopped by such worries. Concerns about others pale into insignificance compared to their bank balance. One way this can be easily achieved is to physically separate those with the problem and the need for the weight-loss drug from those who sell it. By de-humanising the process through devolving all communications to virtual environments means the sellers will never have to meet those they supply. By removing the human factor we remove the potential for empathy. Even if by happenstance the vendor and buyer meet then there is always the default response of 'buyer beware'. The seller can always say "I just sell the stuff, I do not make it". This ignores the fact that they have been providing the buyers with poor information that led to them buying the product in the first place.

To actually write something worthy of being considered evidence means that it needs to be published in a creditable source. To do this, the process of publication means that the work has to go through peer review. Other scientists who are highly trained, independent and anonymous to the researchers must consider it appropriate and worthy of publication. Nearly everything I write goes through this process. Everything on the Internet does not. Frequently, you can find information on the Internet that would violate the law of the country you are in, either advertising or other. All is not equal in the world because good science takes many months and sometimes years to appear in credible publications, while you can write anything on the Internet and publish it immediately. Moreover, all is not equal because the general population do not have access to scientific journals, while most have access to the Internet. Therefore, the only other option to counter the internet is the book. Here, through this medium, it is possible to make the buyer truly aware. To make you fully aware, you need to know some information from a variety of fields. Although it is useful to know why people diet and how the diet drugs work, if at all, it is also important to understand the legality of the process. To understand what can the vendor or affiliate legitimately say without legal repercussions?

To arm the reader with enough information to critically analyse what they read on the Internet requires assessment of eight separate areas conveniently presented in eight chapters. The next chapter concerns how the buyer gets sucked in to buying the specific diet drug. How do the vendors grab the attention of the buyer in the first place and get them to read on to the inevitable 'sell'. They do this through understanding and making specific statements related to the buyer's specific motivation to lose weight, despite their being no evidence to support the claims. The second chapter explores the legal loopholes. It is not necessary to register something as a drug to attempt to sell it like one. There are no fewer than four separate legal approaches that can be taken to registering a product and each route to market is allowed to make certain claims. In fact, most vendors will make nebulous claims that they contain a specific chemical that aids weight-loss. They will not consider any of the above assumptions. They will not consider the 'dosage' required. Indeed, all they need prove is that the dosage given is not detrimental to health. But we will get to this in all good time. Hopefully by the end of chapter two you will know what group any potential product will fall into and what they are likely to say to try and suck the buyer in.

In the third chapter we will spend a little time exploring the differences between Internet (or virtual companies) versus pharmaceutical (or bricks and mortar companies). Regulation between these two companies should be the same, but it often is not. Difficulties arise through dealing with rogue companies situated and registered in other countries. They have instant access to people throughout the world and shutting or blocking a website can be replaced in a matter of hours. It is important that people are aware of who they are buying their dieting drugs from. The Internet is the biggest problem and solution to the field.

After the legal and marketing considerations have been covered, we will move on to how the drugs work. What do we know and how can we target it? Here, you will be given a brief introduction to the complex world of appetite regulation. This will not contain the rubbish pervasive throughout our world put there by those with ulterior motives. This often contains tenuous links to the real process skipping over the integral components to focus on the spurious side-shoots that allows them to blind the buyer with science. This chapter will unblind you.

In chapters five, six and seven we will explore the actual drugs themselves. We will look at the history of weight-loss drugs and consider the previous targets. Here, we will consider what happened to them, why they failed and the lessons learned from them. Then we will look at the reputable weight-loss drugs and discover how they work. Finally, we will consider the pretenders to the throne. Those drugs that are everywhere on the Internet and in the backs of magazines that have no science base at all. Conveniently, these products may report that they have done the science and found rather unsurprisingly that it worked perfectly. They may even show you the 'before and after' pictures of someone who supposedly took their product. These, I need not tell you, are often at best anecdotal, at worst total rubbish.

To complete our journey we have to consider what the odds of success in terms of taking diet drugs to aid weight-loss are and we will do this in chapter eight. Taking a weight-loss drug is not the only way to lose weight. Other methods are available and should be considered alongside the drugs. This will give an indication of the efficacy of diet pills through comparison with non-pharmaceutical interventions against the claims made by those that sell them. Once we have considered all of this information, it will be summed up to give an overview of the field. This will provide you with the mantras to prohibit people sucking you into their sales pitch. You will also be given some final thoughts and a picture of what the future of the diet drug industry should look like.

Chapter 1

OF WHY PEOPLE DIET

You will probably expect the usual health related reasons for why people diet at this point. However, this is not the primary reason for starting a diet for the majority of those people that 'go' on such a regime. Few people are independently told that they need to diet because of health implications/complications compared to those that are actually dieting.

Most people report that the primary reason that they started to diet was for aesthetic reasons [4]. The main motivation is usually brought about by fixation on the visual properties of a particular body part that affects them so much that it provides them with the motivation to alter their behaviour and to restrict food intake and/or increase exercise [5]. This, in the loosest sense, is referred to in the literature as body dissatisfaction. Although many professionals may argue that the main reason to diet is to stem the prognosis of long-term health problems, this is not why the majority of people actually do it. People are much more short-term in nature and we, as a species, struggle with conceptualising an uncertain future. People are much better at dealing with and responding to present problems and things that can be observed. We are not a particularly good species with abstract thought despite the fact that we are the only ones who have shown evidence for it. Until we have tangible evidence we rarely act on anything and dieting to lose weight is no different.

If a health argument was the primary motivational agent then only people who were actually overweight or obese would diet. Specifically, those that have started to experience health complications as a result of their weight. Dieting has become the norm and has been for quite a long-time for women [6] and increasingly so for men [7]. Most women, and increasingly more men, consider the calorific content of their food irrespective of their current weight status. This consideration places an additional psychological control above and beyond the biological drivers to eat. Many theories have been proposed for why this is the case. These constitute perspectives of why people diet. It is important to remember that these perspectives are based on the assumptions of Western society. Many cultures around the globe do not share these values. Increasingly, other cultures are beginning to adopt these views especially once they start receiving Western media and in particular television scheduling [8]. The current Western ideal is for thinness and society collectively implicitly stigmatises obesity as being undesirable because of its opposition to the social ideal. Sometimes this implicit stigmatisation boils over into discrimination by particular individuals; however, this view is implicitly held by all of us.

Overweight people suffer from systemic discrimination within society. This includes all aspects of social life from the likelihood to get married, education attainment and employment. Overweight people will be less likely to get a job, be promoted in one they get, and more likely to be made redundant (receiving less compensation money when they are) [9]. When researchers ask why people engage in this discriminatory behaviour few realise they are overtly doing it. This suggests that the discrimination is implicit within society based on deviation from social ideals. This links directly with attribution theory where we infer personality characteristics and an individual's value based on minimal data (i.e. weight status). In the case of weight status, many people will wrongly associate weight status with numerous negative personality characteristics. These associations include the attribution of poor working habits, emotional problems and interpersonal problems [10].

Attributions to obesity are uncovered if you ask an individual to rate what they think about obese people and then ask the same questions again but ask them to answer them from the perspective of societal norm. Invariably everyone will report that they do not view obesity as bad, but they will say that society does[1]. A person's reported perceived societal view is a form of defense against social repercussions for having a negative view about other groups or people. Although individuals may argue that they do not hold the same view as society (and some may not), most will effectively hide their views behind that of "it is not me, it is everyone else". Therefore, the statement that "you need to diet" becomes that of "if you do not diet then people will not like you". Evidence suggests that obese people are stigmatised by society at every point in life and health professionals often hold the worst views of all [11]. When combined, these factors do not translate into a happy existence for those considered to not be adhering to the societal ideal concerning weight-status.

Weight status is purely a biological concept. It has nothing to do with an individual's personality or character. Simply put, gaining weight is normal and in the current obesogenic environment we inhabit it is abnormal to not do so. Research defines weight status in physical terms through differences in body mass index. Most people in society are comfortable with the concept of body mass index, as it is frequently used. It is a comparison between an individual's weight in kilograms divided by their height in metres squared. This is a very medical explanation for obesity. People, apart from a few University students and gym workers, do not habitually walk around with standardised scales and height measures.

---

[1] Obesity stigmatization is often measured through the help of the fat phobia scale. This is a psychometric questionnaire – psychometric means that it is very carefully constructed to ensure that it measures what it is supposed to measure – that measures people's beliefs about overweight individuals and the personality characteristics associated with it. It is separate into four sections. One half focuses on for females and the other on males. Each half is then further separated by personal opinions and then societal views. Each of these 'opinions' effectively measure the same concept. Societal views obviously cannot be measured, but individually perceived societal view can. This allows the individual to infer what 'society' thinks about overweight people without suffering the potential recourse of being considered discriminatory. General findings from a variety of studies using this scale indicates that the vast majority of people, including overweight and obese people themselves, report that specific personality characteristics are associated with being of a higher weight-status. These reported views generally relate to laziness and other less desirable personality characteristics. It is important to consider that this has no bearing in realty. These are perceived in the same way as all other discriminatory views are perceived. Irrespective of how an individual became overweight, they are generally implicitly believed to have done this because of a personality flaw. The fact that the belief is implicit means it is very difficult to tackle. Before the obvious criticisms about how can implicit beliefs exist as people are unaware of them, this is simply not true. People are generally very aware of implicit beliefs in others they are just terrible at spotting them in themselves. This is because no one wants to suffer social ridicule for holding a negative view of others. To spot implicit beliefs in specific individuals then look to phrases such as "I am not [put in any term here], but..." These often give an indication to implicit beliefs especially when the context of the discussion is more general and about groups of people rather than specific individuals.

Because people do not have a standardised and objective measure with them at all times, they make approximations. They use a strategy of best guess to work out if a person is overweight.

Generally, approximate assessment of adiposity is undertaken through an assessment of comparative 'thinness' or silhouette assessment [12]. The perfect silhouette is often unobtainable for the majority of people, placing them in a state of constant dissatisfaction with their bodies. This dissatisfaction in turn leads to fixation on the part(s) of their body that deviate from this ideal more than others. People then use this criterion to judge others. This can be done in the immediate environment against other people around them (comparative thinness) or it can be done individually through simple visual assessments (silhouette assessment) for adiposity in specific regions of the body (e.g. jaw to neck ratio; shoulder to waist ratio; waist to hip ratio etc...). This makes the assessment entirely perceived and individually determined. People do not wait until they have a BMI of 26 before they decide it is time to diet; they do decide whether to or not based on their own perception of the importance of weight status and relative importance of body image.

Just to deviate from our story a little and to emphasize the point that weight status is entirely perceived and individually determined then this little anecdote may be familiar. I had a student once who explicitly told me they were on a diet to maintain their current weight despite having a BMI of 18.5. When confronted about this she stated that she does not care about what other people thought because that was not what her group of friends do. This little statement has several interesting components to it that are worthy of a little time. Firstly, it would seem that dieting to maintain weight was common among the friendship group. Therefore, current weight status and maintaining weight was considered important by this group. This leads us to assume that if the student was to increase weight they would perceive a loss of social standing or inclusion with the group. Weight status for these young women was indeed important social determinant of those included in the friendship group and those outside of it. This adds another level of complexity to motivations for weight loss. Although weight status is a biological certainty, it also has strong social repercussions in terms of social judgment. This little story may help empathy, but it is anecdotal; similar findings have been offered in the scientific literature [13].

Instead of viewing weight status and dieting in the context of biology, it really should be considered from all perspectives. Dieting has significant impact on every aspect of a person's life both individually and socially. Arguably, it can have a major impact on those around the person, especially those that share mealtimes with the dieter. Therefore, a brief explanation of the perspectives on dieting will be offered. Exploring our little story first, we will start with body dissatisfaction and work our way on to other perspectives after this. Just as a brief note before we dive head long into the next topic, this chapter will not consider why we eat that can be found elsewhere [14]. Eating behaviour is multi-faceted and it would not be right to consider overweight and obese people to be eating because of gluttony. These people are fast becoming the normal weight status so they really cannot be considered deviant in anyway. Holding such views would only further reinforce the negative stereotypes and lead to even more polarised and unfounded discrimination. In this chapter, we will only consider the current theoretical thinking of why people diet. Once we know this we can explore what diet drug vendors say on the Internet and be able to understand their sales strategy.

PERSPECTIVES ON DIETING

Body Dissatisfaction

We briefly mentioned body dissatisfaction at the beginning of this chapter as the principle reason for dieting behaviour. Many studies have linked dieting, body dissatisfaction, thin ideal and eating disorder pathologies. Body dissatisfaction is a simple psychological construct to understand so we will not overly complicate it with needless convoluted explanation. It is simply as the name suggests the dissatisfaction with specific or more global parts of one's body. Body dissatisfaction is a strong predictor of dieting especially in those people who have internalised a thin ideal image [15]. Although body dissatisfaction is an internal cognitive self-evaluative process it is based upon social comparisons. People will invariably directly compare themselves to others irrespective of whether the comparison is appropriate or not.

The most common areas of focus for body dissatisfaction are chests (to be bigger), stomach, hips, thighs, bottoms and overall silhouette (all to be smaller) for women, while men fixate on arms, chests, shoulders (all to be bigger), stomachs and overall silhouette (to be smaller) [16]. Frequently, decisions on whether to initiate a diet are based on dissatisfaction with specific parts of the body and in particular those that they wish to be smaller. This fixation is itself problematic. The desire to alter a specific body part by engaging in a dieting, which is not specific, means that there is a mismatch between desired goal and behaviour. For example, if the objective of starting a diet is to lose weight off of a specific body area such as the stomach, the attempt to alter this through dieting will have an effect on all aspects of the dieter's body. Therefore, the dieter may be happy with the parts of their body that are socially desired to be larger but this is undermined by engaging in dieting behaviours as these areas will shrink alongside successful dieting. Moreover, the loss of weight from all over the body is likely to be proportional. Thus the area of dissatisfaction is not likely to shrink preferentially over any other areas. It is not until a lot of weight is lost that an alteration in the perceived area of dissatisfaction is likely to occur. Essentially, the weight-loss specific from one area goal is setting the dieter up to fail from the start.

Diet drug vendors tap into the body dissatisfaction of the potential consumers by making statements specific to particular regions rather than to weight in general. People who are dissatisfied with their bodies are usually fixated on one or two areas. Often they will want to lose weight specifically from these areas. Simple searches for "lose pounds of fat and" any, and I mean any, body part through any search or decision engine on the Internet will return hundreds of thousands of hits. On the day I did it for this book, the results to the nearest thousand hits were as follows:

- 1,830,000 for Stomach
- 813,000 for Thighs
- 1,480,000 for Bottom (average based on multiple names)
- 401,000 for Arms
- 1,290,000 for Face
- 552,000 for Feet

If we add in the word 'drug' into the search term the results are as follows:

- 753,000 for Stomach
- 275,000 for Thighs
- 894,000 for Bottom (average based on multiple names)
- 164,000 for Arms
- 482,000 for Face
- 255,000 for Feet

For the more Internet savvy among you, it may be suggested that this search does not account for specificity in the statement only that the website contained this information. If we refine the search strategy for specific quote "Lose fat from your ..." then we get the following:

- 40,100 for Stomach
- 20,300 for Thighs
- 10,300 for Bottom (average based on multiple names)
- 12,500 for Arms
- 15,700 for Face
- 1 for Feet

By no means is this a systematic review of the Internet sites, therefore, there may be cross posting between the various body parts. Unfortunately, it would take too long to trawl through every website looking for those that make specific statements about specific body part. Despite this, the number of hits very clearly suggests that making statements about their product that are based on people's dissatisfaction with a specific body part and thus what they want to hear appears to be common practice amongst Internet vendors of diet drugs. As far as I am aware, no pharmaceutical has ever made the claim that their drug or any drug has the ability to specifically aid in weight loss from a specific region of the body. Indeed, if they did make this statement they would be pursued by the trading standards agency to alter any such claim. Weight-loss, in terms of stored fat, does not preferentially come from a specific region in the body. When energy debt occurs and reliance on stored energy happens then the first 'port of call' is the glycogen stores around the liver. After this, it is drawn from all of the fat tissue in the body. Hormones are released in the body that act on all of the fat cells at the same time. Preference for specificity could only be argued for those areas closest to the bloodstream or if a drug was directly injected into the required region. Since none of the diet drugs currently available on the market are administered through injection, no such claims can be made. Indeed, to offer a drug by injection is explicitly prohibited under UK law unless the drug has received testing as a medicinal product. Although we will explore this in detail in the next chapter, very few of the 'drugs' available on the Internet are actually registered as medicinal products.

Dissatisfaction with one's body is not always as straight-forward as a person will report. The obvious assumption is that when a person reports they are dissatisfied with a specific body part, we believe that it is a dyadic relationship (i.e. I am dissatisfied with my nose, it is my nose that is making me dissatisfied). However, body dissatisfaction is influenced by other factors. Individuals with any one or a combination of the following are likely to report dissatisfaction with their bodies: low-self-esteem, depression, friends or peers who report also to be unhappy with their bodies [17]. It is beyond question that body dissatisfaction will lead to both poor self-esteem and emotional consequences; however, the findings that individuals report body dissatisfaction if their associates report not liking their own body adds a layer of complexity to the conundrum. This moves the concept of body dissatisfaction away from the internal personal cognitive domain and into the socio-cognitive arena. Effectively, the desire to start dieting may derive from dissatisfaction with one's appearance or body image, but this stems from a direct comparison with others. Social comparison is a little more complex than body dissatisfaction and we should spend some time delving into it a little, as it is likely to shed light on the strategies of how companies and individuals sell their diet drugs in future chapters. However, before we wonder into this area we should briefly deal with the tricky question of why women tend to diet more than men. To do this we need to turn to the feminists, as they are the originators of the study of body dissatisfaction.

Feminist Ideology

Feminist thinkers have had a long tradition of commentary within the area of body image. From the pinnacle of academic thought during the mid part of the last century, this perspective has fallen from grace and is now often, and wrongly, reserved for introductory, often anecdotal, interpretations of the subject. Many utter feminism in the same sentence as historical examples of subjugation of women. The link between feminism and various grievous popular fetishes such as Chinese foot binding, improbably small corsets or the current pandemic of aesthetic surgeries is pervasive. This link denigrates the field to the point it seems extremist. This is unfortunate and probably created by dissenters to the field latching on to the extremist views within it and perpetuating them as the normal representation of this subject in an attempt to undermine the feminist perspective. Although, the blame cannot be totally outward facing as a popular misrepresentation of a field is ultimately the responsibility of the field itself and its inability to cope under the burden of critical [mis]interpretation.

The reasons for the fall of feminism are complex and multifaceted. Perhaps it is because it did not move often enough beyond historical interpretations to labour its points. Or perhaps it is because its viewpoints were superseded and replaced by social psychological perspectives that were more comfortable with evidence-based positivism. Whatever the reason for its fall, it still remains important in explaining the pressures of women and why they diet more than men. The field also provides valuable insights into the gender inequality within dieting and the social pressures behind it beyond the simple body dissatisfaction perspective. Until such a time when inequality in the propensity to diet disappears there will always be an important role for feminist ideology in this field. In an interesting turn of events, teaching feminist thought to women has been shown to successfully improve body satisfaction, and defend them from media influences, but does not stop them from interpreting thin, specifically underweight individuals, as having the ideal body image [18].

Feminism offers insights into the advertising strategies of a lot of dieting companies, especially those who operate through virtual means. Where sex sells, the feminist follows close behind to point out the inequality in the advertising strategy. While the evolutionary theorist would explain this from a mate selection perspective, the feminist thinker will question the relative gender inequalities on how society stringently reinforces 'worthiness' to breed. Comparatively few criteria for aesthetic beauty are required for, or are specific to, men. This places undue pressure on women to achieve arguably unachievable specific body shape goals. Feminists place the blame for this on men's sexual desires and the need to keep women subservient.

Central to the feminist theme is the notion of a patriarchal society where social interactions are dominated by the needs of men. Women's needs are secondary, or may even be tertiary (after the children's). This would be a somewhat simplistic explanation of a rather complex philosophical school of thought. There are many branches of feminism that place emphasis on different aspects of society that encourage gender inequality. Objects of blame from the various feminist groups range from classist, capitalist and institutional viewpoints. Indeed, internal conflict between the various branches of feminism may have inadvertently weakened this philosophical approach and allowed critics to circle pitting one group against another to define which component is more or less important. In short, it objectified and attempted to quantify the relative merits of a field that never claimed to have roots in positivism. Whatever the reason, feminism descended into a period of identity crisis from which it is only now starting to recover.

Many modern commentators claim that feminism has now emerged from its identity crisis. However, the research on the topic from a body image perspective has focused almost entirely on self-identification of the 'feminist'. The interpretation has turned from the commentary on society to the effect that adhering to the feminist perspective has on the individual in terms of how they view their body and that of others. This regression to simplistic representations of feminism actively disengages from the intricacies of the field. In terms of the view of the female body – which is what we are interested here – feminism would appear to be liberalism rather than explicitly feminist ideals. This relates specifically to the representation of this perspective found in body image research rather than its theoretical commentary, which continues to be rich and detailed.

Feminists would argue that the perceived need to diet is a layer of control placed on the woman. The incongruent body image ideal is created to focus women's energy on achieving the best possible male partner based on biological determinants. It creates impossibly difficult criteria for women to follow focusing on their biological function of having children and caring for them. This actively prohibits women from focusing on societal inequality keeping them under the control of their 'chosen' partners. Thus, the thin ideal is created by men to control women. Research evidence would indicate that this is not the case, as it is women who are perpetuating the thin ideal and not men. This somewhat undermines the utility of this perspective. However, if we consider how diets are sold rather than the underlining motivation for dieting itself, then it comes back into the ascendancy. Throughout the advertising literature, the diet is sold on the grounds of sexual attraction. "Take this and get your beach/bikini/holiday body" brings back the objectification of women for the purposes of sex based on the desires of men. The implicit message is "take this and feel comfortable walking around in mixed company with little on and be desired by the men around you and envied by women in the same environment". All companies are guilty of over using this message to sell their products. It is an implicit component to the sex sells strategy. Sex may sell to men, but it does not to women. For women, it is not that sex sells, it is an individual's insecurity and the need for confidence in their appearance in mixed company, that they are purported to gain from the product, which sells. The pervasive 'made up' shot in the dieting industry is a derivative of this perspective. It never ceases to amaze that people can be bought in with a picture of a person poorly lit, in drab clothes, before intervention compared to a picture after weight-loss, often scantily dressed, taken by a photographer, and wearing cosmetics applied by a professional.

The feminist ideology, if not chronologically, certainly in detail, preceded many other attempts to explain social representations of the human form and the surreptitious attempts to control it. Following analysis from the feminist school, many other approaches attempted to engage with this area. Two such schools were the social psychological and socio-cognitive approaches. It is important to remember that many concepts within these approaches stem from feminist observations. Instead, the replacement of specific feminist terms into more testable components was offered to explain how we judge ourselves and each other in a social environment. However, the roots of feminism are still available within the literature even now. It would appear that dieting for aesthetic reasons is very much the remit of women, so much so that very little research is performed on men. Therefore, the approach that is often adopted and advocated by commentators is that dieting for body image purposes is not important to men. This would be an assumption, as little actual data has been collected from men on the subject. What little is known about men suggests that they are dissatisfied with their bodies too; albeit to a lesser degree. Feminism currently stands resplendent in its explanations because the overwhelming bias in the specificity of research on women. It will remain a credible explanation of dieting behaviour until data on men is published. Only then can we fully understand the unique pressures and the derivation of how and why they exist that are specific to each sex. Researchers are currently rectifying this gender bias in the literature.

Feminist ideological viewpoints are reinforced on the Internet through appealing to people's desire to be attractive to the opposite sex, or more specifically men. Several thousand websites are dedicated to this subject. Some advocate never losing weight to attract men, while others suggest it is necessary. Some websites even suggest that taking diet pills is necessary, while others get flagged up because they sell both diet pills and alleged human pheromones to attract the opposite sex. To further reiterate the stance of the feminist thinkers, the statement "lose weight to attract men" returned one hundred and fifty one hits while "lose weight to attract women" had only ten. Of those ten, four were simply "cut and paste content" websites. "Cut and paste content" websites are those where the designer finds a site that has high traffic (people viewing it) and copies its content word for word. Although this violates copyright laws, on the Internet this rarely matters. Unless the originator spent time hunting these people down and threatening them with legal action, they will get away with violating the intellectual copyright of the creator of the stolen site. This is yet another reason (like the ability to make unfounded claims) that suggests the Internet does not seem to need to follow the same laws as everyone else. In addition, search terms for lose weight to get a bikini/swimsuit/beech/summer body with diet pills will return somewhere in the region of a quarter of a million hits. Swimming trunks/Speedo terms receive only about fifteen thousand hits.

Social Comparison

We all compare ourselves to one another. In contrast to Dr Martin Luther-King's desires, we do not define ourselves by the content of our character; instead, we do it by how we positively differ, in character, visual appearance or adherence to social ideals, from others around us. We do not view the specific positives in ourselves rather we draw self-esteem from what we do better than others around us within our immediate group. This in its broadest sense is social comparison.

We all constantly make snap judgments about others based on very limited information. In social situations where we meet people for the first time we judge someone's 'worthiness' for interaction based mostly on their appearance. Evolutionary theorists would suggest that this is based on some kind of competition for social popularity to ensure that an individual's genes are passed on to the next generation. In effect, the judgment about others is based on whether they are worth breeding with, are significant competition for potential mates or can help us in acquiring a stronger mate.

Social psychologists and in particular those that adhere to social comparison theory have a less individualistic interpretation of this judgment. Instead of basing their argument on biological pragmatism they propose that these judgments are based on a desire to please others and ingratiate themselves into their group. Humans are social animals and require other like-minded people around them to seek solace from a sometimes hostile social environment. It is impossible for someone to define themselves either positively or negatively without a yardstick in which to measure it. This yardstick is their group. People do not compare themselves to the social average.

However, judgments about others are based on social norms and cognitions. Currently, society dictates that being larger is less worthy than being thin. Many authors, especially those who research body image, point a finger of blame for popularising the thin ideal – size zero models – towards the media and lifestyle-based, perfume and high end fashion clothing companies. The constant bombardment of thin ideal images has led to people who are larger being discriminated against. This has not always been the case. Social comparison is a transient process. Subtle changes in social norms are difficult to observe if measured over short periods of time. However, if measured over a period of decades, the norms become much more obvious. If measured from prehistory then the social body image-related ideal to strive for has moved from obese, to overweight, to slim, to arguably disordered.

The first object from prehistory that can be used to infer social ideal for weight status and body image is the Venus of Willendorf. Reported to date from around 22,000 BCE the figurine suggests that the social ideal for a woman during this period was to be obese. The prevalence of obesity within hunter-gather communities is very low. Therefore, this may indicate that our ancestors worshiped a much larger female form than we do today, but share a similar desire for a mate that is incongruent to the possible norm. Today, people are much larger and the prevalence for overweight and obesity is so high it is almost the archetypal form. In contrast to this norm, the social ideal is for thinness. The Venus of Willendorf shares similar incongruence to social norms, albeit in the opposite weight status direction to today. Furthermore, several similar figurines have been found throughout Europe suggesting a shared social ideal for obese women within a large geographical area[2]. By the time of the Greek civilisation, the ideal body image had slimmed right down to a more chiseled (if you pardon the pun) look. The female ideal form as portrayed in Greek art, was slim, but not overly so. This image remained fairly similar right up and past the Renaissance period and

---

[2] Venuses of Brassempouy (France), Dolní Vestonice (Czech Republic), Savignano (Italy), Lespugue (France) and the Russian limestone Venus of Kostenki.

beyond[3]. Relatively recently, the female ideal has become much less attainable. Current societal preference for the female form is for thinness. It would appear that this thin ideal is reinforced by social norms, female peer groups and male sexual desires indicating that body image requirements are multifaceted beyond simple male patriarchal enforcement[4]. Male ideal has changed little since prehistory compared to the social ideal for the female form. Fewer examples of carvings of the male form are found during the same period of the Venus of Willendorf. Those that are available portray an image of leanness. Over time, the inferred social ideal based on artistic portrayals of the male form indicated that a more muscular frame was desirable. The social ideal required muscle mass for males has remained relatively stable; however, it has increased marginally over the intervening centuries[5].

It would appear that through art, our ancestors have offered insights into what they believed should be the ideal body form. Based on the limited information inferred through art, this social ideal is transient. Every body image from obese to overly lean has been offered as the social ideal. Apart from the intervening period between prehistory and modern society, the ideal has been arguably achievable for many people in the population; although it could be argued that during the times of antiquity famine was endemic and so achieving the ideal may not have been possible for everyone. The obvious explanation is that the social ideal is the image held as sexually desirable and thus a preference for mate selection. However, this would not explain why the ideal of the female form, reinforced by females, differs significantly from the form desired by males. If anything, it could be argued that female aspirations actively undermine their mate selection potential. Therefore, the social ideal body should be considered as a social rather than sexual indicator.

Social attributes for success are linked to the weight status of an individual based on the socially desired ideal form. It could be argued that portraying, or attempting to portray, the socially ideal form means that the individual is attempting to link themselves to the positive attributes held by society in order to achieve social success through social standing. The portrayal of the appropriate image is a communicative act to others and is an immediate physical visual marker of success. The communication meant through this image is that the individual is successful and that others should associate themselves with them, leading to social success for the individual. This may go some way to explaining the incongruence between the 'norm' and the social ideal. By making the social ideal hard to achieve, means that only few who really are socially successful can achieve it. In this social domain,

---

[3] For example, Botticelli's Birth of Venus, Titian's Venus with an Organist and a Dog, Brocky's Cupid and Psyche. Then at some point in the twentieth century society started to view thin and thinner as the ideal body form for women. Concomitantly actresses became thinner and thinner. It is important not to suggest that film and art caused the thin ideal. Artists simply reflect their surroundings and so when portraying attractiveness they offer societal perspectives entwined with their own beliefs. Society accepts/rejects the artist's interpretation and perpetuates it further holding up as the ideal. Society is to blame not the 'scapegoat(s)' individual.

[4] Citations in not 14 plus: Dittmar, H., Halliwell, E. 7 Ive, S. (2006). Does Barbie make girls want to be thin? The effect of experimental exposure to images of dolls on the body image of 5- to 8-year-old girls. *Developmental Psychology, 42,* 283-292. Legenbeuer, T., Vocks, S., Schäfer, C., Schutt-Stromel, S., Hiller, W., Wagner, C. & Vogele, C. (2009). Preference for attractiveness and thinness in a partner: influence of internalization of the thin ideal and shape/weight dissatisfaction in heterosexual women, heterosexual men, lesbians, and gay men. *Body Image, 6,* 228-234. Rozin, P. & Fallon, A. (1988). Body image, attitudes to weight, and misperceptions of figure preferences of the opposite sex: a comparison of men and women in two generations. *Journal of Abnormal Psychology, 97,* 342-345. Stice, E. (1994). Review of the evidence for a sociocultural model of bulimia nervosa and an exploration of the mechanisms of action. *Clinical Psychology Review, 14,* 633-661.

[5] For Example: Artemision Zeus (bronze statue from 460 BCE), Michelangelo's David, and the action heroes of the late twentieth century.

achieving a weight status that opposes the social norm reinforces the markers of social success despite them undermining genetic success by being different to the mate selection criteria of the opposite sex. For example, to achieve a low weight for females in an obesogenic environment will require a concerted and constant effort. The person would have to have finite control of their eating behaviour and their nutrition. Furthermore, they are likely to have to exercise frequently. Having access to highly nutritious foods, have the time to prepare them and exercise to a standard to portray to social ideal body image requires consumable resources (money) to designate to them. To achieve this, it is necessary to have spare resources beyond the amount needed to thrive in the current environment. Therefore, by creating a social ideal that is incongruent to the environment allows the opportunity to portray a visual marker for success through body image. The same process could be attributed to males who require large muscle bulk or the Venus of Willendorf type female image in a society that has comparatively scarce food resources.

Gender appears to be an important component to social comparison and in particular the strength of the judgment inferred from food items consumed. It will come as little surprise when you read that females are judged much more on their eating behaviour than males [19]. Due to this gender semi-specificity it is possible to imply that dieting, as an attempt to control social opinions, is more important to females rather than males.

The theoretical combination between body image and social ideal is known as impression management. If an individual portrays a good social ideal image then others may attempt to ingratiate themselves to them by copying their behaviour. This is known as behavioural modeling. In the next two subsections we will consider these concepts a little more. In the context of dieting and the use of diet drugs, the overarching consideration for the need to consider these two components is that the drive to start dieting may stem from a desire to achieve a better social standing (impression management). Alternatively, dieting behaviours may manifest within an individual as a result of their parents or peer group starting to engage in dieting behaviours. In effect, it is a process of 'copy-cat' like behaviours within a social group that leads to dieting (modeling).

Impression Management

Impression management is not only related to body image and the portrayal of a social ideal. It extends to any behaviour that a person uses to portray a positive image to others. This aspect is important to acknowledge because without the intention to portray the positive image to another person it would not be possible to consider behaviours that the person does not usually or habitually express. Therefore, the attempts to portray the social ideal in terms of body image consider dieting in a wider context. This would include more drastic solutions of surgery – both gastric and plastic.

The attempt to portray or maintain a specific impression has several components to it that need to be considered in the context of dieting and dieting behaviours. The portrayal of an impression to another person is simply to condense everything a person wishes to portray into the smallest, simplest, and most straight-forward way possible to manipulate another person's opinion in either a positive or negative fashion. This impression may be true, false or partially true. In the context of human interaction, the impression is likely to be the partial truth offering only the positive attributes; rather than offering a more rounded view of the individual. In order to achieve the desired effect, there must be a shared and accepted list of what is and is not acceptable characteristics, as well as how these attributes and comparative behaviours are expressed. Based on these premises, the impression must have a goal (to control others' judgments about the individual), target (someone to form an opinion about the individual), socially determined marker (a set of rules for impressions), and a system of judgment (determinants of success of controlling impression formation).

In a social environment the determinants of the social impression that are specific to dieting are based on the selection of food and the social view of the food itself. The 'attribute' or 'grouping' of the food, by selection, can be transferred to those that select them. Society has dictated the relative merits of different foods and by preferentially selecting them in a social situation means that the selector is attempting to show to other people that they have that particular attribute. Therefore, food selection extends from simply choosing foods that are palatable and appropriate to hunger levels to become a more complex communicative act. In our society, at this moment in time, dieting and the selection of foods with a low energy value is considered to be 'good[6]'. By selecting these 'good' foods the social attributes of the food are transferred to the individual. Therefore, the selection of 'good' food by the selector condenses to form the social judgment of 'good person'. Food selection is however, not the only way to manage impression.

Another way to manage impression is through quantity selection. Eating ever decreasing amounts is associated with 'good' feminine social ideal, which reinforces the thin ideal [20]. It is not currently known at what point eating ever decreasing amounts of foods cease becoming an ideal and spill over into pathology. There is of course a biological weight status criterion to define this – a BMI ≤ 15 – but no portion size association with it. It is likely that this is an individually determined marker, but it is not possible to offer definitive explanations at this time. If we assume that portion size impression management strategies are individually determined then it may be possible to suggest that, for some people, dieting is in fact the normal state. Such individuals would be considered highly restrained when it comes to food choice. In the field of psychology such people are defined as being restrained eaters. We shall come to this later in the chapter. It will suffice to state at this time that the incorporation of the social cognition of restraint can become ingrained into the individual to such a degree that it becomes more-or-less a component of their personality.

Before we move on to another component to social comparison, it is important that we consider one finial component to impression management. This final part is that the behaviour expressed in terms of food restriction or dieting to portray a positive image is context specific [21]. The communicative act of impression management through food selection or quantity restriction is considered as a social ideal for women. Mixed-sex environments where portraying a feminine ideal is not favourable, then the use of food restriction would not be seen as positive and would not be as frequently observed. The fact that food restriction can be so easily manipulated by social context brings credence to the concept that, at least for women, dieting and the motivation to do so is ingrained, or at least socially indoctrinated, at a

---

[6] Usually determined by its fat content with lower fat levels being considered good foods; however, this is slowly changing as the general population becomes increasingly aware of what constitutes a healthy diet. For those interested on referred judgements between the selection of food versus social positive/negative attribute of the individual see the following: Barker, M.E., Tandy, M. & Stookey, J.D. (1999). How are consumers of low-fat and high-fat diets perceived by those with lower and higher fat intake? *Appetite, 33,* 309–317. Mooney, K. M. & Amico, T. (2000). Food scrutiny: We are all watching what you eat. Poster session presented at the annual meeting of the American Psychological Society, Miami Beach, Florida. Stein, R.I. & Nemeroff, C.J. (1995). Moral overtones of food: judgements of other based on what they eat. *Personality & Social Psychology Bulletin, 21,* 480-490.

very young age. From this perspective, dieting should be seen on the continuum of normality where the frequency of dieting behaviours is proportional to body dissatisfaction derived from the individual's perception of themselves measured against the yardstick of social comparison.

The consumption of food is more than simply putting hand to mouth in the body dissatisfaction/social comparison explanation of the world. Impression management is not devoid of social manipulation just like any other component thus far discussed. To manage other people's impressions of us through selecting specific foods, it is also possible to ingratiate ourselves through other means. The old adage that "imitation is the highest form of flattery" is the lay explanation of this phenomenon. Psychologists call it modeling behaviour.

Modeling

Friendship groups have been shown to manipulate body dissatisfaction. One way this is potentially achieved is through consistent modeling. Each member of the group models other members within it to improve, or maintain, social acceptance, status or a positive impression of themselves [22]. After several replications of the behaviour over an extended period of time, the behaviour becomes habitual. It quite literally becomes a behaviour that is performed without thought.

Humans are social animals and require approval from significant others. In a situation where people meet for the first time, they will attempt to endear themselves to others through copying their behaviour. This extends into the realm of eating and food selection too. People will literally copy another person's eating behaviour both in quantity and selection [23]. There are some caveats to this phenomenon. The person must be a suitable model. Women will emulate other women and men other men in terms of the quantity of food consumed. It is unlikely that mixed sex modeling will occur. Children rely less on the sex of the model. Instead, children will model any individual as long as they are familiar with them. They are less likely to emulate strangers compared to parents, siblings, friends and known cartoon characters. Furthermore, there may also be a competitive element to it. Women in laboratory studies have been shown to competitively under-eat against someone they are trying to model if they perceive them to be close to the thin ideal. Therefore, modeling eating behaviour in women is based on maintaining the social ideal. This is further reinforced by the findings that women will not model another woman who does not adhere to the social ideal. Therefore, if a woman eats large portions, other women will not consider them a suitable model and will not attempt to copy them[7].

Social comparison statements to help sell diet drugs concern making the whole process look easy. Statements like "lose X amount of weight in X amount of days is easy on X drug" are examples of these. They want to make out that their drug is a fail safe way to lose weight.

---

[7] Other factors important to modelling is the sex of the person to be modelled, the suitability of the person to be modelled, the connectedness between the model and the participant, the slimness of the model and the relationship/appropriateness of the behaviour to the body image of the model (i.e. if thin and they overeat, they will not be emulated). Conger, J. C., Conger, A. J., Costanzo, P. R., Wright, K. L. & Matter, L. A. (1980). The effect of social cues on the eating behaviour of obese and normal subjects. *Journal of Personality, 48,* 258-271. Hermans, R. C. J., Larsen, J. K., Herman, C. P. & Engels, R. C. M. E. (2008). Modeling of palatable food intake in female young adults: effects of perceived body size. *Appetite, 51,* 512-518. Salvy, S-J., Jarrin, D., Paluch, R., Irfan, N. & Pliner, P. (2007). Effects of social influence on eating in couples, friends and strangers. *Appetite, 49,* 92-99. Salvy, S-J., Vartanian, L. R., Coelho, J. S., Jarrin, D. & Pliner, P. P. (2008). The role of familiarity on modeling of eating and food consumption in children. *Appetite, 50,* 514-518.

By making it look easy, they are attempting to "let you into their secret" it is an attempt to make the buyer believe that everyone is taking this drug and that is why they are thin. The specific additional components to social comparison (inclusive of modeling and impression management) are also pervasive. Modeling components to the diet drug vendors repertoire commonly include the dreaded "before and after" picture. This is where the advert shows a random person complete with a random quote about how they lost an exorbitant amount of weight while using this product. Usually the statement will also include reference to the fact that they only took this product and nothing else was required. Irrespective if it is true or not (I am sure I am not the only one that thinks this 'evidence' as dubious at best), this makes it seem easy and that everyone need only emulate the person in the advert to lose weight.

Another component to modeling is the celebrity endorsement or 'reported' use of the drug in question. So many celebrities have been linked with various drugs that I am sure they do not endorse or even necessarily know about. In the same way as academics get quoted on such sites for the efficacy of a diet drug, celebrities are used as social comparison or aspiration models to take the drug. The sell goes a little something like "look at how hot X person is, their secret to a hot body is X drug, buy X drug at the exclusive cut down price of...". Impression management is often used by diet drug vendors through the reinforcing of stereotypes. Such statements as depressed, unhappy, unemployed etc... because you are fat are frequently encountered on the Internet. Often vendors will link the drug directly to improving this outlook. However, most of the time this is through a proximity statement such as "lose weight through this drug and x symptom will disappear".

This brief foray into the social perspectives of dieting provides an interesting insight into the normalisation of dieting. We will return to this at the end of the current chapter, however, the information offered here should be enough to provide an explanation into the reason why some people start dieting. In particular, research into the social perspective suggests that there is a gender bias in dieting behaviour in favour of an increased ratio of women compared to men within the wider population. Portraying a social ideal body image would appear to be less important to men. Adhering to this perspective alone would discount all of half of the potential market for diet drugs. Therefore, other perspectives must explain why men, albeit a smaller comparative percentage of them, also diet.

Health-Related

Health-related messages concerning nutrition are everywhere. Companies are constantly telling us that their products are 'healthy' or 'healthier' and governments across the globe are spending some of their budget on health education programmes for instilling better balanced diets in their population. Instead of simply adding to the constant noise of guidance to improve diets and why we should do so, I will keep this section brief. Health related motivations to start dieting come mainly from the medical profession. Periodic health checks or acute episodes of illness often lead to advice to lose some excess weight for those in the overweight or obese category. Alternatively, the manifestation of a chronic problem such as non-communicable diseases associated with excess weight (fertility problems, metabolic syndrome, type II diabetes, cardiovascular disease, respiratory dysfunction, liver cirrhosis and cancer[8]) may also provide the initial impetus to lose weight. Those individuals given the ultimatum of diet or suffer the consequences account for a different group of people compared to the body dissatisfaction group. These people have biological motivations to lose weight compared to the previous social determined group who have more psychosocial-related motivations.

Differences between those motivated by, or started their diet because of, social comparison or health-related problems differ by whether they personally decided to diet or whether they were told they need to. This has the potential to create qualitative differences between these two groups. Arguably, those that have been told to diet rather than have freely come to the conclusion that they 'need' to do so should have differing levels of success. All dieters will have felt the effects of not meeting the social ideal and have received similar social motivations to lose weight. Individuals who have a health-related motivation to lose weight are going to be overweight or obese as measured by their BMI; while those who diet because of body dissatisfaction are less likely to have achieved a higher than acceptable weight status. Therefore, the difference between these two groups is based on their sensitivity to perceived social pressure to attain the thin ideal. Individuals who start dieting only after they have been told they need to lose weight are arguably less motivated by the societal ideal or have not internalised 'ideal' body image. An alternative argument could be offered to the same observation through suggesting that those told to lose weight find it harder to stay on a successful diet. To find relative importance in these different interpretations, one could simply ask whether the person has a history of dieting. The answer may provide yet another gender divide, with males being less sensitive to social ideals (mainly because few of these ideals refer specifically to men and thus are not necessary for them to adhere to) and therefore do not diet while females have a history of unsuccessful dieting. This gender divide may be a rather simplistic explanation of the motivations though as it would appear within the data that progressively more males are dieting to lose weight [24].

Consequential psychological repercussions, or more accurately termed associates, between health-related and body dissatisfaction indicates little differences between the two groups beyond their current weight status. Amongst overweight people the prevalence of dieting is about 3 times higher in males compared to only 0.5 times higher in females. This disparity is due to the fact that around half of healthy weight women report dieting. This gender split adds some credence to the supposition that males are less likely to diet until told to do so or they reach a higher BMI. Beyond actually starting to diet, similar comparative associates between body dissatisfaction and health-related dieting are observed. Both report higher levels of depression and lower levels of self-esteem. These characteristics are likely to stem from the systemic discrimination that overweight and obese people suffer within society.

Healthy-related components to the diet drug vendors' statements are not as well used as perhaps the other approaches outlined above, but they are still prevalent. The reason for fewer examples of using this tactic is due to the potential buyer's responsiveness to health-related information. People always assume that the worst will not happen to them. Therefore the efficacy of this strategy is weaker and thus not used as often. The second reason this health-related approach is in the minority is because it is not the primary reason for attempting to lose weight for the majority of people. Therefore, to target this will inevitably miss the largest target audience.

---

[8] Same as note 10.

Despite its minority appearance, health-related advertising strategies are still available in the advertising material. The important components to this approach are to normalise extreme symptoms complete with some statement from some unknown person saying that it will happen rather than might happen. Associated factors with excessive weight become determinants. What might happen becomes certain to happen. The vast majority of consequences of obesity have only been measured as associates. This does not mean that they will happen only that they are more likely to happen. The whole point to using this strategy is scaremongering. It is an attempt to draw the person into buying the product as a quick way to avoid the possible consequences of having excess weight. It is the old scare and save tactic. This approach has been around since time immemorial and is still used today to sell diet pills.

Evolutionary

If we are to believe the representations of the human form in art, then the evolutionary perspective is somewhat undermined. The fact that throughout recent history the objectification of the human form has changed significantly from one extreme to another undermines the genetic determination of attractiveness and the desire to attain the best possible mate. This is because our genes have not changed proportionally to the social ideals. It would appear that the weight status components to the 'attractiveness equation' are determined by social rather than biological perspectives. There are of course other facets to attractiveness, but the one we are interested in appears to show too much variability to be predetermined.

Weight status attractiveness may not be biologically determined, but our evolutionary heritage provides a different perspective to view the relative success of dieting and how it is both integral and problematic to our current environmental predicament. It is somewhat obvious to state that our ancestors survived and thrived in a very different environment than we find ourselves in today. From this evolutionary perspective, dieting becomes normal rather than abnormal. While other perspectives suggest that dieting is reactionary to our current social demands, evolutionary theorists allow us to consider how dieting can become so ingrained that it could almost be considered a personality characteristic.

The behavioural phenotypes we have inherited from our forebears find themselves redundant in a modern environment filled with easily obtained calories. The hunter-gatherer and early subsistence farming lifestyle does not provide an infinite larder of calories to draw from. In contrast, modern farming practices have allowed us to create vast surpluses of food, which means that the relative price for a calorie has dropped inordinately. Society and social demands has progressed faster than evolution.

For our forebears dieting was normal. That is to say that normal eating was similar to dieting today. In the past where food was a scarce commodity, humans were forced to eat less than they would have liked to from time to time. In order to make food stretch further due to unpredictable food resources meant that obtained food had to be made to last as long as possible. Cognitive restriction of appetite was an evolutionary desirable characteristic to have, as gorging would mean that the people would not have confidence in their food reserves and would have had to search for it more often. Modern dieting to the evolutionary scientist is literally the use of a beneficial behavioural strategy to conserve resources during unpredictable food availability for use in an environment with too much food. This advantageous behavioural phenotype has been high-jacked for use to adhere to an overly complex socially derived criterion about body image. This criterion would quickly cease to exist if we found ourselves in times of food scarcity. Indeed, we would probably revert back to considering obesity as the ideal body image, at least for women.

Evolutionary perspectives also allow us to consider that dieting is doomed to fail. While other perspectives suggest that the presence of social pressures to conform to a perfect human form will lead to dieting, it almost implicitly assumes that this will be successful. This is not true. Dieting predicts weight gain not weight loss [25]. The evolution of the behavioural phenotype was based on a different purpose than it is used for today. While our ancestors employed dieting behaviours to make food last longer, we are using the same behaviour to deny ourselves food. By eating fewer calories than our short-term biological demands will naturally result in a hyper-awareness of food in our environment and an increased desire to acquire and consume it. We will quite literally become fixated with gathering and eating food. This is an inverse relationship. The more we restrict, the more fixated with food we become, and the more internal resources are required to restrict from eating it. Eventually, this obsession will result in the failure to restrict and gorging on food. For our ancestors, this was seasonal living. In the winter months of temperate environments in Northern/Southern hemispheres or the dry seasons in Equatorial regions meant fewer resources and times of calorie hardship. Times of restriction immediately preceded times of plenty. They could, subsequent to the period of restriction, consume calories without having to worry about conserving resources. Thus the beneficial behavioural phenotype for our forebears does not help us diet. It may allows to do so, but it will likely end in over-consuming to compensate for the period of restriction/starvation and undermine our intentions.

Based on the evolutionary perspective new components to dieting behaviour are uncovered. While other perspectives do not engage with the failure of dieting – choosing instead to focus on pressure to engage in the behaviour – evolutionary theory does. Caution must be read within the evolutionary perspective though. The strength of the evolutionary perspective is in its logic based arguments. The argument goes a little something like "We reached this point in time based on the success of our ancestors. We have inherited these successful characteristics from our ancestors. Any failure in our abilities to perform a specific task must be because of something new and unique to our situation that our ancestors never encountered and thus did not have a characteristic to pass on". Some assumptions are made within the evolutionary model that needs to be considered before accepting its logic. Firstly, it suggests pre-determinism. Proponents of the evolutionary perspective indicate that everything is a result of genes. The word 'phenotypic' for example is a word specifically created to explain heritability of everything from appearance to behaviour. Secondly, it makes the assumption that success in an environment is population determined and failure is more individually determined. What is meant here is that those individuals with the appropriate genes will survive and those who do not will fail and die without passing on their genes to the next generation. This suggests that the propensity to diet is genetically determined and as no gene for dieting behaviour has been identified then the genetic marker of this behavioural phenotype cannot be validated. Until such time as a genetic marker is identified, this entire approach is based on supposition. In light of these assumptions, one must be careful to identify dieting as genetically pre-determined. To suggest this would also suggest that some people are better at dieting than others. This undermines people's thoughts about trying to lose weight creating the belief of failure prior to the actual attempt.

The five explanations of why we diet, body dissatisfaction, feminist ideology, social comparison, health-related and evolutionary consider why people diet. However, these perspectives do not show how people diet. Restricting one's food intake is not an easy process. In fact dieting is so hard that those who are successful at it suggest that it has encompassed most of their attentional resources. Successful dieters do not actually diet; they are simply so fixated on controlling their weight status that they develop complex thought processes to help them maintain their weight. For these people, dieting and eating is one and the same thing. These people are known amongst eating behaviourists as restrained eaters. Even amongst restrained eaters, there is more than one type. Some are successful, but most are not. Within the literature, it is now well recognised that restrained eating predicts weight gain not weight loss in the same way as dieting does. In the next section, we will consider how dieting becomes normalised for some people.

DIETING BECOMES NORMAL – FOR SOME?

For some people, often female, the pressure to achieve a desired body image or fear of becoming fat causes changes in the way they view food and eating. They become hyper-aware of the calorie content of food and will selected foods deemed to be 'healthy' or 'good' foods. For these people, 'healthy' or 'good' food refers to those that are low in calories or fat content. Many would associate this behaviour with those who have eating disorders, but this is not always the case. Those considered restrained eaters exhibit similar behaviours in terms of calorie restriction to those with eating disorders, they just will not do it to the same magnitude and will not have all of the other problematic behaviours associated with eating disorders. The criteria of acceptable foods become increasingly narrow and the standards regarding both type and quantity of food eaten will be almost unachievable.

Although this may be the remit of some women, this is the same behaviour expected of all people trying to lose weight. It is also the same behaviour observed within the evolutionary perspective. Those people losing weight will often set unachievable goals/expectations of consistent weight-loss over time and any deviation from this narrow rule set would be considered failure. Due to the similarities between restrained eaters and dieters they have become almost interchangeable within the literature. However, there are subtle differences that should be acknowledged. The concept of restrained eating grew out of the research on dieters. Retrained eaters are not 'dieting' to lose weight like most dieters would be; rather they are 'dieting' to maintain their current weight status or body image.

One way to compare these two groups is to explore how they control their food intake. Both groups impose cognitive rules (thought processes) on how much and what they should eat. Instead of using their biological controls of how much and when to eat, such as hunger and fullness, they use psychological controls [26]. They think about how much they should eat rather than how much they want to eat. In the case of those who are eating disordered, they take this further to ignoring how much they should eat. By not eating to fullness at each meal, both restrained eaters and dieters find themselves in a state of slight energy debt. For the dieter, this leads to using up fat tissue to supplement the disparity between what is eaten in terms of energy value and how much they need to survive. Restrained eaters can fall into a state of energy debt and, like the evolutionary perspective suggests, will become fixated on obtaining and consuming food. For this reason, both restrained eating and dieting predict over- not under-consumption. Successful restrained eaters, and there are not that many when measured over a long period of time, have two components to their behaviour that differs to unsuccessful dieters and restrainers. This successful group will 1) match their energy demands to their energy output much better and 2) will be flexible about their rules around food.

The accurate matching of energy input with output staves off the high levels of hunger and limits hyper-vigilance towards food and its cues. Stopping the hyper-vigilance stops the negative effects of being a restrained eater and ensures that the individual meets their desired body weight maintenance goals. The other component to successful restrainers – flexibility – is also important. Instead of viewing their psychologically-derived control of eating as all-or-nothing, all-encompassing, must-be-adhered-to, self-defining, set of rules, they see them as general guidance. They do not fixate on their rules over a short-term but do in the medium- to long-term. This aids in their ability to maintain their weight as lapses are not viewed as failures. For the more rigid adherents to the restrained rules or dieters, lapses are viewed as failure and a sort of 'what-the-hell' effect ensues. This effect means that a minor short-term lapse leads to the loss of cognitive restraint on food intake and a correction back to energy demands plus a little more. They will basically eat without thinking about their rules. Because they are in a slight energy deficit they will eat beyond what they currently require. They will over-eat. Anymore than a few lapses and the amount of calories consumed in the medium-term is higher than what would have been consumed without such harsh restriction rules. This in turn leads to weight-gain not weight-loss and perceived failure. This can then further compound future attempts at 'dieting' and the inevitable wait for the lapse to occur and weight-gain to follow [27].

Due to the amount of attention the dieter and restrained eater places on eating, any form of distraction can lead to them violating their rules and, compared to their normal mealtimes, over-eating. Any form of task that diverts their attention away from food will undermine their control. There are a variety of tasks that have been devised to do this. For the really interested reader, there is a book out by one of the primary researchers who has devoted his life to doing this [28]. In effect, a lot of psychological control is required if someone wants to undermine their hunger cues. If the body requires energy, it will constantly tell the person's brain that it does, so equally constant psychological controls are required to maintain abstinence. In a world full of food and its cues this is a difficult, nigh on impossible, task.

Another way that restrainers and dieters differ from one another is through a thought process associated with not eating. Restrainers and dieters may differ in their motivations to maintain or lose weight, but they also do in terms of 'fear of fat'. As mentioned earlier in the chapter, overweight and obese people suffer discrimination and arguably those who a restrained are aware of this discrimination and fear both it and the associated body image. Recent research has indicated that this fear is associated with restrained eaters and is the primary reason for their frequency of restriction and dieting behaviour [29]. Those that are dieting are doing so for additional reasons, some of which may be health-related or social comparison-related. Interestingly however, restrained eaters suffer from similar psychological problems as overweight and obese individuals. Like obese individuals, restrained eaters are likely to be depressed and have lower self-esteem; however, they are also more likely to be less emotionally stable, worried about their body image and easily distracted [30]. Each of these behaviours can be linked to being in negative energy balance (i.e. having less energy coming into the system as going out of it) or failure to adhere to their rules around eating.

With the culmination of dieting being normal eating behaviour for some people comes the end to our brief whistle stop tour of why people diet. For most it is motivated by social factors such as body dissatisfaction, the need for adoration from the opposite sex, unfavourable perceived social comparison to immediate others or problems with their health brought about by carrying excess weight. We have also seen that the whole process of dieting is probably doomed to fail due to its reliance on an evolutionary behavioural phenotype designed to over-consume after periods of restriction.

Within this chapter we have explored why people start dieting and what their motivations to diet are. This leads seamlessly into how diet drug vendors use these motivations to sell their wares to people. Irrespective of what the manufacturer says about their drug, those that sell it will invariably say anything to match their product with the buyers' motivations. Some will make supposedly cast iron guarantees that the product will work or you can claim your money back. However we must ask how can something guarantee to work without first knowing all of the individual's circumstances?

This opens up another interesting arena to explore. How do diet drugs come to be? What are the criteria to become a diet drug? What safeguards does one have to overcome before marketing a product as a weight-loss drug? The answer is very little depending on what route is taken. In the next chapter, we will explore this legislation. Most of the drugs available on the market simply circumvent these rules to take a path of least resistance. Of course diet drugs are medicines right? Wrong.

Chapter 2

OF LAW

If we developed a product and wish to register it as a weight-loss product we would have to study the current legislation within the country in question. Within this chapter, we will explore what is required to meet the legal demands to register a substance as a weight-loss product and to legally make the claim that the product results in weight loss. This is actually quite stringent. What is being sold in vast numbers does not meet the legal criteria we are about to discuss. Instead, loopholes are used to get the product to market. Products can be registered in one of four ways. These are: register as a medicine; register as herbal remedy; register as a homeopathic remedy; and register as a food supplement. The first two groups (medicinal and herbal remedy) are related based on their similar method of giving a potentially pharmacologically active substance to the consumer. This means that the substance given to the person has known properties that will elicit a biological response. The second group explicitly contain no known active ingredient or, in the case of foods, do not contain enough to cause a significant clinically-relevant change in biological function. In the next two sections, we will consider the legality behind the Medicine Act (1968) which encompasses the laws on the manufacture and use of medicinal drugs and herbal remedies. Following this we will move on to consider the homeopathic remedies. Understanding the law allows amazing insights into what can and cannot be said, what will work and what probably will not or is not evidence-based, but still can be sold as a weight-loss product.

MEDICINAL PRODUCTS

It is likely that you picked up this book because you have some doubts about the industry. The assumption I will hold here is that you are a good scientist and would want to register your product as a medicine to help people lose weight. The reason you would want to register your product as a medicine is because there are many more requirements including ensuring that the product actually works in humans. To register the product as a medicine we have to become familiar with the Medicines Act (1968). This is a 171 page document with annotations, foot notes and amendments. It is extremely laborious to work through and covers everything to do with developing and selling a substance as a medicine. Thankfully the MHRA, which is the governing body for medicines and healthcare in the UK, has made this more accessible for the lay person to understand. They define a medicinal product through European Laws as the following:

a) "Any substance or combination of substances presented as having properties for treating or preventing disease in human beings.

b) Any substance or combination of substances which may be used in or administered to human beings either with a view to restoring, correcting or modifying physiological functions by exerting a pharmacological, immunological or metabolic action, or to making a medical diagnosis"

Although overly verbose, as most legislation has to be, this definition appears relatively straightforward. For us and the diet drug vendors, the 'devil is very much in the detail'. The interpretation of the word "disease" is important here. Obesity is not a disease; although associates of obesity are frequently referred to as non-communicable diseases. Obesity is an inevitability of positive energy balance (consuming more calories than expended). Moreover, obesity is an expression of your body working normally. Thus, obesity is not a disease and therefore is arguably not covered by the first limb of the definition of a medicine. Obesity may have medical consequences and as such we may want to deal with the problem of excess weight, but this will be done through health policy and interventions at a public level rather than as a medical intervention. Referral for a medical intervention would require the presence of a known medical problem such as diabetes, sleep apnea or cardiovascular disease. Only then would specific medical advice be offered perhaps alongside prescription drugs.

The second limb of the definition is more important to those interested in diet drugs. Reported interpretations of this definition are based on the "function and intended purpose of the product". If statements are made that the diet drug is given to a person with the intention of achieving a medicinal purpose then this definition applies, if they do not then it is less likely to be important.

To provide a fair overview to this piece of legislation, as at this point in time it would appear that we have been able to side-step the need to register any weight-loss product as a medicine, we need to look further into the detail of how it is interpreted by the regulatory agents. Within the MHRA interpretation of this definition they suggest that they are likely to invoke the Medicine Act (1968) in a number of situations. These include: how the product is made; what it is made of; how it is delivered into the body; whether a statement is made about treatment; side-effects of taking it; whether the product or constituent parts are familiar to the public; and what is said on the product's promotional literature including by those documents created by third parties. These caveats suggest that our diet drug vendors have been brought back into the fold of the legislation for medicines; however, this is not the whole story. As long as the product is not sold to a vulnerable person, and unfortunately overweight people would not be considered vulnerable no matter how desperate they are to lose weight, diet drug vendors are allowed to make claims about "maintaining, help to maintain or support health or a healthy lifestyle".

Armed with this basic legal knowledge it should be possible to peruse Internet sites that sell diet drugs. Despite what many people believe, under the law, there is no specific leniency for virtual vendors. Advertising on the Internet was brought into the fold of medicines (advertising) regulations in 1994 and those that violate this law should expect to be prosecuted. Recently, the MHRA have found it difficult to police the Internet for individuals selling 'legal highs'. This is because of the complexity of international law and the extradition of individuals from other countries to the UK to stand trial. Those individuals already in the country are currently hiding behind a screen of those trading elsewhere. Compared to legal highs, diet drug industry is a much larger 'beast' and will be much harder to 'tame'. With additional resources expected to be diverted to aid in stemming the supply of 'legal highs', as a side effect, diet drug vendors should expect more attention from the regulatory agencies.

It may come as a surprise to many diet drug vendors, but there are some specific words that will attract the attention of the MHRA. These words are frequently used when describing diet drugs. Soon, only actual medicines can use them without suffering detailed examination. The actual list of words that will attract attention is quite detailed [31]. Attention from the regulatory bodies for diet drugs should be expected if the following words are used:

- Burns fat…
- Can benefit those who suffer from…
- Can lower cholesterol…
- Clinically proven…
- Medical research…
- Help/Helps with…
- Stops craving for…

Each of these words has been chosen as it is deemed that they make reference to having physiological, pharmacological or metabolic effects. Regulating this field will be difficult; however, it is likely to be more successful with stringent licensing of vendors wishing to distribute and/or advertise diet drugs. Allowing anyone to distribute diet drugs, especially those people that do not fully appreciate the pharmacokinetics or potential pharmacokinetics of their product, is a recipe for disaster. Moreover, increased policing and regulation is required on the Internet as the customers are not verified prior to sale. Diet drugs should only be sold specifically to those individuals with a BMI of at least 28. This is not checked/verified on the Internet and so anyone can buy diet drugs, including those who are below this weight criterion. For example, people with eating disorders frequently abuse drugs for the purposes of losing weight. Virtual sellers could be selling their products to these people. People with eating disorders would be classed as a vulnerable group and thus the vendor is violating medicinal law.

TRADITIONAL HERBAL REMEDIES

Common strategies to avoid medicinal regulation are to side-step into herbal remedies. Until recently, this area was unregulated. Anyone could set up a company and sell herbal substances under the guise of traditional remedies, as long as they were not under the prohibited substances laws. The argument went that people have been using the herb for many thousands of years so it must work. Offering evidence for this assumed use was inconsistent at best, at worst non-existent. Currently, the UK is undergoing a transition process where the traditional herbal remedies are being brought under regulatory control from the end of April 2011. At this time, more evidence will be required to allow the use of herbal remedies for health purposes.

Before we spring into regulation concerning herbal remedies, it is important to acknowledge that there is a fine line between what is considered a medicine and what would be considered a traditional herbal remedy. The flippant comment that often circulates about traditional herbal remedies is that "everything in traditional herbal therapy has been tested and all those found to work are now called medicine/drugs". Without getting dragged into this argument too far, this is partially true and partially untrue. Medical trials have only been performed on herbal remedies that have been shown to have a strong effect on recovery from an illness. Therefore, not everything has been tested and new [re]discoveries are made all the time. The vast majority of these [re]discoveries are significant, but not clinically significant. This means that they have an effect, but it is not strong enough to merit application as a medicinal drug. In this arena evidence is king. If an herbal remedy is legitimately suspected to have an effect it is tested. If an herbalist somewhere suggests an herb has a specific effect, it is not always researched. Remember, to be good scientists, having no evidence or evidence from uncontrolled studies is not a sign of something working. We must conclude that nothing works until good quality evidence is found to the contrary. In terms of the law, there is an important opinion on this subject offered by the MHRA. They state that:

> "Many herbs have an established or accepted use as medicines For example… an appetite suppressant (Hoodia)… the MHRA will generally consider products containing ingredients like these in doses large enough to have a significant effect on the actual functioning of the body to be medicinal products[1]."

Consider the use of the words "doses large enough" and "significant effect". The incorporation of these suggest that the use of traditional herbal remedies in terms of legislation will be for products that do not have a significant effect on the body or are not given in large enough doses. As soon as an herb has been found to have a significant effect, or even found to have one, then it is likely to move from a traditional herbal remedy to a medicine with all of the requirements there in. Most traditional herbalists should welcome this legislative interpretation as it will provide legitimacy to those herbs that actually have an effect; however, the likely outcome will be resistance.

The law on the use of herbal remedies is both simple and complex. Herbal remedies are excluded from the Medicines Act (1968) as long as they meet the following criteria:

1) That the process of manufacture or sale is not done on private property so that the public cannot enter.
2) That the supplier does not use their judgment to prescribe treatment or dosage.
3) That the preparation process only includes drying, crushing or comminuting (making into a powder).
4) That the company or person does not attempt to 'rebrand' the product; they must sell it under the plants name.
5) That the seller does not attempt to sell the product without written recommendations as to its use.

---

[1] The text deleted from this quote is simply a list of other herbs known to have pharmacological properties. It is not a quote taken out of context to prove the point.

Under these criteria, herbal remedies remained unregulated for forty years after publication of the Medicines Act. Following significant problems with safety[2], changes had to be made. These changes were designed to quantify what is considered 'traditional'. Under the banner of traditional herbal remedy, it would appear that a period of only thirty years use in the European Union or, under the discretion of the European Committee for Herbal Medicinal Products, at least fifteen years use outside of the EU is required. In addition, the herb must have met the legal criteria laid out about prior to April 2004. If an herb meets this criterion than it will be added to the European positive list and can be sold in the EU.

One potential problem of this process is that it distinctly prohibits the addition of new herbs to the list. This in itself is not much of a problem due to the simple fact that the herb is designated as a traditional therapy and therefore should have been around for at least thirty years. However, one minor issue with this legislation is that with the movement of people comes the movement of traditional remedies. There is room for additions to the list, but this is quite prohibitive. To get a new traditional remedy added to the list, it must meet the criteria laid out within the law and must be accompanied with an expert herbalist's opinion and a bibliographic review of the remedy to show that it has a long tradition, as well as evidence that it is safe to consume. As part of the safety requirements, it is likely that all future traditional herbal remedies will have to be shown to be safe to take without medical supervision and thus can be sold over-the-counter.

Another significant problem, unlike other substances under the remit of the MHRA, it is perfectly acceptable for celebrities to endorse the use of these products. This is expressly forbidden in medicines and in the next section of homeopathic remedies. This loophole in the law allows 'quack' celebrity 'health professionals' to come into the market and sell these products to people based on their notoriety rather than the drug's efficacy. It would be extremely helpful to the country if this practice was brought in line with other substances under the same regulation. It would be equitable if all of the areas had similar advertising legislative requirements. If pharmaceuticals and homeopaths cannot use this advertising practice then neither should herbalists.

The current trend of side-stepping out of the criteria for medicines and into the unregulated world of herbal remedies will hopefully disappear with the imminent changes to the current laws. However, it is not the use of these traditional remedies that is the current problem. The monitoring of what is written compared to what is legally allowed to be written will be the future of regulation of substances covered under the Medicine Act (1968). With the addition of the new regulated terms, or those that will draw attention of the regulatory body, this will be increasingly difficult and require additional resources to police effectively. All of the words that are soon to be considered associated with medicine rather than other less regulated substances are used throughout the Internet. Until prosecutions are made against specific virtual vendors, it is hard to imagine that changes will occur. They have a system that works and is extremely lucrative through an environment that is hard to track culpability. Without a good 'stick', the 'carrot' is simply too good a prospect to miss out on.

Several avenues are available to the regulatory body to quickly stem the prevalence of vendors of herbal remedies or those active substances that fall outside of the remit of, or are exempt from, the Medicines Act (1968). These include any one or a combination of the following and would apply equally to diet drugs as they would 'legal highs': 1) Police the

---

[2] For example, Hydroxycut.

Internet and prosecute those that violate the law. This would likely be a never-ending quest. It is simply far too easy to shut down a site and reopen it under a different domain name. Ever increasing amount of resources would be required to find, track, locate and arrest those individuals responsible. Moreover, if those people are outside of the country then they will be almost impossible to track and arrest without international condemnation and cooperation. This all seems a little too much for stemming the supply of drugs designed for dieting, especially if they are not considered prohibited substances. 2) Police the borders and prosecute those that bring in these substances into the country. To control the supply of diet drugs from other countries it could be either heavily taxed or banned for import. This would not require alterations to the legal status of owning, selling or taking the drug in the country, but it would give greater control to the manufacture, quality and integrity of the product. This too is probably an unfavourable solution because it will meet very strong resistance from the pharmaceutical companies who would inevitably be affected by this legislation. 3) Strictly control the licensing of distributors of diet drugs. Currently, anyone can sell diet drugs as long as they are not licensed as a medicine. Legislation could easily be altered to not allow the exemption of herbal and other potentially biologically active ingredients from being sold or supplied by unregulated individuals. Indeed, it may be worth placing extra statutory criteria for the wholesale or supply of these substances. Currently, it is not required that the vendor has any pharmaceutical knowledge. By simply changing this requirement would drastically limit the supply of diet drugs. This would legitimise the field and remove the association of diet drugs to human pheromones and other such dubious substances. Again this is likely to be met with resistance, but unlike other areas, it should be more specific compared to other potential solutions. Of course, the obvious problem here is that it would only work within the UK or EU member states. Vendors outside of this jurisdiction would remain unaffected. Furthermore, it may have additional problems of criminalising the buyers alongside the vendors. Heavy taxation on the import of diet drugs alongside the strict control of licensing may elevate the need to criminalise the buyer. If it is much more expensive to import the product it would alleviate the demand for it, making the UK a much less lucrative market. Whatever the strategy taken, it is clear that policing the Internet will be a daunting task for those responsible. Moreover, the legislation against diet drugs is likely to play second fiddle to the more pressing matters of other potentially more harmful substances such as 'legal highs'.

In the last two sections, we have explored the substances that have a known pharmacological effect on the individual. These are not the only drugs available to those attempting to lose weight. Two other legislative options can be taken to get a product to market. One of these is highly specific (homeopathy) and the other much more generic (food supplement). Both have little to do with diet drugs, but they are still advertised and sold as weight loss 'aids'.

HOMEOPATHY

Homeopathy is a difficult subject to talk about openly. Many practitioners of the subject do not welcome open criticism of their profession or analysis of their interventions by scientific means. Discussion about the relative merits of homeopathy can be found elsewhere and interested parties are encouraged to read this[3]. Irrespective of anyone's personal viewpoints of the topic, the legislation of the subject is in itself interesting. This is controlled under the Medicines Act (1968) but with the alterations laid out by The Medicines for Human Use (National Rules for Homoeopathic Products) Regulations (2006). Throughout this legislation, homeopath practitioners are allowed to operate under similar rules as a pharmacist.

Unlike traditional herbalists, Homeopaths have the ability to offer their products to treat ailments that would be considered minor (i.e. ones that could be relieved or treated safely without the supervision or intervention of a medical doctor). Also unlike other 'treatments' for weight loss, homeopaths do not have to adhere to the same criteria as other groups with known biologically active ingredients to their drugs.

Any potential drug offered by homeopaths is required to have safety and efficacy tests performed on them. These however, do not necessarily have to be clinical trials like in our previous two groups. Homeopaths do not need to submit pre-clinical tests or clinical tests for their product and do not necessary have to provide safety checks either. According to the MHRA this is because the scheme is restricted to the use of products that are sufficiently dilute, outlined in the regulations as 1×10^{24}, to guarantee safety. Although it is tempting to infer what the MHRA mean by 'guaranteed safety' they do not state more than this and so the rest will be left to the reader to infer for themselves. The legislation goes a little way beyond the MHRA interpretation and states that such tests are not necessary if the substance is commonly found in food, has a dilution comparable to other over the counter drugs and is considered to be reasonably safe or not of biological origin. It is safe to assume that the MHRA would not allow a homeopathic remedy to become available without safety checks unless it met the criteria it sets out (i.e. sufficient dilution). If a substance is not diluted to the 1×10^{24} then it would require safety tests to be performed.

Special dispensation compared to other groups is also offered to homeopathic remedies for the efficacy testing. The need for scientific investigation is not integral to the efficacy requirements of the legislation to allow registration of a homeopathic remedy. Instead, this group is allowed to infer efficacy from homeopathic provings. Provings are legally defined as the administration of the substance to the human participant in order to ascertain the symptoms produced by it. As this does not claim to be a scientific approach, and is not legally considered as such, it will not be assessed under this remit. However, such experiences when applied to homeopathic remedies are tantamount to nothing more than a medical case study. This is a written form of anecdotal evidence that gives indications for further investigation in the scientific endeavour. Homeopaths accept the provings as their evidence and it would appear that this is legally admissible for their products and only their products.

The provision of homeopathic remedies to aid weight loss is easy to find. Many of those on the Internet make direct claims about homeopathy treating weight-loss.

Although homeopathic remedies have special dispensation for some components of the regulatory process, they have strict rules concerning advertising. According to the EC directive 92/28/EEC homeopaths are not allowed to make claims that they can enhance health. Furthermore, they are not allowed to provide recommendations by scientists, health professionals or celebrities to aid in getting people to use their products. Any homeopathic publications are allowed to describe the use of a registered product but are not allowed to

---

[3] Same citation as note 3.

promote the use of any particular registered product. This relates to any publication available to the public including published books and periodicals. Homeopaths are allowed to offer 'treatments' for minor ailments similar to a pharmacist, but they are not allowed to make therapeutic claims about their products. This leaves the homeopath walking a very tight line in terms of what they can and cannot say. This they do well and it is difficult to find many violations of their advertising criteria even on the Internet.

There are also some other restrictions on homeopathic remedies. These restrictions related to how the remedy is delivered. Homeopaths are only allowed to deliver their remedies orally or topographically (on the skin). This places similar restrictions on the preparation process for their remedies as traditional herbal approaches.

With the completion of the homeopathic remedies, we leave the Medicine Act (1968) and transfer to another piece of legislation. If none of the first three options are available to a particular manufacturer or vendor of a specific diet drug then there is one option still available. Simply make a claim about a specific nutrient or food and then claim that the product is a food supplement. This has long been the strategy of several companies and organisations across the globe. In short, any substance claimed to be a weight-loss 'drug' sold outside of a pharmacy or not prescribed by a doctor will either be a food or a 'drug' registered as allowed to treat, but not necessarily provide therapeutic interventions for, minor ailments. You will notice that 'drug' will, from this paragraph onwards, start to be presented in inverted commas. The reason for this is because if the substance is not registered as a medicine it is not a drug. The use of the word 'drug' on the Internet and elsewhere appears to be a catch all term. Therefore, substances available from vendors referred to as weight-loss 'drugs' encompasses a lot of products, when, in actual fact, very few are registered as drugs. What they should be called is weight-loss supplements. They are given the term 'drug' in order to sell it to the buyer as a pseudo-medicinal product and allow people to associate all of the perceived good efficacy rates of pharmaceuticals. If we enforced the use of the term drug to be used only by substances registered under the Medicines Act, we would change the marketing of weight-loss 'drugs' overnight. Instead of allowing them to associate themselves with medicine, they should be pushed out into the supplement market. Now, if they were called weight-loss supplements they would cease to be associated with pharmaceuticals, by at least the educated amongst the population, and would then become associated with vitamin and mineral tablets. This would be their 'rightful' place. It would also most likely cut into their profits immediately. People would cease to place confidence in the products and see them for the efficacies they can actually have. However, we will return to this later in the book and thus we will save commentary on this until then.

FOOD SUPPLEMENTS

Most of the stuff sold under the term weight-loss 'drugs' are in fact food supplements. They are derived from foods or potential food sources. Registering a product as a food need only comply with four statutory laws: Food Safety Act (1990); Trade Descriptions Act (1968); Weights & Measures Act (1985); and Food (lot marking) Regulations (1996). None of these require extensive testing to make claims about their product. For our purposes of advertising a weight-loss 'drug', the Food Safety Act and the Trade Descriptions Act are of utmost importance.

The Food Safety Act (1990) covers pretty much anything that is supposed to be consumed by humans. It explicitly does not include illicit substances and medicines, but other than that, anything that is reasonably expected to be consumed by a human would count as a food under English and Welsh law. As the name of the Act suggests, it covers all of the legal requirements to ensure safety of food sold to the general public. Adhering to this statute means that companies have to prove that their product is safe for human consumption. Beyond these expectations there is little mention about what someone can say about a food item. One area that is covered in this Act is under section fifteen, which considers aspects about Falsely Describing or Presenting Food. This particular section of the Food Safety Act prohibits the vendor from falsely describing foods in terms of their content or quality. In the diet 'drug' industry falsely describing the content of a product is not a common theme. Making claims about what the product can do is much more common and not considered the remit of this particular statute. To explore what we can say about a particular nutritional supplement we would need to turn to the Trade Descriptions Act (1968).

For the purposes of trade description for weight-loss products, the important definitions are descriptions of:

- fitness for purpose, strength, performance, behaviour or accuracy;
- testing by any person and results thereof;
- approval by any person or conformity with a type approved by any person;

These specific definitions suggest that it is not possible to make definite statements of a product or associate people with their product without their prior knowledge. This is the same laws applied to homeopathic remedies. These criteria only adhere to direct statements of "will help". It is important to consider that it is possible to make statements of "could help", "can help" or "may help" as long as there is some evidence somewhere that allows the backing of this claim. Depending on what category the substance falls under (i.e. medicine, traditional herbal, homeopathy or food supplement) will dictate what is considered evidence for the claim. To emphasize this point, if I ran a study on a group of 100 people on a healthy plan diet and told them all to eat 5mg of chalk before every meal and 30 reported chalk helped them lose weight then I could legitimately set up the "chalk diet" and advertise that this may work as part of a healthy diet for 3 in 10 people. I do not have to provide a control group or run it as a clinical trial, as long as I am not claiming it as a therapeutic intervention or using substances under the remit of the Medicine Act. I am of course being flippant, but the example still stands. Also the fact that I am a professional in the area complete with the doctor title[4] and I am telling someone how to successfully lose weight, I bet more than 30 would suggest the "chalk diet" would help for no other reason than the placebo effect, especially if I give them some random reason for how it may work.

---

[4] I.e. stupid enough to spend at least three years in a room thinking about a tiny component of human behaviour that most people do not care or even ever necessarily think about. For doctorial titles, read diligence not intelligence.

REGISTERED PRODUCT VERSUS REGISTERED WEIGHT-LOSS PRODUCT

Under the two statutes of the Trade Descriptions and the Food Safety Act it is relatively easy to get a product to market. One need only provide evidence that the product is safe and has some form of tenuous efficacy. The product is almost certainly safe if it is found in, or derived from, other food products. The only point the potential product would be considered unsafe would be if we increased the concentration of the supplement to many times above what would usually be consumed as part of a healthy diet. Furthermore, the efficacy of our product need not be significantly effective. Most people do not understand inferential statistics and so revert to descriptive analysis of data. This is why the presentation of X in 10 people is pervasive throughout the field. Presentation of 'efficacy' data in terms of frequency or mean score change tells us very little. We need to know whether a product is significantly effective against a placebo or not. Furthermore, we need to know the magnitude of the effect in order to infer whether the substance is of clinical significance. A placebo-controlled trial is where the participants are placed in one of two groups and 'blinded' so that they do not know what they are taking (either placebo tablets or the 'drug'). Everything else about the participants' experience during their weight-loss regime is kept the same. The amount of weight lost is measured and statistically compared. If the difference between the two groups is high enough or if we tested it on a very large sample of participants then it would be considered statistically significant. The more people that are involved in the test the more likely a significant result will be found even if it is only a very small difference. For it to be clinically significant and useful to the general population then we would need to show large amounts of weight-loss in small groups of participants. Only then would this be considered significant. This is the rules that medicines have to adhere to. Other groups do not. You will soon see in the forthcoming chapters why so few of the 'drugs' available are registered medicines.

With the description of the laws that weight-loss products have to adhere to covered, we have some insight into how effective the product is likely to be. Before we even know the name or the content of the product we can infer quite a lot about the product based solely on how it is registered. The presentation of the products in this chapter runs from medicines to food products. It can be inferred from the order of presentation how much detail, or how much leniency away from medicinal laws, the company has to go in order to register their product. Most of the products available as weight-loss 'drugs' are in fact registered under traditional herbal remedies or food products. Homeopathic variations are specific to their field and are specifically designed under their guidelines. Irrespective of the belief structure behind homeopathic remedies they have a lot of legal leniency as long as they can "guarantee safety". In order to guarantee safety, it is this author's opinion that they must show that their product has no pharmacological effect what-so-ever. It of course can have a biological effect, but this does not have to necessarily relate to the product itself. Most stimuli in a person's environment can evoke a biological response. For example, other people, music, food or anything else you wish to offer can have a biological effect. It does not mean that any of these can be considered therapies and, indeed, cannot legally claim to be one.

If we were to read these laws literally then it would appear that a lot of vendors, or more accurately supposed vendors, of weight-loss products would have to adhere to them. This is only the case if you actually hold the product on their premises or act as an advertiser for the product. There are ways around these laws and the necessity to adhere to them. In short, there are many ways to sell a 'drug'; someone need not do so directly. Thus, there is disparity between how you can go about making money from selling diet 'drugs' if you are on the Internet compared to if you are a vendor selling from a bricks and mortar premises. In the next chapter, we will consider the differences and how the Internet vendors can get away without having to adhere to the laws covered in this chapter.

Chapter 3

OF INTERNET VERSUS BRICKS AND MORTAR

There is a fundamental difference between virtual vendors and those who have physical premises from which they trade. This is not the laws that they have to deal with; the law is equitable. As mentioned previously in this book, the Internet vendors are not excluded from the same laws as other sellers. They do however have the ability to use a different strategy to recruit people to do their advertising on their behalf. These people are known as affiliates. Operating in a virtual world compared to a physical world has additional benefits. Selling products from a specific site means that the agencies responsible ensuring compliance to the law of the land knows where to find them from one day to the next. For those operating through the Internet, the freedom to move around is much easier. Although there are requirements under the provision of the wholesale license to provide details of the premises of sale, as well as detailed requirements for storage and movement of medicines [33], other 'groups' or 'drugs' require less stringent criteria. For example, most medicines have a detailed requirement for temperature storage, which must be adhered to even in transit from one site to the next. The transport of herbs follow similar criteria but have less stringent requirements for transit and storage compared to medicines in most cases.

With the freedom of movement inherently conferred upon the virtual seller comes the ability to move outside of jurisdiction of governing bodies. In such cases they can recruit 'distributors'. These people are supposed to become the distributors of the substance within the country they are located. These 'distributors' then accept the risks of receiving the substance to their premises. If it does not turn up or gets confiscated then that is the distributor's not the vendor's problem.

The law of the land only extends to the ends of that land. Once beyond it, the vendor is able to pretty much ignore the agents of the law in another country. The Internet does not respect boundaries without governments forcing filters on the Internet providers or large Internet-related multi-national companies. This is done in China, but it is considered an infringement of civil liberties in the West. This attitude means that our population is left to consider what is and is not acceptable knowledge and make up their minds about what to do with their money. Individuals are left open to abuse from the less reputable end of the diet 'drug' spectrum, as well as a host of other problems well beyond the scope of this book. The balance between civil liberties, health and criminal activities is a fine one, especially when it comes to the Internet. Personally, I am with the civil liberties camp, just so long as we have a strong, effective and rapid regulatory agency that will deal with criminality and review the regulations in the light of modern developments. Key to this fine balance is ensuring that the population is sufficiently educated to be able to recognise what is happening or being done to them. An uneducated populace is easy pickings for those with weaker moral fibre irrespective of the current legal situation.

In this chapter, we will consider how diet 'drugs' are sold to the public. First, we will consider how the Internet vendors sell their wares and then how the more traditional groups do it. Only then can we arm ourselves against the tactics of the more surreptitious vendors of diet 'drugs'.

AFFILIATES

Circumvent the law, become an affiliate to the company. In the UK, it is actually illegal to advertise a medicine to the general public. The statute concerning this is detailed under the Medicines (Advertising) Regulations (1994). Companies, with exception of drugs aimed at preventing neural tube defects or part of a vaccination programme, are not allowed to advertise to the general public directly. Specifically:

> "no person shall issue an advertisement which is likely to lead to the use of a relevant medicinal product for the purpose of the treatment, prevention or diagnosis of any disease specified in, or any disease falling within a class of disease specified in, Schedule 1."

Instead, these companies are only allowed to advertise to health professionals with the power to prescribe medicines. Thus in the UK we are safe from being bombarded with messages about prescription drugs. In contrast, the advertising requirements of homeopathic products are significantly different and have already been covered in the previous chapter. Herbal remedies are not currently involved in the regulations about advertising and are allowed to advertise to the general public. This should give you a good indication of the relative merits of what a product contains. If you see it on television in the UK then it is an herbal remedy, has special dispensation and is probably not a medicine (without the said dispensation) or homeopathic remedy. Despite the best efforts of the advertisers to portray a product as a medicine, if you see it, then it is not a medicine. Any adverts for medicines are illegal in the UK. There are no arguments, no wriggle room or caveats. Companies making medicinal drugs cannot develop marketing strategies aimed at the general population to ensure that they buy them.

The Internet is a different 'kettle of fish' altogether. This forum is where everyone can openly 'discuss' and post information about all sorts of weight-loss 'drugs'. All of it is opinion devoid of most, if not all, evidence. It would be nice to say 'fact' here, but we do not have this luxury. Science is not a pursuit of the definite. It is the collection of evidence assessed by learned people for relationships, differences and patterns in data. Science is, and will always be, progressive. One piece of knowledge builds on the next through circulation of the seven stages of: review of previous work; formulate a suitable question; formulate an appropriate method; collect data; appropriately analyse said data; evaluation of outcome; formulation of next question. Lines of scientific argument can fall out of the cycle at any stage. There are gatekeepers to this knowledge through the peer review publication process found in scientific journals. Access to these journals can be gained through the World Wide Web, however, so can access to a wide range of other pieces of information devoid of any real merit. It is a place where the human race unguardedly offers its opinions and commentary without filter or thought for quality. Some opinions are shared, most are not. Some of those shared are accurate, others are not. Without a quality filter the information, no matter how good it 'looks', is meaningless and could even have an ulterior motive.

The affiliate is an individual who has such a motive. They set up a website for the purposes of diverting Internet traffic to a specific vendor. They themselves do not sell the 'drug' but they do collect a commission from people who buy the product after being diverted to the vendor by them. In many cases they will receive 40% of the total amount of money that the buyer the affiliate diverted to the vendor actually spends. In short, the drug was nearly twice as expensive as it needed to be thanks to the middleperson who gave information that was mostly, if not wholly, scientifically, and intellectually, inaccurate.

Becoming an affiliate is easy for those with a little Internet savvy. All that is required is to buy a domain name – one that makes sense to the product being 'advertised'; depending on the name, these are relatively cheap. As well as the name, the affiliate will also need to find a host. The host is the most expensive part of the process, but this can be done for as little as three pounds a month. Expectations for set up and running costs are about seven hundred pounds, but it very much depends on the Internet and IT skills of the affiliate. A well skilled affiliate can set up a good website for much cheaper than this. They would expect to recoup these costs within the first two months. Beyond the set up costs of the website, an affiliate must also understand search engines in order to get Internet traffic to their sites. Simply setting up a website will not be enough to start drawing in the commission fees from the diet 'drug' vendors. This is the true art to the process and what differentiates the affiliates that make an awful lot of money out of the desperate people wanting a quick fix to their weight-related problems from those that do not make much. Setting up the website is easy, but understanding how people search the Internet and read information will ensure that buyers will flock from the affiliate's website to the vendors'.

Deniability is important in this process. Remember, what is being done here is skirting close to breaking the law. It is illegal to advertise medicinal products and there is heavy advertising regulation on many other forms of diet 'drugs'. These people need to disclaim responsibility or culpability for directing people to take a particular substance to aid their weight loss. If they do not then they are culpable to the laws of the Medicine Act (1968) and will soon find themselves under the watchful eye of the MHRA if not a probation officer. Deniability allows the affiliate to state that they have nothing to do with the actual product and do not have to adhere to the statute laws outlined in the last chapter. Although what these people are doing is a form of marketing and advertising for the product they are 'discussing' on their web pages, they are not strictly considered part of the company that sells the diet 'drugs' and so both groups can more-or-less deny any real association or culpability with one another. This ability to deny association with one another is more necessary for the affiliate than the vendor. For the company, these affiliated people are considered simply other companies that endorse their product; while the affiliate is claiming to be a member of the Press.

MEMBERS OF THE PRESS?

Of course, affiliates are not paid up members of the Press and are not usually part of any organisation associated with the Media. Instead, these people claim that they are operating under the bounds of the media. In a sort of version of law top trumps, affiliates operate through freedom of expression laws that state under article 10.1 of the Human Rights Act (1998) that:

> "Everyone has the right to freedom of expression. This right shall include freedom to hold opinions and to receive and impart information and ideas without interference by public authority and regardless of frontiers."

Using this statute, the affiliate suggests that they are simply sharing their opinion and thoughts with the world and do not endorse the use of the drug they are talking about. Some affiliate websites will even state this somewhere in very small print or an infrequently visited webpage somewhere on their site. Although they are quick to invoke this right, affiliates are usually not particularly familiar with the law. Instead, they will often simply state that it is a free world with freedom of speech. Unfortunately, no such dictate exists and people have the right to freedom of expression not the freedom of speech. For those who are familiar with the Human Rights Act they would quickly counter any such claim with the very next point in article 10.2:

> "The exercise of these freedoms, since it carries with it duties and responsibilities, may be subject to such formalities, conditions, restrictions or penalties as are prescribed by law and are necessary in a democratic society, in the interests of ... for the protection of health or morals..."

In this statute, making the claim that the affiliate has the right to freedom of speech (expression) is fine as long as they accept the responsibility for it. If it was deemed by government to be an infringement of the protection of people's health then any such activity would not be covered under the Human Rights Act (1998). In such situations where these statements fail, the affiliate would find her/himself invoking another Human Right under article 6 – the Right to a Fair Trial.

Another approach that many affiliates take is one of not accepting duty of care or differing responsibility to other more appropriate people. Here, the affiliate will make some remarks about the substance in question and then say that the reader should consult the vendor or their general practitioner prior to taking any such drug. Although this is an appropriate attempt at ensuring safety, it is used as a strategy to avoid accepting any culpability or legal repercussions of taking a specific diet 'drug' based on their advice.

In short, this is a tight line on which to walk; one which, based on the copious amounts of websites I have read on the matter, and the affiliates I have spoken to, I am certain most affiliates do not fully appreciate. The real issue of why these people can get away with this activity is because of the practical problems policing the Internet. With filtering the Internet being considered an encroachment on civil liberties and the difficulty locating the perpetrators, this activity has been left more-or-less light-touch regulated.

Irrespective of the legal status of the activity of writing affiliate websites, it is still being done and we should appreciate how this is done. As suggested above they are acting like a member of the press by offering the reader their opinion or review of the field. Of course, this view is marred by the fact that they are attempting to guide the reader into buying the product but that is neither 'here nor there'. Such activities are not subject to peer review or evaluation so it is moot. The affiliate's blog will follow a process of considering 'the evidence' of the effects of diet 'drugs' (most often of other bloggers or newspaper articles), comparing and contrasting different diet 'drugs' based on some apparently important factor to taking it or simply writing a news-type article about the 'drug' in question. The information considered is rarely, if ever, based on scientific evidence even if the drug itself is actually controlled under the Medicine Act. There is one simple reason they will not consider the scientific evidence, but this will all come in good time. The point of the affiliate's article on their website is to convince the reader that the product they are discussing is the best one available on the market. By the end of the article, there will be, by some miraculous happenstance, a link to a place that these 'drugs' can be bought. It is advertising masquerading as 'news'.

Tactics of the affiliate are complex including the especially complex strategies of website optimisation. This author is not an expert in this arena and would never claim to be. Some of the tactics are however much easier to understand and observe than these unwritten information technology requirements. The first is staying 'ahead of the game' and keeping their 'finger on the pulse' of society. People will hunt for subjects on search engines that are 'of the now'. Legitimate news articles or interviews by eminent experts will capture the public's conscience and they will search for the story or the people involved. Affiliates will latch onto these and quickly write about them too. Then when the potential buyer types in these search terms into the engine it directs them to their 'news' coverage of the area and eventually to the vendor. I have personal experience of this, as has many of my colleagues. Quotes from my colleagues and I can be found littered throughout affiliate websites. More-often-than-not, these 'quotes' are taken out of context, misunderstood or misrepresented on most of the affiliate websites I have seen. By quoting perceived experts in the field it provides perceived legitimacy to their coverage of the topic to the potential buyers and also captures search terms under our names. Affiliates quite literally cash in on the reputation of the experts. Those drugs registered as medicines are not included in this statement as they have gone through the full process to achieve legitimacy in the marketplace. Amongst patients with eating disorders, diet 'drugs' are a real problem and are of a large concern for professionals. If eating disorder patients can get hold of diet 'drugs' then I feel they are not being appropriately controlled and are being sold to vulnerable people. This, in my opinion, violates the Medicine Act and should be prohibited.

It would appear that there is a general reluctance and/or view that the activities of affiliate writers are considered unacceptable in our current society and should be limited. This probably stems from the close links that they have managed to thus far forge with civil liberties and that the curtailing of their activities would perceptually require an attack on the 'people's' freedom of expression. This is not really the case, as it could be viewed that the expression of these views are undermining the health of the nation and/or miss-selling the potential effects of the diet 'drugs' offered. Affiliate websites are unlikely to stop anytime soon without some form of institutional intervention because the money obtained through this activity is relatively easy. Although the affiliate will not make vast sums, it is possible to make a significant contribution to their income through simply updating their website from time-to-time with popular search terms. This is easy money, but it is definitely time-consuming. With a general reluctance or ignorance to legislate against this activity, the worst that could possibility happen to the affiliate is to suffer the wraith of a rival vendor or manufacturer of a competitive 'drug'. The likelihood of receiving this negative attention increases with the success of the affiliate's websites or if they say something particularly untrue or misrepresentative of another product. Brief searches on the Internet will quickly reveal that every drug is both supported and attacked by different affiliates and so tracking and contacting affiliate's can quickly become a full-time occupation. With the only viable option available to stop the affiliate's activities being a legal 'cease and desist notification', it becomes an equally rapid 'fool's errand'. In most situations, initiating contact with the affiliate will be fruitless. They will simply state "freedom of speech" as a defense for their website. A company can then attempt to contact the host, which will invariably result in the host contacting the affiliate to temper their website rather than change it. As the general message does not change, the best business decision for the manufacturer or vendor is to join in and start recruiting their own affiliates. Often these are one and the same people they sent the 'cease and desist notification' to, as affiliates can have several websites for several drugs. After all, what is the point of putting all of your 'eggs in one basket'? It would appear that affiliate websites are practically, if not theoretically, above the law.

It is not all 'sweetness and light' for the affiliate. Skirting the law means that they too can be subjected to violation of their rights. Professional affiliates can spend a lot of time optimising and updating their website. Indeed, to make the real meaningful money they have to capture a significant proportion of the market share. Once they have done this, other affiliates can simply copy their websites and repost it under another domain name. This instantly takes a large part of their share of the market. The lack of legal knowledge shared by affiliates, or more accurately where they are in the world so they can avoid prosecution, one affiliate may threaten another based on the Copyright, Designs & Patents Act (1988). If the affiliate is in a country that respects this law then they may be successful, if not, then they will suffer a loss in profits and will eventually have to start again with another website. This constant risk to income posed by reposting successful affiliate sites means that it makes a lot of business sense to keep multiple sites with multiple vendors running simultaneously. By operating in the grey area of law means that they are not always afforded its protection.

It would be unfair to lump all affiliates into one category. Affiliates can be differentiated based on the morality of their 'review'. Some are fairer than others. Affiliate websites that use the word 'supplements' instead of 'drugs' is an indication of an individual that has some grasp of the complexity of the area on which they are writing. Some affiliate websites offer more balanced view than others, using the best information that is available to them. However, this is not the case for all of them. Some will make information up, simply omit important information or create an extremely biased view towards the drugs they are affiliate members of. Frequent examples of this are "reported" side-effects. In a system without peer review, one piece of made-up information can quickly spread amongst affiliate websites, especially if it is a side-effect that will back their viewpoint and allow them to direct readers to their vendors. The whole point of the peer review system in science is to limit the impact of these practices. On the Internet, there is no filter other than the person controlling the mouse.

Based on this section, it would appear that we have demonised the affiliate. However, is what they are doing truly wrong? After all, these people are providing a 'free' service to the world. Their income is not guaranteed and/or proportional to the information they offer.

Without descending into arguments about the cost of publishing, the simple fact is that most science based publications are not free to access. The average price of a single article is around thirty American dollars. Alternatively an individual can subscribe to specific academic journals; however, the cost of this varies from a few hundred to a few thousand pounds per year. In a world where the access to the credible scientific information is prohibitive, it is not possible to demonise people for providing free-to-access-for-all information. Even if people did have access to this information it is unlikely that the average person would understand it. Scientific papers on diet 'drugs' are written from a pharmacological or psychopharmacological perspective. This often necessitates the use of very subject specific language. Without education in the meaning and use of such language means that the average lay person will not understand the specifics of what is being discussed within the paper. Of course, they will be able to read the words, but they will not be able to derive meaning from them. This means that the population is reliant on other expert people, who do understand the material, simplifying it into common language for them without using subject-specific words. Most scientists are reluctant to do this. The reasons for this are many, but the principle reason is, I believe, the fear of being viewed as a 'pseudo-scientist' – an individual that does not write peer-reviewed papers. There are many individuals who write on topics for consumption among the wider population. Many do not have the appropriate qualifications and/or experience to write about what they do and their works are often riddled with mistakes. Instead of relying on their ability and knowledge, they create a media image of an 'expert' that is controlled, defended, fed and sometimes attacked by the media. Against this backdrop, many scientists refuse to engage with these types of publications in an attempt to avoid being associated with the 'quackery' type 'academics'. There are many out there and you will know some of them. I would personally encourage everyone to thoroughly research the background of any individual before they personally consider accepting them as an expert. The individuals the media sometimes parade as an expert are worse than your average secondary school student. Therefore, is the affiliate any different to a variety of individuals that are arguably doing more harm than good within different media? Personally, I would suggest that they are doing harm, but they only exist because of variety of exclusionary tactics operated by those with the credible information. Based in this environment, it really is not possible for us to demonise anyone who offers some information no matter how biased it is.

Avoiding affiliate websites, which will inevitably cloud the judgment of any individual that has not spent time learning the intricacies of the subject, is relatively easy. Such sites exist because people visit and read them. They actually exist because the only real competition with them is the online newspapers. A simple search about diet drugs on any search engine will find that the top few hundred results will be either affiliate sites or creditable news sites. The obvious answer is to avoid the affiliate sites and only read the newspaper sites. Although this is often an overly simplistic representation, it is not knowingly wrong and does not attempt to sell the reader anything. The second way to get free information is to go to the manufacturers' website. Although they are not allowed to advertise, pharmaceuticals are allowed to provide educational material. This material is carefully monitored and the company is culpable for it. Therefore, it will be more-or-less devoid of miss-selling practices; however, it will obviously be somewhat biased. Finally, ask the professionals. Talk to independent experts or read their work. Some of it will be free and some can be sent if requested. This will give a much more balanced perspective and the expert is likely to be very happy to tell you about their work – in the right forum of course.

Unsolicited emails will likely be ignored by the horrendously over-worked academic who has to effectively write full-time and teach full-time to maintain their standing in their chosen professional field.

MANAGING THE PROCESS

Deniability is important in this process. It is likely to place any manufacturer of substances regulated by the MHRA in difficulty if they are explicitly linked to the strategies employed by affiliates. The common process to avoid direct association with the actions of an affiliate is to allow a middle management company[1] to control and pay them. These companies are, by their own admission, marketing strategists or consultants. They propose to increase traffic at a specific website irrespective of its product. In effect, the principle role of the management company is to monitor and improve Internet traffic (i.e. people clicking on and reading a specific website) to the vendors purchase area and increase sales.

These companies will do everything from recruiting, motivating, assisting and paying the affiliate members. Within this arrangement, the vendor of the diet drug simply employs the second company as marketing consultant to increase Internet traffic. They then leave it to this company to deal with how they do this. Potential affiliate writers then join the consultant company and write for them. The actual vendor then does not have to worry about the strategies their consultants use to get people to the site as they have total deniability in this process. Most of these companies are situated in the United States of America. European Laws obviously do not extend to companies situated in the US. Interestingly, within the US, pharmaceuticals can freely advertise to the public and therefore they are not overly bothered about engaging in this practice.

Managing the affiliates and their activities in this manner means the vendor of the diet 'drugs' can have total anonymity and deniability of any potential violation of the law in any given country. The vendor employs an independent consultant to deal with their marketing, which, in turn, employs independent consultants to actually write the material. Therefore, in the same way as the affiliates have multiple websites for directing people to their vendor, the affiliate management company has multiple affiliates in numerous countries working indirectly for the vendor. The only person in this process who is truly culpable under UK law is the affiliate. Stopping this activity is therefore completely impossible. Closing one website down because of violations would probably have a minor impact on the affiliate, a minute impact on the management company and a miniscule impact on the vendor. If the country decided tomorrow that this activity was wrong, then the only way to stop it would be to literally pull the plug on the Internet itself. In this way, it is perfectly possible to advertise pharmaceuticals on the Internet totally against a Nation's laws.

To explain how this occurs, consider the following line of argument. Under section 25 of the Trade Descriptions Act (1968) the vendor of the 'drugs' can claim that they:

---

[1] A quick search for such companies revealed three – Madhatterconsulting.com; hitpath.com; indiumwebmanagement.co.uk. There are many more, but if you visit any of these companies' websites, you can get an indication of their activities, company profile, what they do and how they do it. None of these companies are expressly related to diet pills in any way, they are simply successful affiliate management companies.

"In proceedings for an offence under this Act committed by the publication of an advertisement it shall be a defense for the person charged to prove that he is a person whose business it is to publish or arrange for the publication of advertisements and that he received the advertisement for publication in the ordinary course of business and did not know and had no reason to suspect that its publication would amount to an offence under this Act".

Sending information to affiliates detailing good practice would constitute due diligence in this situation. Policing the enactment of the information is not required. For the legal minded amongst the readers, they could of course point towards section 24(3) which states:

"In any proceedings for an offence under this Act of supplying or offering to supply goods to which a false trade description is applied it shall be a defense for the person charged to prove that he did not know, and could not with reasonable diligence have ascertained, that the goods did not conform to the description or that the description had been applied to the goods".

This is why deniability is integral to the Internet marketing process for the vendor and why they employ the management company. If an accusation was ever made about miss-selling practices then it would be passed around like a hot potato to eventually land at the door of the affiliate vindicating both the vendor and the management company of any wrong doings. They will claim that under section 24(2):

"...involves the allegation that the commission of the offence was due to the act or default of another person or to reliance on information supplied by another person, the person charged shall not, without leave of the court, be entitled to rely on that defense unless, within a period ending seven clear days before the hearing, he has served on the prosecutor a notice in writing giving such information identifying or assisting in the identification of that other person as was then in his possession"

So as long as the finger is pointed at the affiliate within seven days before the hearing they are safe from prosecution. The affiliate would then claim that under section 24(1)(a) of the same act that

"that the commission of the offence was due to a mistake or reliance on information supplied to him or to the act or default of another person, an accident or some other cause beyond his control"

The "reliance on information" the affiliate will use is other material on the Internet. This will be allowed because they do not have the expertise or access to the material in suitable scientific journals, but they do have the right under the freedom of expression laws to give an opinion on it. Moreover, they will claim that they wrote a story on it rather than an advert so it was not 'selling' the drug at all. So begins the never-ending circular legal argument using up valuable court time and reaching little conclusions.

The affiliate management company views their role in the process as being responsible for controlling the payment of its affiliates through analysing the origin of how a particular buyer came to end up on the vendor's website. They are not interested in the actual product bought only the origin of the sale. By tracking how the buyer got to the website, the management company finds which affiliate website directed the buyer to the vendor and pays them a percentage of how much the buyer spent. This is usually 40% of the purchase price. Depending on the company, this arrangement will differ; however, for the selling of diet 'drugs' through affiliate websites, the most popular method is a percentage in the successful purchase of the product. In this 'underworld' of the Internet, it appears that being the top of the search engines and owning the appropriate domain names is the key to success. If you wish to see how successful these affiliate sites are at doing this then simply type in any word associated with the medical field. Do not do this in the search engine, just write www, followed by the word, and add on the suffix .com or .co.uk etc... They are all there selling diet 'drugs' and other non-medicinal products. It is a truly brilliant, intelligent and potentially lucrative strategy and one that a lot of the world is oblivious to, especially those who actually end up buying the product and indirectly end up paying the affiliate for the information they read. In a newspaper article, the buyer gets a lot of information for 50p; for the affiliate's information, they will pay many hundreds of pounds over the long-term.

DISTRIBUTORS AND WHOLESALERS

Before we conclude the way the Internet vendors of diet 'drugs' operate, there is one rather concerning strategy that is being employed. When all else fails and the vendor wishes to sell the 'drug' or drug to a buyer directly and they are not allowed to, then they can sign them up as a subsidiary distributor or wholesaler. In the UK, this is illegal, but in other countries this is not the case. The newly signed up 'distributor' than accepts the risks involved in accepting the substance and pays for it up front. These are then sent through the post in the most inconspicuous manner as possible. All medicines in the UK are considered controlled substances. The distribution and selling of any substance regulated under the Medicine Act (1968) requires a license from the MHRA. If the substance is found during routine examination of the post then it is often confiscated. Depending on the amount bought, this may result in additional criminal proceedings for the buyer. There are allowances in the Medicine Act to import unlicensed medicines for private use, however, the MHRA can object to its import if it believes the substance is unsafe, that the person can get the substance in this country or they are not satisfied that the individual needs the substance. Without overtly knowing what they are doing, the buyer can literally become embroiled in criminal activity. This seems somewhat unfair for a person that was simply completing what they believed to be a legitimate transaction for the purposes of obtaining a weight-loss product.

At the end of the 'members of the press' section, I offered some possible solutions of how someone can protect themselves from the affiliate websites. What was not discussed was how we could possibility legislate against this activity. Although we will never stop it altogether there are ways that government could hinder the efforts of these online 'marketers', 'news writers', 'columnists' or whatever name they wish to trade under. The most draconian and improbable solution would be to ban all affiliate activities or online market consultancies (middle-management companies). This will be a never-ending quest and will simply move the problem from one country to the next rather than solve it. Less drastic measures could be to ban the linking of 'news articles' to vendor websites. Professional journalists do not do this and so it will not harm them in anyway. Alternatively, the government could force the display of 'health' warnings on the affiliate sites so that the reader will know what the objective of the website is and be able to make an appropriate decision about its content. All of these solutions will require concerted international negotiation and enforcement. One weak link in the chain and it will revert back to square one. The final and perhaps most effective solution to this problem would be to chase the Hosts. Companies that provide Hosting Platforms for others to work from are the gatekeepers to the Internet and its content. By forcing these groups to be culpable for the content on their server it will create the same peer-review process that is available in other knowledge transfer mediums. The potential punishment for allowing this form of activity will simply be banning the server from allowing access to the population. This would also create a system of vigilance and pressure from other credible websites situated on the same Hosting platform so that they do not also get banned along with the affiliate websites. Whatever the desires for the government to get involved in legislating against material on the Internet, there is one golden rule that everyone should follow. Affiliate websites will disappear if people stopped reading them and clicking on their links to buy the dieting product. By all means read the information on the website, but do not believe a word of it if you see any link in any way to a place where you can buy the product. If by happenstance you want to buy the product, go and find the wholesaler yourself. Eventually this will lead to lower prices and the removal of the 'two-stage' middle people that are increasing the costs of selling the substance to the public.

TRADITIONAL MARKETING STRATEGIES

It was very briefly mentioned early in this chapter that pharmaceutical companies in the UK are not allowed to talk to the general public other than to educate them about a product. The MHRA are very vigilant to this activity and monitor the educational outputs of these companies. They can however talk to the professionals. The biggest group that bear the brunt (and rewards) of talking with pharmaceutical companies are medics. Medics, including nurse practitioners for some drugs, have the power to prescribe. They also have the power to choose which drug to prescribe. It is not too much of a stretch to see where all the advertising money goes. Much of the advertising funds go on supporting academic conferences and knowledge transfer opportunities. Therefore, being associated with the right individuals is also important. Top pharmacists from all sub-disciplines will receive a lot of funding for their work from the pharmaceutical industry. Certain top medics and academics will turn up to international and national conferences having had everything paid for including top quality travel and accommodation arrangements. These will include entertainment at the conference destination under the guise of 'sandpit thinking'. This is simply getting people together to come up with novel ideas for future research themes. For the mere lowly mortal medic or academic they do not get such bonuses. This activity has waned in recent years, but it still continues for the top individuals in their respective fields. These top academics and medics are those that write most of the material and undertake the research on the topic and so they really are the gatekeepers to keeping a healthy bottom line amongst the pharmaceuticals. It makes good business sense to keep them onside and a disproportionate amount of the marketing budget goes on these activities.

Another large chunk of the advertising budget is spent on 'drug reps'. These are individuals that try to talk to medics at all levels of the profession with limited success. Once a medic finds a drug that they 'trust' (i.e. delivers what it says it should at the level it said it would) they will continue to prescribe it. This will be the 'go to' drug for that individual and no amount of 'selling' will get them to change it. Medics will be more amenable to changing a drug it if it is ineffective or has large side-effects, but will often rely on the writings of the top individuals to change to another drug rather than the rambling sales pitch of a drug rep. In this situation, you can quickly appreciate that spending vast sums of money on a very few individuals to get them to attend conferences (a pursuit that is not associated with the research and so the researcher does not have to declare it when writing for journals) is worthwhile.

All of this information although very interesting is very much a moot point in the field of diet drugs. The medic actually has very few drugs to choose from and so the decision of which one to use is relatively simple. All will become clear later, but they have an effective choice of one in the EU and UK and only a couple more outside of this geographical region. The whole host of other 'drugs' are actually not drugs at all and so cannot be prescribed by a medic. There are others available to them, but they are not registered for the prescription of weight loss and so are therefore of little interest to us. This simple fact means that the pharmaceutical companies do not have to spend much money on trying to get medics to choose their drug. They need only ensure that the medic chooses to prescribe a drug for the condition rather than relying on non-pharmacological interventions.

'HALFISH'-TIME

At this point, it would be helpful to consider how far we have come. In the first three chapters of this book we have discussed how companies have hazed the line between diet 'drugs' and drugs. Despite explicit laws to the contrary in the UK, it is extremely difficult to discern the difference between registered medicines, herbal remedies, homeopathic remedies and food supplements. All of these substances are cleverly traded under the guise of a pharmacological intervention to attempt to convince the potential customer that the product they are buying will have a biological effect to stop them eating. By cleverly portraying their product to the population to the limits of the laws they must adhere to, or simply using the Internet to actively disregard these laws, they have managed to sell their product trading on the medical profession.

How diet 'drugs' are sold to the general population vary considerably. Most will make outrageous claims about what their product can do. They implicitly employ theoretical components to why people want to lose weight and directly appeal to them even though the product can never deliver it. Let us be honest, the writers of affiliate websites do not really understand either the theoretical underpinning to why people want to lose weight nor do they understand how the drug they are selling works. They may have a rough idea of why people want to lose weight based on media representations, anecdotal evidence given from friends or information given to them from the affiliate management companies, but they will not be doing this with any understanding. They will judge the success or failure of what their writing based on the sales they generate. In such an environment, promising the Earth is easy because they do not have to deliver anything. Promising the Earth is also more likely to generate sales because a lot of the customers are desperate to lose weight and would love to hear of a miracle cure. Ironically, the vast majority of the Western population believe that medicine can provide the miracle cure despite it being based on science rather than theology. The reason people mix up medicine with miracle cures is primarily because they do not understand how it works, only that it does. In short, these companies and individuals are selling the dream. They prey on the hopes of the people desperate to lose weight and attain a socially acceptable body image in an environment it is improbable to achieve. Selling any product in this manner would in any other situation be tantamount to a violation of the Trade Descriptions Act if not for a technicality. Now, we must consider this technicality.

So far we have considered the processes of law and regulation of diet 'drugs' and how they are sold. We have not yet considered how they actually purport to work and therefore have not fully justified that what the advertising material is saying is in fact untrue. The next half of this book is dedicated solely to this pursuit. Before we consider the actual substances found on the Internet, we must first understand what is and is not possible under current biological/medicinal knowledge. With the advancement of drug delivery methods this may change (and there are some truly interesting and novel approaches being developed in the frontier research), but for the subsequent pages of this book we will base what is possible on the substances available to the population. This is probably the stuff you really wanted to know, but it was important to understand how diet 'drugs' are sold, what is and is not allowed and why someone puts the substance into their body in the first place prior to considering the biology and pharmacology. If there was no desire for them, or regulation of them, then there would be no reason to develop them.

Chapter 4

OF PHARMACOLOGICAL TARGETS: HITTING THE BULL'S-EYE

Firstly, let us state that there is no free-for-all anything goes potential targets for a drug to act on in the body for the purposes of weight-loss. Pharmacologists and medics are bound by doing no harm to the person, which effectively denies some potential targets. To get rid of one potential target straight away, targeting fat cells (or to give them their correct name adipocytes) is not credible. It is a pointless pursuit. The targeting of fat cells to denature (kill) them would mean that the fat that they contain would be released into the blood stream leading to heart disease and strokes. You would be thin, but dead. Even targeting the fat cells to stop them from absorbing fat from the blood stream would have the same effect. Therefore, any statement made about specifically targeting fat cells is either untrue or useless. Stopping them from working or destroying these little cells will quickly kill you to. This, at the very least, does not make good business sense. To get rid of fat cells requires a surgical, rather than a pharmaceutical, intervention. If we wish to destroy a fat cell the only safe place to do it is outside of the body. There is one potential pharmacological target within the fat cell that is viable and that is how this cell communicates with the brain. By mimicking this communication pathway we can trick the brain into thinking it has more fat in storage than it actually has and therefore make someone feel less hungry. Current attempts to do this have met with very limited success. It appears that obese people have much higher levels of this communicative chemical (it is called Leptin and it is a hormone) and their eating behaviour seems to be unresponsive to increasing it any further. Like the drug addict, they become increasingly tolerant to the Leptin in their system receiving fewer effects from it and requiring increased dosages of it to achieve similar outcomes over time. I am sure you are all thinking of addicts in terms of abusive drugs, but I would consider this in terms of coffee. Think back to the first time you had coffee and the first time you drank too much of it. I am sure you suffered with the side-effects of too much caffeine. I also believe that your current daily intake of coffee exceeds the amount you first experienced the side-effects with. In short, you are now tolerant to it. We will come back to caffeine later in the subsequent chapters as it is supposedly a potential active ingredient of some weight-loss 'drugs'. In truth, most weight-loss drugs rely on the effects of caffeine to get their product to market.

Viable targets for weight-loss drugs are limited to two real regions of the body. These are either the appetite-regulation areas of the brain or the intestines. The objective here is to either stop the individual's desire to eat or to stop their body from absorbing macronutrients, preferably fat, into the blood stream. Stopping the desire to eat can come in two forms, either make the person think they are full all the time, despite there being no food in their digestive system, or remove their ability to feel hungry. Arguably there is a third mechanism and that is to remove people's enjoyment of eating food. However, this third term is not a particularly valuable or potentially useful target because it is the same region of the brain that heroin works on. These are called opioid receptors. Please do not make the same mistake as the newspapers did and think that opioids in eating behaviour are addictive. Heroin is an opiate and works on the same system of the brain as endogenous (found inside the body) opioids. Opioids are natural chemicals found in the brain, opiates are exogenous (found outside the body) chemicals found in the wider environment that mimic the effect of opioids. Artificial activation of opioid receptors by exogenous chemicals is addiction through the misuse of a substance, endogenous activation of opioid receptors by the opioids in the brain is simply how your brain's reward pathways work. Anything that a person likes activates this pathway (e.g. listening to music, sex etc...). The addictive nature of chemicals created to work on opioids receptors effectively curtails their use. They are simply too easy to abuse. Moreover, the administration of any drug that activates this pathway does not stop a person from feeling hungry and will not stop them from eating. It simply decreases the amount they consume during a meal by artificially decreasing the endogenous reward for eating.

This high fat food is addictive concept is still widely pushed by the dieting industry. It comes under the remit of "it is not your fault you eat a bad diet, you are addicted to it". You can even see rather idiotic statements that fat has the same effect as hard drugs throughout the wider media. Depending who says this I will role my eyes or shake my head in quiet resignation. In another book I wrote about eating behavior[1], I explained that food is not addictive. It cannot be, as it is an essential need. We have evolved to deal with our environment and we are given little endogenous rewards for achieving energy security and, gram for gram, you get more calories from fat than from other macronutrients. Therefore, we receive more endogenous reward for eating a gram of fat compared to a gram of other macronutrients (protein or carbohydrate), although there is room for individual preferences in this relationship[2]. Being addicted to something means that you are reliant on an exogenous substance that causes irreparable harm to the biological integrity of the individual yet it is perceptually still needed to function. Food is an essential need and in its absence it causes irreparable harm. You need a proportion of fat as part of a viable diet; you do not need a proportion of heroin. Eating too much fat is simply an expression of the food available in the environment combined with endogenous reward, not an addictive motivation to consume it. Of course we have evolved to choose energy dense foods over less energy dense foods to achieve energy security, but this is not the motivation of an addict. Moreover, you get the same reward for going to the toilet as you do from eating. Unfortunately, going to the toilet does not affect our impression management like being overweight; unless of course you do it in front of everyone or in the wrong designated location. I am still waiting for the day when

---

[1] Same citation as note 15.

[2] For example, some people and animals prefer carbohydrates over fats, while others prefer fats over carbohydrates. Despite this preference component, there is more energy in fat over carbohydrate, so more energy is available from a gram of fat compared to a gram of carbohydrates. Moreover, messing around with the endogenous reward system via pharmacologically blocking its effects results in reduction of fat compared to other macronutrients. Taha, S. A. (2010). Preference for fat? Revisiting opioids effects on food intake. *Physiology & Behaviour, 100*, 429-437.

the media report "Beware: Using your toilet is addictive" or "Beware: Hide your teenagers from the addictive nature of music". I am still waiting.

In this chapter, we will explore what are the current potential targets for weight-loss drugs. These will be appropriately restricted to the digestive system and the appetite regulation areas of the brain. It is assumed that you will not need to know all of the pharmacokinetics of the system because we do not have the space in one whole book, let alone one whole chapter, to discuss this. Instead, we will talk about the targets by their designated name and the location where they can be found. You will be given a brief introduction of what they do and what changes in behaviour can be observed if we activate or mimic them but for the in depth detail you will have to turn to the more pharmacological texts. The reason it will not be covered here is that it is assumed that you will not need to know it. In the pages of this book we are concerned with diet 'drugs' and how they are alleged to work. To know this, we must have some grasp on the endogenous targets that the 'drugs' are attempting to access. If affiliates or vendors do not offer these targets, offer a different target outside of the appetite regulation pathway or it is misunderstood/misrepresented then it can be concluded that the drug is nothing better than a placebo. It is possible to blind someone with science and scientific language but when interpreted based on our current knowledge is totally meaningless. I will state again here, that no evidence means that the 'drug' does not work, not that it is "unknown how it works" or "might work" or "does work" until proven otherwise. The rest of this chapter will be broken down into biochemical targets of the brain and those of the body specifically the intestines after we consider the possible ways of "burning fat".

"Burning Fat"

The term "fat burners" is used a lot by affiliate websites as both a descriptive term and an explanatory term for the products they are attempting to sell. It is neither descriptive of any process in the human body nor is it a credible explanation of how any 'drug' works. The human body does not 'burn' fat. Without dragging you all kicking and screaming back into secondary school biology class, humans receive energy from Adenosine triphosphate or ATP. It is not necessary to understand Kreb's cycle or the metabolic pathways of how sugars and fats are broken down to provide energy; instead one need only understand simple energy balance to understand what is meant when the term fat burner appears as descriptor for a product.

Energy balance refers to one of three states: Positive energy balance, where more energy is consumed then is used on a daily basis; Negative energy balance, where more energy is used then is being consumed; and energy balance or maintenance, where energy coming into the system equals the energy going out of it. 'Fat burning' invariably refers to being in a state of negative energy balance. It is often linked to a specific type of negative energy balance – the increase of energy expenditure. In order to lose weight through negative energy balance, one may decrease the amount consumed (i.e. push down the energy intake side of the balance) or increase activity (i.e. lift up the energy expenditure side of the balance). 'Fat burning' essentially refers to an individual that has reached a state where all of their glycogen stores have been exhausted and the body has started to use fat tissue to maintain them.

Although it has no basis in reality, the name fat burning does 'sound' good. It meets the objectives of the consumer and is an instant, very graphic and easy-to-understand 'branding'. It is a great marketing ploy.

Different weight-loss strategies attempt to manipulate energy balance in very different ways. Some are direct and unrefined, while others are harder to understand and attribute to the balance. Simple dieting, that is restricting food eaten, and simple exercise interventions have obvious effects on the balance. Dieting effectively means the control and restriction of eating behaviour to force the body into a state where less energy is consumed than is required to perform the daily functions. Although our bodies are adaptive to short periods of time without food, there are several mechanisms that have evolved to force the person to eat again in the presence of food. In the modern environment, where food is convenient and immediately available, restricting food can be extremely difficult. Our brains are hardwired to become obsessed with finding, preparing and eating food when we are in energy debt. The longer this form of negative energy balance is maintained the more obsessive an individual will come and therefore exponentially increasing amounts of attentional resources will be required to refrain from eating. It does not take long before the psychological restriction of food becomes all encompassing. In contrast, increasing activity is relatively straightforward as long as the dieter has the time and fitness to devote to it. However, there is another fundamental flaw with increasing activity to maintain a negative energy balance. This is that the majority of the energy we consume is not used up by motor movement. Most of the energy we consume is used in maintaining the activity of our organs and metabolism. Metabolism in this case would be our mammalian warm blooded core temperature. Increasing activity will have a relatively minimal effect on overall energy output. One would need to exercise for many hours to 'burn' off the calories of breakfast, effectively denying the body the net energy profit taken in at that meal.

The 'drugs' available through the Internet are roughly characterised by affiliates as appetite suppressants or fat burners. Appetite suppressants aid the dieter through removing the impetus to eat supposedly allowing the individual to force the energy intake side of the energy balance further down than would be allowed without pharmacological help. Fat burners, as a term used by vendors and affiliates, are those 'drugs' that supposedly increasing metabolic rate in order to 'burn off' more calories than would ordinarily take place without them in the system. They are purported to function through inhibition of a variety of enzymes to increase body temperature or metabolic function (see figure 4.2).

Figure 4.1. Diagram of energy balance.

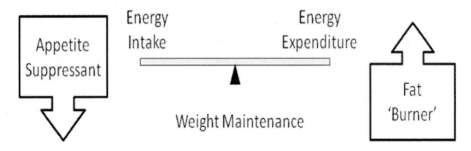

Figure 4.2. Diagram of how the words fat burner and appetite suppressant work with energy balance.

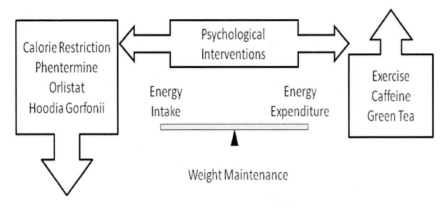

Figure 4.3. Diagram how the various interventions for weight-loss work on energy balance.

Beyond fat 'burning' and appetite suppression, there are also other mechanisms to aid in weight-loss. Orlistat, for example, inhibits the absorption of fat and so also limits energy intake without interfering with appetite. Behavioural interventions, although sometimes include simple dieting, generally refer to psychological interventions or peer support groups that uncover the barriers to losing weight. These psychological tactics are able to affect either side of the energy balance equation through optimising the motivation to engage in other weight-reduction behaviours. The majority of these behavioural approaches are related to triggers that lead to violating the calorie restriction component to the diet (see figure 4.3). In summary, the term "fat burner" is a nebulous term with little scientific merit. It is used in the context of energy balance and specifically in reference to a weight-loss drug that increases energy expenditure side of the energy balance equation.

TARGETING THE BRAIN

Any claim that a 'drug' stops someone feeling hungry means that it is targeting the brain. Making them feel full would potentially involve either the body or the brain. Targeting the brain directly means trying to mimic or increase the effectiveness of neurotransmitters. 'Neurotransmitter' is the specific name for the communicative biochemicals in the brain. In contrast, biochemicals outside of the brain that serve the same function are known as hormones. Both biochemicals provide communication between two cells by being released from one cell and generally activating receptors on the target cell. Receptors, as a quick recap, are small protein structures on the surface of the cell specifically designed to link with neurotransmitters and hormones. Success of activation is generally through increased concentration of the biochemical in the blood (hormone) or synapse (neurotransmitter). In effect, increasing the concentration will increase the likelihood of interaction between active biochemical (neurotransmitter or hormone) and receptor. The synapse is a small enclosed 'gap' between two brain cells (aka neurons). Communication between brain cells is done through a cascade effect. Therefore, activating one cell will have limited impact on the person. To maximise impact we need to ensure activation or inhibition of the whole pathway. For those struggling with this concept then return to the second assumption section of this book and have a little reread of the series of rooms analogy. Increasing concentrations of an active biochemical in the brain can be achieved through several means and therefore diet drugs can work in any one of these approaches. Brain cells communicate with one-another through a process known as neurotransmission. Those of you that took A-level biology this process should be familiar, for those that did not I will provide a very quick crash course. For those who already know this then simply skip ahead, but it may be worth having another little recap on it.

Neurotransmission is the passing of a chemical message from one brain cell to the next through an electro-chemical reaction. All brain cell surfaces (aka cell membranes) are electrically charged. Activating the biochemical receptors of the target cell by release of neurotransmitters from the previous cell in the pathway causes the target brain cell to depolarise (lose its charge). This change causes a chain reaction in the cell resulting in the release of its neurotransmitters to communicate with the next cell in the pathway. Once the cell has depolarised, it will quickly repolarise and reabsorb a proportion of the neurotransmitters released into the synapse. Getting the cell back to its original state as fast as possible allows for faster processing of information. To do this, the cell must not only repolarise, but also remove all of the active neurotransmitters from the synapse as fast as possible. This speed in removing neurotransmitters means that brain cells are not activated unintentionally. To speed up the clearance of neurotransmitters from the synapse, there are a number of methods for clearance on all of the cells that create the synapse (these include both the brain cells and their supporting cells – known as glia cells). There are also enzymes (complex protein structures) in the synapse specifically designed to 'deactivate' the neurotransmitters left there. This, as you can imagine, is an extremely fast process. Any drug designed to increase the activity of a brain cell can target any number of locations in the process of neurotransmission. Some mimic the neurotransmitter, some make the cell create more neurotransmitters, others target the enzymes in the synapse and yet others stop the brain cell from reabsorbing its neurotransmitters after release. This causes the biologically unintended but pharmacologically intended activation of the target brain cell. Diet drugs therefore have numerous potential targets to achieve the increase or decrease of the concentration of a specific biochemical – in this case the neurotransmitter.

Understanding the process of neurotransmission is good; however, we must go further than this and transcend into the macro world. Cells and their various interactive agents comprise the microscopic world. Their pathways are large enough to inhabit the macro world. Although a variety of structures and pathways are involved in the control of eating behaviour, by far the undisputed ruler is the hypothalamus. This is a region of the brain that is responsible for a variety of functions and has all of the main neurotransmitter pathways running through it. Most of these functions are those that require interaction with the rest of the body. Mostly, the brain processes information from the wider world. In situations where the body requires a hormonal response, it will invariably involve the hypothalamus at some point.

The anatomy of the hypothalamus is quite interesting. Well it is fascinating to me, but most people do not share my nerdy predispositions. Essentially, the hypothalamus comprises of lots of nuclei (this is not to be confused with the nuclei of cells). All cells have nuclei that contain their DNA. These are microscopic cell organelles. Macroscopic nuclei are regions within the hypothalamus responsible for looking after different actions. The easiest way to explain how the hypothalamus looks after eating behaviour is to run through a quick example that I use with my first years.

If we start with boxes in figure 4.4 and attempt to put in arrows to show how the various hypothalamic 'nuclei' interact with one another. Invariably, most of my students will complete it by putting in arrows in a circle as in the figure. The completion of a diagram that accurately represents the reality of how the hypothalamus operates is shown in figure 4.5. As you appreciate from this arrangement the interaction is much more complex than what most people would ordinarily understand. In fact, the representation of the hypothalamus in figure 4.5 is a very simplistic offering to explain how the region functions and interacts. Therefore, interfering with this system is not as easy as targeting one biochemical that would be responsible for hunger or fullness.

In terms of structures within the hypothalamus responsible for eating behaviour, these are the Arcuate nucleus, the Lateral Hypothalamic Area, and the Paraventricular nucleus. There are also some arguments to include the Ventromedial nucleus, but this is debatable. It really is not important that you understand all of various names of all of these various structures. What is important to understand is that the Arcuate nucleus along with the stomach is responsible for hunger (it starts eating) and that the rest of the brain and body, through a very complex interaction, tries to stop you from eating. Neither starting nor stopping eating is controlled by a single biochemical, which further complicates any potential pharmacological intervention. This complexity is the main problem in attempting to define, rationalise and create a viable weight-loss drug under the term the affiliates declare as appetite suppressants.

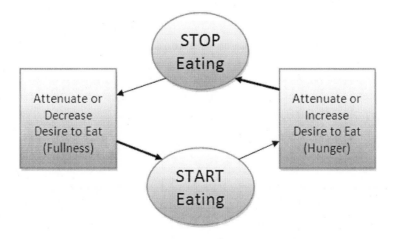

Figure 4.4. Control of appetite.

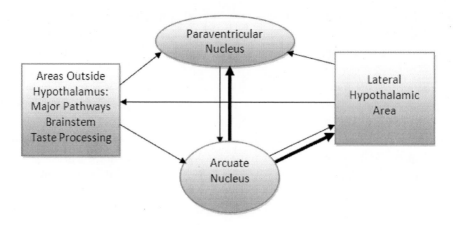

Figure 4.5. Hypothalamic representation for the control of appetite.

Just when you thought that the complexity could not get any worse, there is one more thing that anyone attempting to understand how weight-loss drugs work also need to know. This is that the receptors the neurotransmitters bind to also come in variations. These various structures for the same biochemical allow the same neurotransmitter to have multiple functions. Receptors that bind with the same neurotransmitter are called receptor families. Numerous members of the same family can exist, which for the body and brain in its normal day to day functioning is totally appropriate. Each receptor sub-type is generally in different regions of the brain and do not interact. However, when any drug, pharmaceutical or otherwise (e.g. herbs or nutritional supplements) is put in the system to increase the action of a specific pathway thought to be responsible for a specific behaviour, it will invariably activate many of the receptors in the same family. This will lead to inadvertent side-effects unless the action of the drug can be refined to work only on one receptor within the family or is directly targeted. Unfortunately, we are not allowed to inject drugs directly into someone's brain so all drugs that travel in the blood are delivered indirectly. Although we could spend an awful long time on this subject, it is not necessary to understand it in its entirety. What is integral is that there is an appreciation that simply putting a chemical of any kind into the body will have significant problems and interfering with appetite is an extremely complex process. It is not a case of quashing or suppressing it.

There are numerous potential targets in the brain that could be used to create an effective drug to aid weight-loss and they are shown in the table 4.1; however, not all of them are preferred targets due to how they function. The vast majority of the potential targets in the brain are episodic rather than tonic signals. Episodic signals are those that precede and respond to each meal. They naturally fluctuate to make someone feel hungry, search for food, consume it and digest it. Tonic signals in contrast respond to stored energy. These signals fluctuate over a longer period of time and only if the person alters their weight-status. In terms of brain targets, it is pharmacologically preferable to trick the body into artificially terminating a meal. Although this is not the most preferable strategy overall, that is reserved for targeting the body, terminating a meal is better than stopping a person from eating altogether. From a pharmacological perspective it is much more effective to taper a biochemical reaction then it is to try and stop it altogether. Instead of working against the system, which is likely to have much larger side-effects, it is better to work with it in some manner. Furthermore, stopping eating altogether may eventually have problems with reinitialising it once the target weight has been reached. If effective, this would result in the individual skipping past a healthy weight and into an under-weight weight-status. Terminating eating altogether would also result in rapid weight-loss, which will result in an increased likelihood in weight regain. Therefore, working with brain targets that increase the likelihood for terminating a meal early will result in more controlled, healthy weight-loss that will be easier to maintain upon completion of the intervention.

Considering the preference for artificially terminating a meal and signals that are tonic rather than episodic, the chemicals that would be of most interest are those found in the left hand column of the table 4.1. Specifically, it is serotonin and dopamine. The reason for this preference is that these two chemicals appear to be related to the sensation of fullness. In contrast, the other biochemicals in the list (Cocaine and Amphetamine Regulated Transcript (CART); Alpha Melanocyte-Stimulating Hormone (αMSH); Coricotropin Releasing Factor (CRF)) are competitors to undermining the feelings of hunger. These other three biochemicals actively interact and are in competition to the neurotransmitters in the right hand column while serotonin and dopamine provide a suppressive effect on the whole appetite regulation loop. Brief forays have been attempted to manipulate the CART system by using the substances that bear their names, but because of their highly addictive natures they quickly became drugs of abuse rather than of use. Weak appetite related effects have been found with αMSH; while CRF is complicated and confounded by its integral role in initiating the stress response. High levels of stress hormones in the bloodstream lead to obesity rather than weight-loss. Messing around with the brain, it would appear, is not without its consequences. However, that story is saved for the next chapter when we look at the fall from grace of the previous pharmacological attempts to intervene with people's appetites.

Table 4.1. Biochemicals (neurotransmitters) in the Brain Involved in Eating

Stops Eating	Starts/Increases Eating
1. Cocaine and Amphetamine Regulated Transcript	1. Neuropeptide Y
2. Alpha Melanocyte-Stimulating Hormone	2. Agouti-Related Protein
3. Corticotropin Releasing Factor	3. Melanin-Concentrating Hormone
4. Serotonin	4. Orexin A
5. Dopamine	5. Orexin B
6. Noreadrenaline	6. Endogenous Opioid Peptides
	7. Gamma-Aminobutyric Acid
	8. Noreadrenaline

The link between serotonin and feelings of fullness has been known for over thirty years and has been the target of pharmaceutical interventions for weight-loss above any other potential alternatives. It has been consistently shown that serotonin, or to give it its real name 5-hydroxtriamine, increases feelings of fullness no matter how you interfere with its neurotransmission. Direct injections into the brain of animals, or tricyclic (that increases production and release of serotonin in the brain) and selective serotonin reuptake inhibitors (SSRIs – that stop the brain cell reabsorbing serotonin after realising it into the synapse) administration in humans decrease meal size without interfering with hunger and the initiation of a meal [33]. The most important component in the function of serotonin is that interfering with it does not result in compensatory behaviours or biology. In short, it is pretty effective on first glance.

One of the most frustrating and yet beautiful components to the human brain, and any animal brain, is its ability to compensate and function even without specific chemicals. Just when we think that we have isolated the right biochemical responsible for a specific behaviour or role, our understanding is unraveled when we knock it out. Knocking out is a genetic research model of investigating the actual impact of the loss of a particular biochemical or one of its receptors. The gene required to create a biochemical or one of its receptors is selectively removed from an animal's DNA. If a particular biochemical is required to make you eat or stop you from eating then when it is knocked out it should result in anorexia or obesity in respect to its hypothesized effect. Time and again we find that our best guess for what a specific biochemical is supposed to do does not result in what we expected to happen. Often the animal ends up living a normal healthy life. Something in the living animal compensates for the loss of a specific gene by using something else in its place. It is important to be mindful of these genetic models when making absolute statements about the function of a specific biochemical. It would appear that the living organism is reliant on DNA for coding what it does and what it is, but there is some flexibility in the holistic system with either 'redundant back-up systems' that can be reactivated when required or the existence of a 'count as' where the gene expressed in a particular location can be replaced at will if damaged or mutated. Some of our genetic make-up is definitely integral to our existence, however, others are not.

Before we declare success and all hail serotonin as the 'King cure' for obesity and as the pharmacological target for diet drugs, there are some important observations that we should acknowledge. Firstly, it has been 'weaponised' in numerous forms since its discovery and has been found wanting in every case. Recently, the last vestige of serotonin-related drugs for the treatment of obesity was removed from the European market. Following the steady removal of its sibling drugs, Sibutramine was removed under the auspices of the MHRA in late January 2010. It was not unexpected. All of the previous serotonin targets had significant problems with side-effects, in particular heart complications, and the European Medicine Agencies decided that the risks of this drug outweighed the benefits for taking it. It would appear that any complications that place the person at risk of death, no matter how small, were not considered appropriate for weight loss interventions. The King has died and has left no heir.

There are also some honourable mentions required for some other targets. In a rather backwards about coming forwards manner, Gamma-Aminobutyric Acid (GABA) has also been believed to have been investigated through the administration of the anti-convulsion drug Topiramate. How this drug works is unknown, but it has been shown to decrease food intake. Until such time as the mechanism of how it works is uncovered, and whether that is actually GABA or something else, it will not be used for the treatment of obesity. This can be evidenced in the fact that the Phentermine/Topiramate mix (called Qnexa) was rejected outright over safety concerns. Phentermine is an amphetamine for those interested and we will come back to discuss this drug in detail later in the book. Obesity is not immediately life-threatening, so regulatory bodies are less tolerant to unknowns and potential side-effects.

Another honourable mention for a potential diet drug target that does not appear on our appetite regulation list is Cannabinoids. Allegedly, smoking cannabis leads to cravings for food popularly known as 'the munchies'. Scientists thought that if they blocked this receptor then it would also block cravings for food. This led to the development of the drug Rimonabant. This drug got close to being a viable target despite our understanding of its role in appetite regulation being quite poor. Alas, as soon as it was released, it was withdrawn. It would appear that targeting this neurotransmitter pathway had similar co-related problems as smoking cannabis does – namely the increased risk of psychosis. This was a 'double-whammy' finding. Not only was cannabiniods effectively deleted as a viable target for appetite interventions, it also provided strong evidence against the proponents of cannabis as not increasing the risk of psychosis.

Targeting the brain (known as targeting central mechanisms) appears to have fallen from its very high pedestal following its initial investigations. Let this be a warning to us. What we think we know about the human brain is not enough to attempt pharmacological interventions. When it is necessary to intervene to save someone's life or lift their quality of life out of an unbearable situation, then messing about with neurochemistry can be defended. For the purposes of weight-loss it would appear that our attempts have been judged wanting and certainly needlessly risky. Thus, it would be hoped that people who state that their products are interfering with the brain understand what they are saying and the potential impact on someone's life who is taking them. The risk to reward calculation for taking the drug is inevitably up to the individual. However, most people are that desperate and will believe that the worst side-effects will not happen to them. For most people taking these substances that judgment will be vindicated; however it is risky. The best chance of not suffering adverse side-effects is to not take it. No matter the size of the odds, taking pharmaceuticals that act on the brain for the purposes of weight loss come with risks and they should be fully understood and reported by the vendor and their advertisers at the point of sale. Advertising products as 'all sweetness and light' or playing down the potential effects means that any negative side-effects are on the hands of those that sold the substance not on those that created it. Onus of responsibility really cannot be stated any stronger than this.

Do these supposed failures mean that we should stop investigating the targets in the brain – certainly not. Understanding the brain and how it functions is one of the frontier sciences. Once we comprehend how our brains' function, a lot more medicines and cures will subsequently be identified. Understanding how a relatively few cells manage to perform so many functions is truly bewildering. Sometimes we, the professionals included, get so caught up in linking 'A to B to C' that we fail to appreciate the awe and splendour that is our brains and what they are capable of. Perhaps the failure to step back so infrequently has led to some of these failures in the development of diet drugs; as well as a lot of neuromyths[3] that have

---

[3] For some of the best neuromyths read the articles by neuroscientist and educationalist Dr Paul Howard-Jones. Most of his material can be found on the University of Bristol website. His book Howard-Jones, P. (2010).

sprung up in various sectors particularly the education sector. Stopping all investigations into the brain based on a few failures would not bode well for the resilience of the human race. Furthermore, no matter how well we formulate our hypotheses and carefully plan and rationalise our belief models about the inner workings of our brains the simple fact is a lot of what we know was serendipitous[4]. Tinkering with a system is how we understand the governing principles of its inner workings. Sometimes when we are tinkering we pull on the 'wrong wire' and, as a natural part of the learning process, there will be more failures than successes. By its very nature, there will only ever be one true success. Everything else, in terms of theoretical explanation, will inevitably end in failure.

The best possible outcome in the pursuit of a weight-loss drug is actually in not targeting behaviour at all. This would mean avoiding the brain altogether. Instead, it would be preferable to target the peripheral structures of the body. The best possible solution would be to ensure that the drug does not enter the bloodstream at all and therefore have less chance of serious side-effects[5]. In the next section, we will consider these targets.

TARGETING THE BODY

Targeting biological structures in the body is likely to have a larger impact on eating behaviour than targeting the brain. This may sound counterintuitive and controversial but the logic of the argument is strong. Undoubtedly, the human body is an intricate machine with the brain surpassing all of the other organs in its complexity and energy demands. Using comparatively crude pharmacological interventions on the most complex organ is likely to have significant problems. The reason for this is partly the requirements of the ability to patent a drug and partly our inability, or perhaps our general reluctance, to attempt to manipulate the system with multiple drugs. There are also significant problems with the 'laziness' of our biology too.

In order to copyright a drug and allow a pharmaceutical to have the sole rights to its manufacture, relatively large complex supposedly inert tags are added to the active part of the chemical. This practice provides two beneficial components. The first is that it makes it significantly more difficult to back engineer the product and then allow a rival company to create a similar active substance. The creation of the complex addition to the active site also gives the pharmaceutical company something to patent. In the UK, it is not possible to patent a naturally occurring substance. If it was than the first thing I would patent is analogue of caffeine. I would be extremely rich overnight as anyone who wished to grow or use caffeine would have to pay me. Although an extremely simplistic non-viable example, the creation of the 'extra' part of the drug means that the chemical is not naturally made and therefore can be considered 'created'. This creation can then be patented. The second benefit for adding on large extra components to the drug's structure is that it gives the substance survivability in the hostile environment of the human body. Loads of barriers exist that will stop the active drug

---

Introducing Neuroeducational Research. Abingdon: Routledge also makes an interesting read and well worth a look.

[4] I would like to take credit for this statement but I have to admit that it is borrowed from my old PhD supervisor. All I can say is that it is something that was passed to me that I am now passing on to you.

[5] Well actually the best possible outcome would be not to use pharmaceuticals or 'drugs' for the purposes of weight loss. No drug, no side effects.

reaching its destination. The complexity will give the drug a chance of reaching its destination and having the desired effect. There are several promising strategies currently in the very early stages of development that may render this practice redundant, especially for targets in the body rather than the brain.

There is also a general reluctance to 'hijack' a biological system for the purposes of medical interventions. Instead, medical interventions will either replace a missing component to the biological pathway, as in the case of insulin in diabetes, or 'nudge' the pathway into increased activity, as in the case of the SSRIs mentioned in the last section of this chapter. 'Hijacking' the system would require controlling all aspects of the pathway necessitating the use of multiple drugs in a carefully controlled dosage placed at the site where they are supposed to work in an extremely finite time period. Minor deviations from this complex arrangement will likely have dramatic negative effects. In the complex environment of the human brain, 'nudging' is definitely preferable to 'hijacking' – if only for practical rather than the obvious moral issues of pharmacologically 'hijacking' someone else's brain. Multiple drugs are usually only given to treat a patient with a complex medical problem with multiple symptoms or a life threatening condition where the essential requirement is to administer a potent drug that has large side-effects. These then must be managed for the individual to have any form of quality of life.

The final problem is that our systems are biologically 'lazy'. If it is at all possible, the same biochemicals will be used to do multiple jobs in multiple locations and organs around the body. Therefore, without specificity of activating only one receptor, the drug administered is likely to have unexpected effects. It was mentioned in the last chapter that a lot of the Serotonergic drugs (e.g. Sibutramine) have significant side-effects with heart complications. This is because the heart uses Serotonin to control some of its vital functions. Administration of a Serotonergic drugs for the purposes of altering brain function will also have an effect on the heart, hence the increase in heart attacks while taking them. Appreciating the multi-functional role of a biochemical, as well as discovering new biochemicals and their receptors, in the human body is very much the frontier of biological sciences.

Deciding whether or not to use a pharmacological intervention based on these unfortunate limitations suggests that engaging with the least complex component of weight management is preferable. Another preferred strategy is crossing the least amount of biological barriers. This would suggest that pharmacologically intervening with the digestive system is preferable. It is not as complex, often has less secondary functions and is anatomically situated behind fewer biological barriers than the brain.

The principle process of the digestive system is to break food down into something that can be used by the body and transported by the blood. It is separated into different stages and in each of these stages there is a hormone that signals the rest of the body that the region is actively 'digesting' food. The relative overall function is to break very complex material into its composite parts so our body can use them for its needs. Therefore, the hormonal signals that the various stages in the digestive system release are variants on the theme of 'stop eating' or 'do not eat'. This is reflected in the amount of hormones that have been identified and the markers they are associated with, as shown in table 4.2. These are all episodic biochemicals. They are released in the presence of food to let the rest of the body know that either that 'energy is coming' or that the system is 'in use' and more food is not required. It is a finely controlled machine that is relatively easy to overload. If too much food is put into the system then there is only one exit – the way it came in[6].

The order of the release of the different hormones from the gut happens in a pseudo-set order, indicating that they have some form of anatomical specificity. Ghrelin is released from the stomach and is the only known hormone that actually makes someone hungry. It is believed to have the ability to 'override' the brain's control of appetite. Our stomachs can quite literally rule our heads. Ghrelin is the only exception in the body in terms of its ability to induce, rather than interfere with, hunger. After the stomach, all of the other appetite related hormones released from the intestines create the feeling of fullness.

The intestines are, when put together with the rest of the digestive system, just a really long tube. The intestinal organs extend from the base of the stomach starting at the pyloric sphincter[7] and ends at the anus. There are two separate organs that make up the intestines (the small and large intestines). The small intestine extends from the pyloric sphincter to the ileal break. The smaller intestine (in size rather than length) can be broken down into three sections for the purposes of dealing with food. These sections are known by the names of duodenum, jejunum and ileum. In each of these areas there is a predominant intestinal hormone and generally, but not always, it is the extension, stretching or presence of nutrients in this area that leads to their release into the blood. Cholecystokinin is found in the duodenum, Glucagon Like Peptide 1 and 2 look after the jejunum and Peptide YY is found in the ileum. This is a rather simplistic explanation as the various hormones extend outside of these areas, but these areas are where they are first encountered or predominantly found for the purpose of appetite regulation. It makes sense that the body does not start the next meal until it is satisfied that there is room in the 'production line'. Therefore, most of the hormonal drug targets for appetite have been appropriately aimed at these areas. There are of course, hormones released from fat tissue and other areas of the body in response to food, but these are involved in dealing with the food once it is in the system or to tell the body how much energy it has in storage. Once in the circulatory system, the nutrients must be dealt with and so these would constitute inappropriate targets for diet drugs as they are likely to cause harm to the individual.

Table 4.2. Hormones of the digestive system

Stops Eating	Starts Eating
Cholecystokinin	Ghrelin
Glucagon Like Peptide 1	
Glucagon Like Peptide 2	
Peptide YY	

---

[6] As an interesting side note, this is opioid mediated and the primary mechanism for why heroin addicts do not eat. They literally feel sick. This is an interaction between the reward mechanisms of the brain in the brain stem and the vomit reflex controlled by the gustatory cortex. Both use opioids as their chief neurotransmitter.

[7] Sphincter is not only an American slang term for the anus; sphincter muscles are any muscles that open and close around a tube for the purposes of keeping liquids or semi-liquids in or out of the tube.

Injecting each of these intestinal hormones into a healthy subject has had some significant successes at decreasing food intake during a single meal and when administered over a long period of time has led to weight loss. Cholecystokinin administered to humans results in lowered food intake by around nineteen percent in both lean and obese participants [34]. However, pharmaceutical attempts to exploit Cholecystokinin as a target have failed. Two of the large multi-national pharmaceutical companies have not developed their drugs beyond the trial stage. This means that any 'drugs' that suggest that they work through this system, would be untrue in the strictest sense. Presence of any food in the duodenum will release CCK, so any suggestion that a particular drug works through this system would have to do so in the absence of food. It is a shame that Cholecystokinin has not done well in drug trials, as it is, in my opinion, the most credible intestinal candidate that we know of to pharmacologically target.

Similar effects to Cholecystokinin have been observed with food intake and weight loss when Glucagon Like Peptide 1 is administered, but not to the same degree. An overall decrease in food intake is in the realms of twelve percent compared to Cholecystokinin's nineteen percent [35]. Recent attempts to use Glucagon Like Peptide 1 hormone as a drug target suggest that it is not strong enough to result in enough weight-loss to be registered as a diet drug [36]. Glucagon Like Peptide 2 has received even less support as a viable diet drug target. Finally, administration of Peptide YY has also shown to be very effective at decreasing food intake, but was quickly rejected as a straight-forward target because of large side-effects and its weak effect in obese participants [37]. The side-effects of Peptide YY include nausea, heat flushes, sweating and generalised discomfort. Despite this, two pharmaceuticals have each developed diet drugs using peptide YY as a target, one a nasal spray and the other a pill. Neither company have realised any data about the safety or efficacy of their drugs. It is unlikely that we will see a diet drug any time soon using either Glucagon Like Peptides or Peptide YY as targets.

Compared to other hormonal drug targets in the intestine, Ghrelin is a relatively recent discovery, which is reflected in the lack of drugs targeting it. Despite this, it is comparatively common to see diet 'drugs' advertised on the Internet suggesting that they have some form of effect on Ghrelin compared to any other potential targets. This is probably due to the evidence pointing towards Ghrelin having a role in hunger rather than fullness so it would make more sense to the lay person as a 'good' explanation as to why that particular 'drug' would 'work'. Currently, there is no data available for a viable drug that targets Ghrelin. All we currently know is that Ghrelin injections increase hunger in both lean and obese people and blocking its effect has little effect on eating behaviour. It would appears to have a strong effect when present but is quickly compensated for in its absence probably through brain related control of hunger and meal initiation [38]. Until there is some evidence, preferably independent evidence, all of these claims are unfounded. Personally, I would claim them all unfounded until independent research is completed and published. Data detailing the efficacy of a pharmaceutical company's drug and how it works is eventually found wanting within the scientific literature far too frequently. Often this is because of the natural progression of scientific investigations to lead up to a clinical trial, rather than anything surreptitious. Many potential drugs show initial successes only to fail to reach clinical significance in the blinded drug trial.

Diet drugs devised to interact with the hormonal control have been attempted with varying levels of initial success, but all, so far, have failed to reach the market[8]. Despite these failures, these are the only viable and known direct targets for affecting appetite and successful weight-loss. If a 'drug' does not report to affect one or two of these hormones or neurotransmitters, they are not considered effective. Therefore, if they are not considered effective they should not be traded and will not be registered as a weight-loss drug. There is only one other potential target outside of the hormonal and neurotransmitter control of appetite that could still be considered a diet drug. This particular target does not affect appetite in any way and cannot be considered as affecting hunger or fullness at all. In fact, it would likely lead to increased hunger through less calories making it into the system. This drug target refers to stopping the food actually being absorbed into the body.

TARGETING ENZYMES

There are numerous complex protein structures floating around all areas of your body. These structures all come with the suffix 'ase'. Those of you that can remember far back to your GCSE, O level or high school days will remember that this refers to little proteins called enzymes. There purpose is to break down complex structures into their constituent parts without having to raise the temperature. All complex structures will breakdown if heated high enough. The unfortunate side-effect of increasing the temperature would also be the breakdown of the cells in the body. Thus, enzymes perform an integral function in the human body that would likely result in very significant consequences if they were absent.

Food for humans is essentially the consumption of other forms of life. Our food is made up of the cells of plants, animals and fungi, which must be broken down to their constituent parts so that our bodies can use it for its purposes. Like all apex predators, humans literally steal their energy and nutrients from other life forms. The complexity of the cells in our food is little different than our own. Furthermore, it is important that our bodies have several strong barriers that will deny access to any possible threat to our biological integrity. This threat often comes in the form of single-celled organisms, which also differ little in terms of their composite constituent components from our food. We have a difficult biological conundrum. Both threat and energy come from other organisms. This problem is solved by ensuring that only the smallest possible structures are absorbed into the body.

Absorption of nutrients occurs in the intestinal track. Breaking down the various complex biological materials that form our food falls to the acidic environment of the stomach and the enzymes of the intestine. It is therefore possible to target one or two of these enzymes to prohibit the breakdown of macronutrients, effectively stopping their absorption into the body and thus utilisation or storage. The macronutrients of food fall into one of three categories – protein, carbohydrate and fat. Carbohydrates are essentially different forms of sugar. Fats (usually termed lipids) come in a variety of forms, but are primarily used as a way of storing energy in the human body. Proteins in contrast to the other two groups work through 'a use it or lose it' philosophy. Proteins are consumed, absorbed move around the circulatory system, taken by cells and used or excreted by the kidneys. There is no strict 'storage' site or cell in the human body for proteins. However, arguably one could consider excess muscle mass as a

---

[8] Combined citations from note 55 and 57.

form of protein storage. The two enzyme targets for diet drugs are therefore those responsible for energy storage – carbohydrates and lipids. The enzymes in question are specifically called lipase and amylase. Drugs that stop these two enzymes from working are called lipase inhibitors and amylase inhibitors.

To date, no application of the inhibition of amylase has been attempted for the purposes of weight-loss. The basic science for identification and purification of amylase inhibitors has yet to be completed to a satisfactory standard. All that we currently know about these enzymes is that they are involved in the breakdown of carbohydrates, that there are some natural amylase inhibitors available in nature and that the concentration of the enzyme may be a proxy-marker for hunger between meals [39]. Lipase inhibitors have received much more attention with the development and significant success of the lipase inhibitor Orlistat. It is expected that more drugs will be developed from the vast untapped potential of lipase inhibitors [40]. However, as we will learn in later chapters, this will not be without significant problems of treatment adherence for this group of drugs targeting these enzymes.

Targeting the brain or the body requires an understanding of appetite regulation and the biochemicals within it. 'Drugs' that purport to be effective aids to dieting must target one of the biochemicals outlined in this chapter. If they do not then they are not diet drugs, they are something else altogether. Understanding, developing and trialing a diet drug is not easy, but it is necessary so that information on safety and efficacy can be presented to the medicinal and regulatory bodies. Rushing a product to market without understanding how it works or what it does is not helpful. Most of the time, the true drugs will have significant side-effects that will result in its withdrawal; while the 'drugs' will have limited to no effect on weight-loss at all. Of course, the usual defense found on the Internet is that 'scientists do not know how it works'. Simply put, if we do not know how it works then it is not safe or effective as a diet drug and therefore is not a medicine. To get a diet 'drug' to market under a different term other than a medicine need only show that it is safe. Evidence about effectiveness is not necessary or is watered down to the point that it is a pointless product or, at best, a placebo.

In the next four chapters, we will consider the functional efficacy, reported targets and active ingredients of 'drugs' sold to the world as weight-loss aids, fat burners or any other generic pseudo-scientific names. The chapters are broken down into the past, the present, the pretenders, and efficacy of all of the drugs. We must know what has been tried and failed before we explore the credible diet drug candidates. It is important to know where we have come from before we know where we are or going to. After we have discussed the past and the present in terms of the credible candidates we will finally be in a place to discuss the pretend diet 'drugs' based on their own purported active ingredients. We will also by now appreciate how they got to market and how they are sold. Hopefully with the identification of the less credible 'drugs' we can look more critically at what they are actually saying and the selling strategies they have employed to get buyers to part with their money for them.

Chapter 5

OF THE FALL OF A DYNASTY

The desire to be thin is neither a novel nor recent pursuit. Concomitantly, the pharmacological intervention into obesity is also not particularly new. Before and during the initial explosion in the prevalence of obesity across the globe, the attempt to intervene in appetite regulation and weight status using the pharmacological tools available to the medical profession was commonplace. The first reported widespread pharmacological intervention for obesity was in the 1930s. This intervention related to the use, and subsequent abuse, of a class of drugs called amphetamines. This was not particularly exciting application though, as amphetamines were readily prescribed for all manner of ills following its isolation forty or so years before. In the early to mid part of the last century amphetamines were given to people for everything from combat fatigue in soldiers to attention deficit hyperactivity disorder in children. Obesity was one of many problems believed to respond to the administration of amphetamines. At first they believed it was because of significant panacea like effects of pharmaceuticals. However, some scientists would suggest this to be nothing more than a placebo effect, while others would point towards the generic effect of amphetamines on a wide variety of areas in the brain.

AMPHETAMINES

Amphetamines, when used as a drug, are really quite crude in their target accuracy. They are the drug equivalent of playing darts with howitzers. They will hit the target but will also take out the walls, the house and probably the whole street. Indeed, even when a pharmacologist suggests that they are targeting the effect of a specific neurotransmitter and they are 100% accurate they are still playing darts with bazookas. There are four big neurotransmitter pathways in the brain and to just target one only is likely to have large effects on the whole brain. These four pathways are serotonin, dopamine, noreadrenaline and acetylcholine. Serotonin is by far the largest and is a likely reason why the targeting of serotonin by Sibutramine and its predecessors has met with such poor long-term outcomes. Therefore, explanations such as that a particular drug X targets a particularly neurotransmitter pathway Y may sound interesting and meaningful to the lay person, but to any neuropharmacologist it is tantamount to just about targeting the brain. We demand more specificity in our target explanations. We need to know which receptors, or preferably receptor, the drug targets, how effective it is compared to the natural endogenous biochemical and the effect on the specific receptor it has (i.e. block it or activate it). Amphetamines target three of the big four neurotransmitter pathways – dopamine, serotonin and noreadrenaline.

The principle neurotransmitter that amphetamines work on is dopamine. Dopamine in terms of eating behaviour is a very important in sensitivity to reward and the wanting of food. Effectively, changing levels of dopamine in specific regions of the brain will decrease the desire to want food. Wanting food is an important process to eating. Without the motivation to acquire and consume food the person will not eat no matter how hungry they become. This can be a little hard to grasp, but as a brief explanation, it is best to think of it in terms of your brain having different neurotransmitter pathways for hunger (Neuropeptide Y), fullness (CRF, Serotonin, CART), wanting to eat (Dopamine) and liking the taste (Opioids).

In terms of how amphetamines work on the brain in terms of dopamine function, they do this through increasing the amount of dopamine in the synapse. This affect means that it will increase the amount of dopamine in all dopamine producing brain cells. This is not helpful to a weight-loss drug, as wide spread activation will mean that other dopamine mediated behaviours will also increase. This will result in the person being less risk averse, feel less pain, and be more restless. Mirroring this is the stereotypical behaviour portrayed in films and the media of amphetamine users running around with a vacuum cleaner in the small hours of the night. For effective use, a drug must be specific to the behaviour it is attempting to target. In relation to eating behaviour, the receptor that we are after is the second receptor of the dopamine family or D_2. However, the picture is not that straightforward. Different appetite related weight statuses, as well as the food offered, may have a differential effect on the relative efficacy of amphetamine-induced weight-loss. Every permutation from increased intake to chronic weight-loss has been observed in experiments exploring the activation of different dopamine receptors. The reason the D_2 receptor is implicated is because of the development and subsequent rejection of the selective D_2 activator (known as a receptor 'agonist') diet drug 'Ergoset' showed the most consistent weight-loss outcomes. There is also some evidence that the differences in D_2 receptor distributions in the brain results in obesity [41]. As mentioned above, the action of amphetamines on the brain is not specific to even dopamine; it also works on serotonin and noreadrenaline. Amphetamines appear to work on the serotonin and noreadrenaline neurotransmitter pathways in the same way as it works on dopamine. However, the exact mechanism is still being debated with some resolution to the theoretical models required to explain the experimental data. Irrespective of the theoretical resolution, the official sanctioned use of amphetamines for the purposes of weight-loss has been consigned to the history books in most, but not all, countries. They simply activate too many cells in the brain to be anywhere close to being specific. Hopefully, you now appreciate the howitzer analogy when it comes to the use of amphetamines as a diet drug.

In the previous chapter we marveled at the brain's ability to adapt to the loss of a gene in knock-out experiments. Here, we shall do the same at its ability to adapt to even very high amounts of drugs in circulatory system. Amphetamines may have a large effect on the individual initially, but this decreases over repeated use. Humans become increasingly tolerant to amphetamines following frequent use after only a few weeks. This is not helpful to the continual use of any drug for therapeutic reasons. The brain adapts to this by down-regulating neurotransmitter production. It adapts to expect the surge offered by the pharmaceutical. The presence and action of amphetamines on the brain cell means that it keeps pushing the neurotransmitters out into the synapse. The cells register this increased amount of the neurotransmitter in the synapse and decrease production proportionately.

Although this gives the individual the ability to tolerate the drug, they also become dependent on it to function. The loss of the drug from the system will mean that the neurons will not have enough neurotransmitters to function properly. What follows is the 'crash'. The patient then falls into a cycle of appropriate functioning, crashing and then the desire to take the drug to function again. In other words, they are biologically dependent on the drug. They are addicted.

This tolerability and addiction are not the only problem with the use of amphetamines as pharmacological interventions. They are also fleeting in how long they last. A drug that causes such dramatic effects on the brain will undoubtedly suffer a backlash in the biological need to clear it out of the system. This is reflected in the fact that the effects of amphetamines lasts only a few hours before completely disappearing. This means that the individual will have to take them continuously throughout the day further undermining their future efficacy through increasing the speed of tolerance and addiction [42].

All in all, amphetamines are addictive, become more-or-less ineffective after a few weeks, have to be taken every few hours and cause significant and sometimes permanent alterations to the neurochemistry of the patient. It is no wonder then that they were made illegal in so many countries. However, despite the illegal status of the amphetamines, they have been reported to have been tried by just under a third of obese people in an Italian study. This study also reported that people who have a childhood history of obesity and binge eating disorder are slightly more likely to have tried amphetamines to try and lose weight [43]. It would appear that the use and abuse of amphetamines for the purposes of weight-loss has not totally left our society. This is a shame because it really does have a poor efficacy profile and can do such limitless damage to the person.

The use of amphetamine-like substances is not restricted to the pharmaceutical industry. The original form of the drug was isolated from several species of the plant family ephedra which is commonly found in hot dry climates. The isolation of the natural plant-based form of amphetamine shares the name of the plant family from which it is derived – ephedrine. It has precedence as a traditional herbal therapy and has been used in China for centuries. In the West, ephedrine is used as a nasal decongestant. Its use for controlling appetite does not have the same precedence and it is likely that the application of amphetamines for the purposes of controlling weight dragged the use of ephedrine along with it. Much to the annoyance of traditional herbal vendors across the Western World, the use of ephedrine is restricted. In the UK, it can only be sold by a registered pharmacist who is in direct face-to-face contact with the buyer and they are forbidden to sell more than 180mg in total at any one time. From the beginning of April 2008, legislation made it illegal for anyone else to sell ephedrine. Despite this, it is still easy to buy ephedrine for the purposes of weight-loss on the Internet, costing from around £12 for fifty tablets. The content of ephedrine in diet pills has gone down since the inception of heavy regulation, but it is still relatively easy to find illegal forms of the drug that even boast that they have a high success rate of avoiding detection and delivering the drug to the buyer. Buying ephedrine without prescription restricts the unit of sales to below 180mg in total. This is around 22.5 tablets containing 8mg each or 6 tablets with 30mg in. A simple search on the Internet will reveal that this restriction is not common practice. You can freely buy ephedrine in unrestricted quantities as long as you accept the risk of interception. Some ephedrine tablets are even sold on the Internet as dieting products despite having oral nasal decongestant written on the product. The legislation to limit the sale of ephedrine in pharmacies may have pushed those that wish to buy the product to the Internet. Ephedrine derivatives are also sold under the Chinese herbal name of má huáng.

No matter what evidence is offered in other non-peer reviewed sources, the efficacy of ephedrine is the same as amphetamines. Most Internet sites suggest that between one and two tablets of either 8mg or 30mg are taken before a meal. This would constitute a daily dosage of between 24mg and 180mg. Research indicates that a dose of at least 60mg a day is required to achieve weight-loss. However, research also varies between doses of 60-150mg of ephedrine per day split into equal doses taken thirty minutes before a meal. If someone was taking the higher doses then they would have to visit the pharmacy every day to buy more. At this point, they should be confronted by the pharmacist for inappropriately using ephedrine and banned from buying it. It is, after all, supposed to be sold as a nasal decongestant. This would place further restrictions on the buyer and likely force them to vendors in the virtual environment.

Exploring the best clinical trial[1] on ephedrine performed to date, we find that half of the people that started the trial did not finish it, most choosing not to continue. Both placebo and ephedrine users lost a significant amount of weight over the six month trial with the drug group losing an extra 2.7kg in that time. Ephedrine in this trial was also taken in conjunction with caffeine. In trials where ephedrine was taken alone, these are: not peer-reviewed; do not meet worthiness of including in a meta-analysis; or written in a language that is not English. A meta-analysis [44] indicates that the most likely outcome of taking ephedrine with or without caffeine is the additional loss of 1kg. Putting the person at risk of significant harm by taking an amphetamine-like substance will benefit to the sum of just one kilogram. Moreover twelve out of twenty-three studies did not even achieve this average loss[2].

The last vestiges of the group of drugs called amphetamines are still hanging on within the pharmacological treatments of obesity. With a brief banning from April 2000 to May 2001, phentermine is the last of this dying breed. As Phentermine is still around and is indeed reported to be the most frequently used drug for treating obesity in the US [45], we will come back to it in the next chapter. In the UK, phentermine is not recommended for weight-loss under the National Institute for Clinical Health and Excellence (NICE); instead, they prefer to rely on the lipase inhibitor Orlistat.

Prescriptions of amphetamines from the 1930s quickly reached epic proportions. From a status of a panacea prescribed for all manner of ills, the utility of amphetamines for the purposes of weight-loss has been inconsistent at best. All manner of outcomes from weight gain to weight loss has been reported by obese people taking this group of drugs. Although it is still the preferred drug elsewhere in the world, evidence from the pharmaceutical derivatives and the natural herbal remedy indicate that very small additional weight-losses will be observed by people who are using them concurrent to restricting calorie intake. Although amphetamines will restrict food intake in the short-term, the medium- to long-term prognosis is poor due to problems with increased tolerance and relatively short lasting effects. Phentermine is the last derivative of the amphetamines and was for a time prescribed in

---

[1] The 'best' was defined here under the Jadad score system. This is a short questionnaire that allows scientists to judge the value of the trial in terms of how biased it is. The study in question was Boozer, C. N., Daly, P. A., Homel, P., Soloman, J. L., Blanchard, D., Nasser, J. A., Strauss, R. & Meredith, T. (2002). Herbal ephedra/caffeine for weight loss: a 6 month randomizied safety and efficacy trial. *International Journal of Obesity, 26*, 593-604. This study scored 5 on the Jadad system.

[2] Studies were run between 8 weeks and 6 months. Those that ran for longer did report less weight-loss on average, but there does not appear to be a dose dependent effect.

conjunction with fenfluramine. Fenfluramine is a drug that targets serotonin releasing brain cells and will be the subject of the next section.

FENFLURAMINE

Fenfluramine was the serotonergic drug of choice for many medical practitioners responsible for helping people to lose weight. It was not alone and arguably was not the first of these drugs designed to selectively target the serotonin system. The development and use of serotonergic drugs for the purposes of weight-loss was, like the use of amphetamines, not intentional. Many authors noticed and reported that overweight depressed people prescribed serotonergic anti-depressants lost weight during the course of their treatment. With the high percentage of obese people presenting with symptoms of depression, it was not long before medical professionals were prescribing serotonergic drugs specifically for the purposes of weight-loss. Fenfluramine quickly became the serotonergic drug of choice, but was found, like the first amphetamines, to not be specific enough. This led to the replacement of Fenfluramine with d-fenfluramine, which was shown to be more specific to serotonin targets.

Both fenfluramine and d-fenfluramine have been shown in numerous studies to be effective at reducing food intake. The effect is roughly around a twenty percent reduction in food intake during a meal. Different studies have however, reported differing effects on the amount of food consumed, but all seem to be in the same direction. The drug is purported to work through disrupting the storage of serotonin in the brain cell and then forcing serotonin out into the synapse. Interestingly, this is also the most favoured theory for how amphetamines work on their targets too.

With both phentermine and fenfluramine having similar modes of action on the cells in the brain, it will come as little surprise that the preferred method of treatment was a combined pharmacotherapy nicknamed phen-fen. In a series of seminal papers by Weintraub and co-authors [46], they showed that the use of the combined phen-fen drug was better at inducing weight-loss than either drug in isolation. The use of Fenfluramine for the purposes of weight-loss lasted for around twenty-five years before being withdrawn in 1997 amid patients developing serious cardiac complications and concerns. In particular, there was an increased report of heart complications[3] amongst those people taking it. Subsequently, it was declared that a world-wide ban on the use of fenfluramine was merited.

Making fenfluramine illegal did not remove it from the market. In order to make their product effective, some traditional herbal remedies were found to include a pharmaceutical grade of fenfluramine. This of course was an illegal additive to the product. This has resulted, in some extreme cases, in admission to accident and emergency rooms and even organ transplant [47]. The MHRA are aware of this problem and have identified at least thirteen herbal products sold in the UK that contain illegal fenfluramine. In a letter sent out by the MHRA on 28th April 2004, they required vendors of thirteen different herbal products to surrender all of their stocks. It would appear that the stereotypical vision of an illicit drug dealer does not always fit. Sometimes disreputable companies simply add illegal substances

---

[3] For indicative meta-analytic review see Sachdev, M., Miller, W. C., Ryan, T. & Jollis, J. G. (2002). Effect of fenfluramine-derivative diet pills on cardiac valves: a meta-analysis of observational studies. *American Heart Journal, 144*, 1065-1073.

to their products with little care for their impact. It is indeed a very scary thought that in the world of traditional herbal remedies, some individuals will simply add pharmaceuticals in a surreptitious attempt to avoid regulation. Therefore, there must be a continual vigilance concerning the addition of fenfluramine, or any other pharmaceutical grade drugs, into products to recreate the now banned phen-fen product. Phenermine is still legal with a prescription.

With the loss of fenfluramine and d-fenfluramine from the legitimate pharmaceutical market came the opportunity for another serotonin-related drug that works through a different mechanism to take its place. The side-effects of fenfluramine were well known soon after its inception and all manner of attempts were made to create a drug that works in the same way without the unwanted problems. From these attempts came the rise of selective serotonin reuptake inhibitors (SSRIs). Where fenfluramine and d-fenfluramine interfered with the storage of serotonin and forced it out of the cell, SSRIs simply blocked the cell from reabsorbing serotonin when it was released from the cell. The net effect was the same with more serotonin being in the synapse and thus activating the required neuropathway. With SSRIs came the ability to still target serotonin cells for the purposes of weight-loss despite the loss of fenfluramine. The SSRI of choice quickly emerged from amongst several competitors – its name was Sibutramine.

SIBUTRAMINE

Before we consider the relative effects of Sibutramine it is probably more appropriate to start with its predecessor. Better known amongst the wider population under its trade name – Prozac – Fluoxetine has been prescribed for weight-loss and tested for the relative merits for reducing food intake since the early 1990s. This allowed it to 'pick up the slack' that Fenfluramine left behind following its withdrawal. Comparable decreases in food intake were observed between Fluoxetine and Fenfluramine, so it was effectively its natural successor. However, all was not perfect with the Fluoxetine argument. In obese individuals, Fluoxetine was not always successful at aiding weight loss, especially over longer trials [48] and there were also indications of weight gain amongst some patients. The final death nail in the coffin of Fluoxetine for the weight-loss was the longer standing history of administration of this drug to eating disorder patients; although, it was found that these anorexia patients did not gain weight as fast as those on other drugs [49]. This supposed illogical outcome may have meant it was hard for regulatory bodies to advocate the use of Fluoxetine for the purposes of weight-loss at the same time as it being prescribed to eating disorder patients. An alternative explanation could have been the desire by professionals to target more than just the serotonin system in the brain as they had with amphetamines and the phen-fen products.

Although Sibutramine inherited the mantle from Fenfluramine, it is not totally specific to the serotonin system. Sibutramine works on both the serotonin and noradrenaline systems through a similar reuptake inhibitor action. Where other studies reported a lower level of hunger on other serotonergic drugs, Sibutramine showed signs of affecting fullness. This may be important for the long-term efficacy of diet drugs. While hunger is transient and very episodic, fullness works both during and between meals. Feeling fuller may make it easier to stay on a lower calorie diet; this is especially the case when obese people often eat in the absence of hunger [50]. Sibutramine lasted as an acceptable weight-loss drug until January 2010. It was withdrawn from the market due to similar safety problems concerning heart complications as the other serotonergic drugs that preceded it. Although arguably not as serious as its predecessors, it was considered by the EU to be unfavourable in a cost benefit analysis. With the lost of Sibutramine, it really was the end of the dynastic rule of serotonergic drugs for the purposes of weight-loss and the group that derives the name of this chapter.

The use of serotonergic drugs for the purposes of weight-loss has thus far been a failure. Messing around with serotonin receptors may have implications for appetite, as well as numerous other behaviours, but it also appears to have significant repercussions for heart complications. This long-known problem, along with the desire to target serotonin for the purposes of weight-loss, has led to extensive research into serotonin receptors. The objective has always been to identify the specific serotonin receptors involved in appetite regulation and create a pharmaceutical drug to target it. This led to the identification of many different types of serotonin receptors throughout the human brain; in fact more have been identified than any other neurotransmitter. While D_2 receptor was important for dopamine and appetite regulation, for serotonin it appears to be $5\text{-}HT_{2C}$; although there is some indication for a role for $5\text{-}HT_{1B}$ also. Selective activation of either of these receptors appears to have significant side effects. Therefore, future serotonergic compounds will have to be highly specific in exactly which 5-HT receptors they activate. Based on the consistent complications with serotonergic drugs it is unlikely that significant pharmaceutical research and development resources will be ploughed into this target anytime soon. Even if a successful serotonin-related drug were to be developed, it is unlikely that it will receive backing from the regulatory agencies until such time it could prove to have no effect on the heart.

By now it should be apparent that the loss of a pharmaceutical drug, or even concurrent to the release of it, the food supplement market will attempt to offer something that is supposedly similar. Often it is the derivative biochemical that is taken from the diet and then metabolised into the active neurotransmitter. For serotonin this is called 5-hydroxytryptophan. This food supplement is now pervasive across the Internet and sells for roughly £7 for thirty 50mg capsules. The emphasis of this food supplement is an attempt to do the same thing as the pharmaceutical drugs without supposedly taking drugs. Personally, I have never quite worked out the logic of this 'natural' ingredient selling strategy. Drugs are simply refined versions of naturally isolated biochemicals. Sometimes they are manipulated in an attempt to make them more specific to the task at hand, while others are not changed from the natural ligand. These food supplements follow the exact same process to attain a purified form of the natural ligand. In essence, they are exactly the same as a pharmaceutical just a cruder form. This crudity can take it to a point where it does not work at all or makes it too generic.

In the case of 5-hydroxytryptophan, the supposed logic is that if you consume a higher amount of the natural derivative of a particular chemical it will increase that chemical in the body and in particular in the location where it is allegedly low. The very early kinetic studies of the administration of 5-Hydroxytryptophan do not suggest this. If the idea is to take 5-Hydroxytryptophan to increase the levels of serotonin in the brain, then it would only do this once it has distributed equally throughout the body. Many organs have receptors for serotonin and consuming the pre-cursor 5-Hydroxytryptophan will result in the vast majority of it being stored in the kidneys and liver. Of the amount consumed between 47-84% of the total amount consumed will reach the blood but will have been eliminated after about four hours; however, this is highly responsive to inter-individual differences. Due to these inter-individual problems, a medical professional is required to work out an effective dose. Because this diagnosis and drug concentration manipulation is only allowed with registered medicines, the efficacy of 5-Hydroxytryptophan is going to be, at best, inconsistent [51]. Recently, some scientists have reported that dosage studies should be carried out on 5-Hydroxytryptophan as they too appear to be inconsistent. The closest dosage available to anything like something considered effective would be in the region of 200-300mg taken 5 times a day [52]. Most Internet vendors suggest that a person should only take 50mg (or one tablet a day). Maximum dosages for an adult per day are recommended by most vendors to be 150mg. This is way below scientific reports of effective doses. The disparity between the two is probably due to the vendors' fear about the side-effects of serotonin. There is a phenomenon reported in the literature called serotonin syndrome. This syndrome has many characteristics including dizziness, disorientation, hypertension, hyperthermia, and hyperreflexia/myoclonus (overly sensitive reflexes leading to muscle spasms). In some cases it can lead to death. For 5-Hydroxytryptophan, serotonin syndrome has not been recorded yet. The only reason that could possibly explain the dose set by Internet vendors at 150mg must have been derived from rodent data, which shows serotonin syndrome at doses above 100mg/kg [53]. Alternatively they may be confusing other serotonergic drugs with 5-Hydroxytryptophan.

The most damning component to the use of 5-Hydroxytryptophan as a weight-loss tool is that it has not been tested for this purpose. In all papers that are available in the scientific domain undertaken through detailed searches in specialist forums, nothing has been returned about the effective use of 5-Hydroxytryptophan as a weight loss diet 'drug'. Thus the use of 5-Hydroxytryptophan for this purpose is highly questionable. It will require higher doses to be considered effective and the dose has to be tailored to the individual. Taking this food supplement for the purposes of weight loss, at least in the recommended doses, is likely to be wasted money.

Finally, we have come to a point where we can say serotonin in all of its forms is done with. It has had its time in the sun as the drug target of choice for viable weight-loss interventions. It will remain there until such time as our understanding of targeted drug delivery has improved. The potential side-effects of taking serotonergic drugs far outweigh any potential gains they can deliver. These gains will be discussed, but not until chapter eight.

Before we continue into the next chapter, we need to briefly consider one last drug that has also been left in the past. We really should only spend as much time on it as it has existed for – that is very short. This drug is Rimonabant and, as shown in the previous chapter, targets cannabinoid receptors.

RIMONABANT

Rimonabant is a cannabinoid antagonist (meaning that it blocks the effect of endogenous endocannabinoids in the brain) that preferentially targets the CB_1 receptor. It was approved for use across Europe in June 2006 and was withdrawn mid October 2008 amidst safety concerns about psychiatric side-effects. In particular, it was believed that taking Rimonabant led to increases in depression and suicide. Initial drug trials revealed that Rimonabant had favourable drop-out rates compared to other drugs and had similar weight-loss properties compared to other centrally acting drugs. Rimonabant had other comparative benefits over pre-existing weight-loss drugs. It lasted in the system much longer (about 16 days) and only required one tablet taken daily at a dose of 20mg.

The fleeting existence of Rimonabant has not stopped other less reputable companies from creating a similar product and selling it over the Internet. Although there are some concerns over the authenticity of the products, it has been shown that some of the illegal weight loss products available through the Internet contain Sibutramine, Ephedrine and Rimonabant irrespective of what was on the label [54]. It must be acknowledged though that these were illegal dieting products and so are different to those sold under brand names legally. What should be taken from these governmental findings is that people must remain vigilant to claims made by Internet vendors that a particular product supposedly works 'like' another known drug. It may actually contain that exact drug irrespective of the claim, especially in cases where the product name is unfamiliar. Another lesson we can learn from these findings is there is a vibrant market in counterfeit weight-loss drugs. Buying a drug from an unknown Internet vendor may actually be counterfeit containing different doses or unknown and tested polymorphs (pharmaceuticals that are similar in chemical structure to the now illegal drug). Taking these drugs may have dangerous repercussions. Most worrying, is that these drugs will probably look enough like the genuine article to fool the lay person. With the known safety problems with Rimonabant, taking drugs of unknown provenance may have serious consequences for the buyer's health.

FROM THE PAST AND HEADING INTO THE PRESENT

The conclusion drawn from each of these past credible targets gives us a clear understanding of what could be the credible candidates for weight-loss drugs. It would appear that, for the time being at least, serotonergic and cannabinoid drugs are off the list. The side-effects of these drugs far out-weight the benefits.

When it comes to the human brain, it would appear that crude pharmacological interventions designed to target specific neurotransmitters are not going to have the efficacy we would like them to. Our brains use the same chemical to do numerous tasks and therefore hoping to affect a specific behaviour by targeting a specific neurotransmitter is going to have significant side-effects. As obesity is not a life-threatening illness in itself, regulatory agencies appear to be far from tolerant of any potential side-effects to treat this weight-related condition. Gone are the days when we can use howitzers or bazookas to play darts. Instead, we are going to have to get better at targeting specific neurotransmitter receptors in specific areas of the brain or face targeting the non-psychological components to eating behaviour. Instead of making people feel less hungry we would have to simply stop them from absorbing the macronutrients into the blood stream. As we will see in chapter eight, this does not appear to be as effective. To survive in the world of increased regulation of medicinal and herbal products, proverbially speaking, psychopharmacologists are going to have to play darts with darts. For pharmacological interventions to survive they are going to have to get specific to the appetite-related region of the brain, to specific neurotransmitters in that region and, most importantly, specific neurotransmitter receptors. That is, of course, if the assumption that behaviour is totally biologically controlled by specific biochemicals in isolation, over a more interactive theoretical viewpoint, holds up to the rigours of future scientific testing.

Now we know what has happened in the past it is possible to understand the present and eventually the likely outcomes in the future. In the next chapter we will start with the last vestiges of the amphetamine drugs and move on to other potentially credible targets and drugs. Those that do not appear in the next chapter will of course appear in the subsequent chapter – selling dreams.

Chapter 6

OF CREDIBLE CANDIDATES?

We have flirted with the topic long enough and are now in a position to understand the difference between what is said, why it is said and what has failed in the ongoing pharmacological treatment of obesity or those attempting to lose perceived excess weight. It is time to assess those pharmaceutical drugs claimed to have an effect and likely to be true. There are other types of 'drugs' that have been shown not to work but are still purported to be effective on the Internet, but we will save these for the next chapter.

Before we start, we should mention that we are not dealing with absolutes. This is not a cop-out. It is a statement of truth. The movement between chapters five, six and seven is fluidic. Any given drug can move from one group to another relatively easily. The obvious and easiest movement is from chapter six to chapter five. All of those drugs found in the previous chapter did, after all, start out as credible candidates. It was only after cost/benefit analysis that these credible candidates were dropped. Moreover, some of the drugs found in the previous chapter are still used elsewhere in the world despite their banning in the West or Europe.

Many of the drugs that we will discuss in this chapter have already shown hints of moving into chapter five. However, as they have not officially moved yet, they are still credible candidates. The least likely move is from the next chapter into this one. Remember, everything starts out under the assumption that it does not work – this is the application of the null hypothesis and relates to the first sanctioned rule of science. If it has not been found to work in past experiments then it will only start to work again through the combination of study findings under a test called a meta-analysis. This particular analytic technique legitimately combines the findings of numerous studies to uncover smaller effects that could not be observed in studies with small numbers of people in it. Small effects are not helpful in weight-loss interventions. These effects are important in life-saving interventions, where small differences determine the difference between life and death, in weight-loss interventions, small effects are the difference between losing an extra pound over the course of a year. Therefore, this effectively denies the probability of moving from the next chapter into this one.

The candidates that will be discussed in this chapter are those that are currently sold as effective diet drugs. Many brands of diet drugs will tell the world that their diet drug is unique and fares better than all their competitors. Of course they will say this, it is sale's patter. The truth of the matter is that even if they contain a novel compound or element, it is unlikely to be an active ingredient. The active ingredient is always the ingredient(s) that allows the company to get around trade description laws. After all, there must be evidence for something in the product that has scientific merit as a weight-loss agent otherwise they will suffer the backlash of litigation. Looking through the ingredients on any packet of diet drugs will quickly reveal what is the active agent and what is simply 'fluff'. 'Fluff' in this instance is ingredients believed to aid weight-loss in some indirect manner but have no scientific efficacy. Most of the ingredients in non-pharmaceutical drugs contain a lot of this 'fluff'.

In this chapter, we will consider the pharmaceutical drugs first. This is not because they are necessarily better or that we are biased towards these drugs, rather it is because they have to achieve a higher standard to be registered as a medicine. This inexorably leads to more available and credible scientific investigations. There are numerous claims made about diet drugs by all pharmaceutical or supplement companies, but invariably it is drawn from their own data or research that is not published in the public domain. It is not beyond the realms of possibility that testing their own drug is a conflict of interest.

Of course, they will find their drug is better; after all, if it does not reach market then the developers will be out of a job. With the increased scientific testing requirements for a drug to be marketed as a medicine then more independent research is often conducted on it. It would be somewhat pessimistic to assume that people will always find their drug to be effective. There must be some attrition in the development process where refinement to the active ingredient will improve weight-loss; therefore, we should not totally discount non-independent studies in their entirety. Instead, we will consider such research in the context it was taken and place more emphasis on independent findings. The focus on the pharmaceutical products will start with Phentermine.

PHENTERMINE

Of all of the drugs available to people attempting to lose weight, phentermine is the longest standing. It was first registered as an appetite suppressant in the mid part of the last century and as such has had over forty years of unadulterated use. It was briefly banned alongside its eventual combination chemical – Fenfluramine – but was reinstated after a legal challenge. Despite its long history, limited information about its efficacy is available.

Unlike other weight-loss drugs, few long-term studies have been undertaken with phentermine. Findings on studies that have been carried out suggest that Phentermine results in a significant drop in reported hunger and a resultant drop in weight [55]. Like other amphetamines, Phentermine is a controlled substance and cannot be bought legally without prescription. Despite it being a controlled substance, there are surreptitious attempts to trade under this name on the Internet. Affiliate websites talk about the effects of Phentermine and then direct buyers to the product Phentremine. For those that missed it, the product has the two letters swapped round. Phentremine does not contain Phentermine. It contains Hoodia Gorfonii and caffeine as its active ingredients.

We will come to these two later. For now, it is interesting to take a moment to reflect on this practice and consider how diet 'drugs' are sold over the Internet. Surely that must be miss-selling if there ever was such a phenomenon? The vendor has also apparently attempted to optimise their website in the attempt traffic people to them who spell Phentermine wrong. This company is not alone. Another drug Phentemine also exists with calcium as its active ingredient. And as I write this book, I was sent a spam email offering a product called Phentermin that allegedly costs $210 for sixty tablets. I could not find any information about its ingredients anywhere. This all offers a clear warning for the 'Lazy Typer' trying to buy a pharmaceutical diet drug.

Phentermine works through activation of the α1-adrenoreceptors, one of the receptors of the noreadrenaline system. It is theorised to work through activation of neuronal cells in the paraventricular nucleus, the site of the known appetite suppressant peptide CRF. This cannot be the only mode of action as administration of CRF to humans does not result in altered eating patterns [56]. This difference indicates that Phentermine acts on some other Paraventricular-related neurotransmitter to elicit suppression on food intake. One potential unsubstantiated explanation may be an interaction with Urocortin, which is a sister chemical to CRF that also has potent appetite suppression effects. CRF has a known role in eating behaviour; CRF is also responsible for initiating the stress response. Phentermine is therefore activating the Paraventricular nucleus in an attempt to eliminate feelings of hunger. Stress and eating are intrinsically intertwined. It makes perfect sense that activation of the stress response, the neurobiological pathway responsible for fight or flight, overrides desire to eat. It would not be helpful for an animal to be concerned about eating when attempting to avoid a threat to their psychobiological integrity. A deer does not want to attend to the grass when a predator is bounding up behind them. It would be counterproductive to their survival. Phentermine probably works through hijacking this neurocircuitry and interfering with the desire to eat.

All is not simple in the world of noreadrenoreceptors. It has been shown that activation of the α2-adrenoreceptors induces eating in animals [57]. In addition, long-term activation of the stress response pathway can lead to obesity. Cushing's Syndrome (a disorder characterised by the over-expression of the stress hormone Cortisol) is characterised by truncal obesity and atrophy of the arms and legs. This may lead to long-term problems with Phentermine when long-term efficacy studies are actually run on the drug. In particular, experiments exploring peripheral muscle physiology may provide initial evidence or eliminate this obvious potential problem. For now we will leave it as a cliff hanger and wait to see what happens. Currently, in the UK, it is not advised that Phentermine be prescribed for weight-loss purposes. Moreover, it is an amphetamine and as such is a controlled substance. The likelihood of getting Phentermine legitimately for the treatment of obesity is quite small.

Attempts to bring back Phentermine into the UK market was recently attempted through its combination with Topiramate – Qnexa. Topiramate has been used effectively for the treatment of Bulimia Nervosa, binge-eating disorder, preventing weight-gain in schizophrenic patients and Prader-Willi Syndrome (a genetic disorder characterised by the over-production of Ghrelin, insatiable appetite and subsequent morbid obesity [58]. The primary use of Topiramate is as an antiepileptic agent. However, it was quickly noticed that the action of Topiramate appeared to differ from other antiepileptic drugs by decreasing rather than increasing the weight status of the patient. As a target, Topiramate is tentatively believed to operate through $GABA_A$ receptors. Animal data appears to be portraying a very positive efficacy for Topiramate [59] but little data is offered about its efficacy in obese humans. For obese binge eating disorder patients, Topiramate, in a dose of 400mg, resulted in comparable weight-loss to Sibutramine and Rimonabant [60]. Qnexa, the combination of Phentermine and Topiramate, was rejected in the summer of 2010 for use as an anti-obesity drug. The potential side effects reported by a second-hand organisation suggested that the drug had significant side-effects including depression, memory-loss, increased heart rate and birth defects. The need to rely on a second hand organisation was because the company has not released their data into the public domain. Moreover, they only presented data for a period of just over one year. With the presentation of more long-term data and the potential to eradicate the attribution of the negative side-effects to the drug itself, Qnexa may come back in future years. For now, Topiramate may only be prescribed for more threatening medical conditions rather than obesity.

If Phentermine works through activating the stress response, then we have a direct conflict between this pharmaceutical agent and what are popularly known as Cortisol blockers. Cortisol blockers are sold under a wide variety of trade names starting at about £7.50 for thirty capsules. Cortisol is the last hormone released in the stress response, while CRF is commonly considered the first. Thus Phentermine purports to work through activating CRF and by proxy Cortisol, while Cortisol blockers claim to suppress appetite by blocking it. Both cannot be right. The answer to this is complex and both yes and no. On balance, the Cortisol blockers are flawed in their assumption that high levels of Cortisol are responsible for weight gain.

The scientific assumption that Cortisol Blockers make is that high levels of Cortisol is associated with lots of other abnormalities in obesity, making it harder to lose weight. There is some evidence for this claim in people that have abnormal stress responses. For the majority of people however, a higher basal level of Cortisol is associated with being healthier. Thus, blocking high Cortisol levels for most people would be inappropriate. This formulates the "no" part of the answer between the accuracy of Phentermine over Cortisol blockers. In terms of obesity related to Cortisol function, it is the pharmacokinetics that is important. Pharmacokinetics of Cortisol relate to how fast it is cleared away, as well as concentrations in the blood. More appropriate abnormalities in Cortisol would be derived from problems with how fast it is deactivated in the body rather than looking at total amounts. Increased Cortisol levels are related to stress not eating behaviour. Indeed, abnormal Cortisol readings in an individual point towards lower levels in the morning rather than elevated levels. This would suggest that Cortisol blockers would be harmful to those with abnormal Cortisol levels that results in weight gain and obesity [61].

For the "yes" answer in favour of Cortisol blockers we must turn to the noreadrenoreceptors. So far we have treated receptors as pretty much static structures that are either there or not. This is not strictly true. The amount of receptors on the surface of a given cell can change. As we have mentioned already in this section, α1-adrenoreceptors are the target for appetite suppression and α2-adrenoreceptors for appetite stimulation. In the presence of Cortisol, α2-adrenoreceptors concentrations in the hypothalamus change. There is complex interplay between Cortisol and α2-adrenoreceptors that will alter the concentration of the receptors and thus their effect on appetite [62]. This is not the whole story however. In order to fully explain the potential effect of Cortisol blockers on appetite we must understand that an interaction between the stress pathway and Serotonin occurs. This interaction leads to the net effect of increasing Serotonin levels which can potentially induce weight-loss. This would then explain the reason why so many Cortisol blocker products also contain 5-hydroxytryptophan – the serotonin-related food supplement. The mode of action of Cortisol blockers is in fact not to actually target Cortisol; it is an indirect attempt to target Serotonin. As there are products available that already target serotonin (albeit no pharmaceutical drugs, as these have all been withdrawn), it would suggest that indirect measures are not appropriate until it is possible to identify those individuals that actually have a problem with the stress pathway and Cortisol levels. When this identification of abnormal Cortisol levels is eventually uncovered, it will be under the remit of medical professionals. As these diet 'drugs', or more accurate supplements, cannot change their dosage in response to a diagnosis their attempts to emulate pharmaceuticals will mean they are further relegated to the periphery. This information, when assessed as a whole, would suggest a balance in favour of a "no" response to whether Phentermine or Cortisol blockers are correct. The action of Phentermine is direct and appropriate, Cortisol blockers are indirect and on 'shaky' scientific grounds.

Phentermine remains a credible candidate for pharmacological interventions to aid weight-loss. The principle reason that it remains on this list is because of its longevity without suffering regulatory backlash. This longevity suggests that the drug is relatively safe. Phentermine also remains credible through the pharmaceutical companies' desire to link new potential candidates with this drug to create a combined pharmacological therapy. All is not rosy though as this appetite suppressant drug does have a black mark against it. For many years, the drug hid behind the preferential use of serotonergic drugs avoiding detailed scrutiny as scientists were more interested in other compounds. With Phentermine being the last vestige of the amphetamines, as well as the loss of viable serotonergic drugs, it will mean more focused investigations will home in on this substance. Under this additional scrutiny, Phentermine may follow its sister drugs into the pages of history. Precedence would suggest that a ban will be the likely outcome. Phentermine does have two things going for it however. It is still heavily preferred in the US and is also the last centrally acting drug available for the purposes of weight-loss. Unless serious concerns over its safety are uncovered, it is likely to remain as a credible target until something better is developed. Even then it may hang on as a combined therapy in much the same way as it did through the serotonergic dynasty.

This concludes our discussion of this candidate and also concludes the pharmaceutical targets aimed at the brain. There is one known credible pharmaceutical candidate still left to consider. It too is not without its controversy. It is only known potential candidate that does not target appetite regulation. Instead, it simply interferes with the absorption of fat.

ORLISTAT

Orlistat is alone in its class. Where other drugs attempt to interfere with appetite, Orlistat prohibits the absorption of a percentage of consumed fat ($\approx$ 30%) from passing through the intestines and getting into the circulatory system [63]. This drug works by blocking lipase enzymes, which are created in the pancreas and released into the duodenum section of the small intestine. Orlistat binds with these lipases to stop them from breaking down fats into a size that can be absorbed. The end product is that the fat remains in the intestines and eventually passes out of the rectum. Because of the effect on lipases, some fat-soluble vitamins may not be absorbed (i.e. A, D, E, K, and β-carotene). To counter this, some authors advocate vitamin supplementation. This would be a little premature as it has been shown that this is not necessary for all identified vitamins in all cases. It would be more appropriate if vitamin levels were monitored for those people taking a higher dosage of Orlistat. Of all of the vitamins identified, E and β-carotene would probably be the most likely candidates for monitoring as these have been found to significantly alter following administration of Orlistat [64].

The inhibition of lipase defines the remit of the potential side-effects. Due to the fat remaining in the intestines, it can lead to stools with high lipid content. Stools high in fat are often loose and hard to adequately control and hold within the colon and anus. Therefore, the potential side-effects for Orlistat are loose stools, faecal urgency (the need to immediately go to the toilet accompanied with an inability to hold it), oily discharge or spotting, faecal incontinence, flatulence, diarrhoea and abdominal pain. Due to the nature of these potential side-effects, there have also been reports of high levels of anxiety, headaches and fatigue. At this moment in time, it cannot be discounted that this may be a pharmacological effect, as a very small proportion of Orlistat does make it into the blood; however, anxiety, headaches and fatigue is likely to be more psychosomatic in nature and related to the stress of the biological side-effects. The potential for social embarrassment for those people taking Orlistat will mean that some will discontinue the course.

Orlistat is traded under two brand names. These two brand names refer to the dose content of the drug – 60mg and 120mg. Although both are essentially the same drug, the lower dose is available to people over-the-counter for sale from a pharmacist for people with a BMI over 28. Orlistat as a drug has the least controversy surrounding its administration; however, the recent addition of the over-the-counter prescription practices has been the subject of some problems. In particular, sufferers of eating disorders, members of eating disorder associations and media organisations have been able to legally buy Orlistat as a weight-loss drug without meeting the BMI requirements. In the bricks and mortar pharmacy undercover reporters have found it difficult to obtain Orlistat and it is held behind the counter to prohibit direct access to the drug without help from a customer service representative. The same company's online shops have been less diligent. On these Internet shops, they only ask the question if the buyer is above a specific BMI. Despite requests from eating disorder associations, these companies are reluctant to alter this practice. In truth, other online vendors do not ask any questions about a person's weight prior to sale, so altering the manner of how one company functions online will simply move the buyer to a different vendor.

Unlike other pharmaceutical interventions, Orlistat is the only drug that can be given to children. The principle reason for this is that the drug has very limited effects on any other organs beyond the small intestine and stomach. Very similar side-effects are observed between adults, adolescents and children suggesting that the drug works in a very similar and highly specific fashion [65]. The ability to prescribe the drug to children means that Orlistat is here to stay. No other drug has had this potential and any future diet agent that has to enter the blood in order to function will find it difficult convince regulatory agencies to allow its use on children.

The comparative ease in access to Orlistat over-the-counter and on the Internet has meant that it is widely available with few legal problems. With the increased popularity of the product has come a different illegality issue. There have been reports of some people creating counterfeit capsules for Orlistat [66] for sale through Internet vendors. This counterfeit version contained both Orlistat and the now withdrawn Sibutramine. Regulatory agencies have asked all consumers to be vigilant about the type and quality of the product when buying from online retailers. In particular, some commentators have asked consumers to be wary of Orlistat being sold at cut down low price. Orlistat starts from around £20 for 42 capsules of the 60mg version and £35 for the 120mg version. For the 120mg version a prescription is required in the UK.

The success of Orlistat has sparked a lot of nutritional supplements and traditional herbalists to add what they claim are natural versions of lipase inhibitors to their products. The most commonly claimed addition to diet 'drugs' that provide the purported same effect as Orlistat is an extract from the leaves of the plant 'Cassia Nomame'. To date there is very little scientific data to back this claim [67]. It is believed that these claims are based on two scientific papers [68]; neither of these papers suggests anything other than a chemical property that could inhibit lipase. Instead, they are studies of enzymes in isolation and in a Petri-dish. At this time, there are many plant derivatives that have been shown to have lipase inhibitor properties [69], but these are a long way from being tested to explore their utility as a drug. To say that they can have an effect based on this data is a very large leap of faith. It is tantamount to saying that there must be a pot of gold at the end of the rainbow because I cannot see it from here. Until such time as the extract is tested on humans, or even animals, little conclusions can be drawn about its efficacy. The addition of this compound in diet 'drugs' is yet another attempt to emulate the pharmaceutical industry without having to go through the same regulations and necessary efficacy tests. To give an indication of the potential efficacy of 'Cassia Nomame', thousands of chemicals are tested by the pharmaceutical industry and the vast majority do not make it to clinical trials let alone to the market itself. Moreover, the extract of the plant will contain numerous chemicals that need to be isolated and tested individually for inhibition of lipase. Only once the specific chemical is identified can it be tested for efficacy as a drug and then, upon successful outcome, be considered a true competitor to Orlistat.

With the conclusion of Orlistat comes the conclusion of pharmaceutical interventions for obesity. The rest of the biochemicals that will be considered are from the traditional herbal, food supplement or homeopathic field. We will return to the efficacy of all of the drugs in the penultimate chapter, but that is later. It is important to remember that all of the 'drugs' from the non-pharmaceutical fields do not require the same stringent testing prior to coming onto the market. This makes the independent review of them difficult. Instead, we must rely on limited information and have to infer information based on efficacy. In the rest of this chapter, we will consider three potential candidates for use as a diet drug. These are those that have been considered and evaluated within the scientific domain. Some have been around longer than others and as such have received more research focus. The three potential candidates are Hoodia, already considered a potent appetite suppressant by the MHRA, caffeine and green tea.

Hoodia Gorfonii

Hoodia is a traditional herbal remedy. It is/was used primary by the San people of Southern Africa for suppressing appetite and replacing fluids on long journeys. As a plant, Hoodia Gorfonii is hardy. It exists in a climate with extreme temperature variation (-3-40C) preferring stony/sandy soil. Although Hoodia Gorfonii is found in the Kalahari Desert, it is not a cactus. Many media, affiliate websites, vendors and information databases wrongly suggest that it is a cactus. The BBC even reported it as the Khalahari Cactus Diet. Hoodia

Goerfonii is in fact a member of the milk weed (Asclepiadaceae) family. It does share one similar property with cacti – it is slow growing and takes a long time to reach maturation. Due to its life-cycle and recent public interest as a dieting aid, it is at serious danger of being harvested into extinction [70]. The harvesting and packaging of Hoodia is prohibited in South Africa and Namibia due to its rarity and as an attempt to save the poor plant from desperate people.

Hoodia is used as an example by the MHRA for a compound that has led to stronger regulation of traditional herbal remedies. This is not because it is currently considered unsafe, although it has recently been shown to have the potential to interact with other drugs [71], but because it has such a potentially strong effect. It is currently unknown how Hoodia suppresses appetite, but it is believed to do this through some interaction with the central nervous system or peripheral organs. In short, it is not an intestinal enzyme inhibitor. This is assumed from its binding properties with the blood and its breakdown by the liver.

Hoodia Gorfonii extract has been analyzed and the chemical believed to be responsible for its appetite suppressant effects has been identified by at least three different groups [72]. The current name of the isolated chemical is P57AS3 or P57 for short. All drugs start out as number and letter combinations until they reach the latter stages of clinical trials. It is only at that point that they are given an actual name. Several patents based on compounds isolated from Hoodia have also been submitted by the pharmaceutical industry, indicating a strong interest from these companies in the potential application for derivatives from this plant. Unfortunately, initial pharmaceutical exploitation of the P57 compound has indicated that its use as an effective appetite suppressant drug is limited. Phytopharm obtained the rights for the harvesting and application of Hoodia in 1997 from the South African government. They then went into collaboration with Pfizer to develop the plant for pharmaceutical purposes. Pfizer discontinued collaboration with Phytopharm and their exploration of the compound in light of problematic side-effects in liver metabolism in 2003. This was all hearsay though and no official communication has been offered as to why the company stopped development. Unilever then took over from Pfizer in 2004, but also discontinued development in 2008. Phytopharm still own the rights to develop Hoodia Gorfonii for pharmaceutical purposes. In their most recent press release they suggest that they have had favourable outcomes in a clinical trial with a different variation of the drug than the one used by Pfizer and expect to publish at some point in 2010. To date, no scientific papers have materialised from their labs on the subject. It is unlikely that a pharmaceutical company would make such a claim without a strong intention to publish. Therefore, we should expect notification of the efficacy of P57 at some point soon.

The rarity of Hoodia Gorfonii in its indigenous environment is not only reflected in its protection by African governments. In fact few diet 'drugs' actually contain the active ingredients of Hoodia – as little as 33% actually contain P57 [73]. This notable absence seriously undermines the efficacy of diet 'drugs'. Instead, these supplements often contain extracts from other Hoodia plant species that are common and thus cheaper to manufacture and are not under the protection of governments in their native countries. Just because a diet product says it contains Hoodia Gorfonii does not necessarily mean that it contains the active component of the plant. The odds are not in the buyer's favour that the products they are buying actually contain the biochemical they are after. If the product does not expressly say that it contains P57 then its efficacy is likely to be pharmacologically non-existent.

P57 is currently a credible candidate for the future use in pharmaceutical drugs. However, a lot of its credibility lies in the fact that it is a traditional herbal remedy that has shown to have an effect on animals and in unpublished studies on humans. If at any point in the near future that there is a serious effect on liver metabolism are uncovered, the usefulness of Hoodia will move straight into the previous chapter. It will also result in diet 'drugs' having to remove it from their product in the same way as they had to remove ephedrine. As a word of warning, many similar drugs have been identified and reached similar levels only to be removed prior to publication. Over the years, many potential drugs under various letter and number combinations have emerged, been tested and then not pursued any further. P57 may be another one of these compounds. Its lack of development and published research since its initial registration in 1997 and the withdrawal of two separate companies does not bound well for the application of P57 as an anti-obesity agent. It is likely that any potential pharmaceutical application of Hoodia is a long way from the open market.

CAFFEINE

Caffeine is the most common constituent of diet 'drugs'. It is considered so important to most supplements that it sometimes appears in numerous forms. Those that claim some other active ingredient in their 'drug' will invariably use another name for caffeine. Usually this is guarana, but it can be numerous other names too. Irrespective of what is advertised or discussed on affiliate websites, the 'active' ingredient is caffeine. If the drug advertises that it increases metabolism it is invariably saying that it has high levels of caffeine.

Just to place the credible use of caffeine for the purposes of weight-loss in context allow me to state that the vast majority of scientists who write on the topic of drug targets for obesity do not mention the utility of caffeine. There is some evidence to indicate that caffeine may interfere with eating behaviour, but it is conflicting convoluted, indirect and limited. This has not stopped the vast majority of the diet 'drug' market from loading their products up with caffeine and making claims about weight-loss through it. The reason that caffeine is placed in this chapter is the fact that it is the less 'credible' candidate that allows a lot of diet 'drugs' to be advertised as such rather than for any scientific reasoning about efficacy. Within this section we will consider just how viable caffeine is.

As the reader may have already inferred, the role of caffeine in weight-loss is highly speculative. Caffeine is a stimulant that for most people is consumed as a beverage under the intention of reducing fatigue, increasing clarity/attention and placating cravings. Caffeine, unbeknownst to most people, has had a turbulent past with regulatory agencies. In the US, repeat attempts have been made to create legislation against the use of caffeine and in recent years, the interaction between caffeine and other drugs have brought its ubiquitous use back into question [74].

The side-effects of caffeine are well known to most people. The majority of the population have suffered from the effects of caffeine at some point usually through the overconsumption of caffeinated drinks. The most common symptoms of caffeine are nausea, headache and insomnia. In higher doses, it has been reported to result in restlessness, excitement, muscle tremor, tinnitus, scintillating scotoma, tachycardia, extrasystoles and gastric ulceration. A dose of about 10g of pharmacological grade caffeine is fatal for everyone, but smaller doses can result in death depending on the size and sex of the recipient. This has led to the US regulatory agency limiting the intake of caffeine to 200mg per three hours without prescription. The limitation of the use of caffeine means that it is actually a controlled substance in some parts of the world. This also appears to be specific to medicinal applications of caffeine, as the restriction on the sale of coffee is not enforced. Coffee shops would likely not limit the repeat custom of buyers even if they went over the 200mg in three hours. In some coffee shops that would only be two cups.

The effects of caffeine are not without their benefits. Habitual consumption of caffeine is associated with lowered blood pressure and risk of heart disease [75]. Moreover, the long history of few reported problems with sensible usage of caffeine, along with many commercial endeavours being reliant on caffeine, means that any regulation on the substance will likely meet ferocious and successful legal challenges. In the medicinal industry, over three thousand separate products contain caffeine [76].

The pharmacological effects of caffeine specific to its utility as a treatment for obesity are twofold. Caffeine works on both the peripheral organs and the brain. The brain targets for caffeine are the adenosine pathway. The adenosine pathway is responsible for maintaining wakefulness through controlling a region called the sleep-wake flip flop[1]. The effects of caffeine on this pathway are very short-lived and if the active dosage drops the endogenous neurotransmitter will quickly reassert itself. In short, the effects of caffeine on the brain does not create a strong or long-lasting biological dependency and recovery from even heavy consumption is very quick – measured in hours rather than days or months [77]. Moreover, the habitual use of caffeine results in high levels of tolerance. In the same manner as amphetamines, caffeine will have exponentially less effect over a relatively short period of time. Tolerance to the administration of caffeine will take between one and four days in the dosage offered by most diet 'drugs [78].

The central effects of caffeine are not the pathway that most diet 'drug' companies claim how their products work. Instead, they rely on the effect caffeine has on the body to make their claims. They suggest that caffeine induces increased thermogenesis. This is effectively true, but more for lean people. Caffeine has a dose dependent effect on thermogenesis in habitual low consumers of caffeine resulting in an increase of about sixteen percent of activity. If activity is low, a sixteen percent increase is pretty minimal. There is also evidence that caffeine reduces food intake by about twenty-two percent, but this is in men only [79]. Furthermore, the effect of caffeine on obese people has to be matched to their weight, requiring a diagnosis and manipulation of dose, something a diet 'drug' is explicitly not permitted to do. Even when dose is matched to weight status, the effect in obese people is reduced by around a third on average [80]. Finally, trials have shown that caffeine does not result in weight-loss compared to placebo [81]. The scientific case is closed with very little wiggle room.

We already know that the development of tolerance to caffeine is relatively quick. The tests on the effect of caffeine on thermogenesis thus far have only been done on habitual low consumers. We can only imagine that this effect is further diminished in those who have a higher tolerance to the substance and those that are overweight or obese. This evidence-based information should successfully discredit the role of caffeine in inducing thermogenesis for

---

[1] I know scientists get bored too and this sometimes spills out into imaginative names for phenomenon and structures.

the purposes of losing weight until such time as more evidence becomes available to discredit everything we already know about the subject.

In addition to the wide array of positive and negative effects, caffeine in relatively high doses is a potent diuretic. This action effectively means that caffeine removes fluids from the individual. As any researcher who has performed a study exploring caffeine and eating behaviour can attest, the ingestion of high levels of caffeine will result in the participant running to the toilet within twenty minutes. Therefore, any observable benefits will likely be the loss of fluids not excess adipose tissue.

Exploring the actual information that many diet 'drug' websites claim to be the scientific merit of the efficacy of their product they often refer to two studies: Dulloo et al. [82] and Acheson et al. [83]. The total sum findings of these two papers for the utility of caffeine as a weight-loss drug was an increase of 79kcals of energy expenditure for obese people and no effect on free fatty acids except in the lean controls. That is about as much energy in an apple or less than a third of a bar of Snickers. It's about 4% of the recommended daily allowance of calories to maintain weight.

The effect of caffeine on food intake and thermogenesis means that it has just about made it into the credible candidate chapter rather than the next one on selling dreams. Considering the actual implications and long-term effects of caffeine on body weight suggests that it is no better than offering a placebo inert substance. The ubiquitous use of caffeine throughout the diet 'drugs' industry really should be investigated; especially in light of the claims that are made. The evidence on which the efficacy of the 'drug' is based does not match the advertised outcomes. That is, if we only consider the independent research on the topic.

In many of the diet 'drugs' available on the Internet, the only active ingredient is caffeine and it has been effectively shown that administration of this substance does not elicit weight-loss or many effects in obese people. Due to how these 'drugs' are advertised suggests that it can really help people lose weight. Based on the interpretation of the data in the public domain this would appear to be completely unfounded. Rigorous application of the Trade Description laws should be adopted in the case of caffeine to ensure that consumers are not misled. In light of these findings concerning caffeine, it would also be helpful if this industry were forced to explicitly state their supposed active ingredients on the product and ensure that the consumers are informed of the appropriate energy lost as a result of using it. This should be presented as an average weight loss of the independently published data not an amalgamation of their own work or of cherry-picked studies.

GREEN TEA

Of all credible candidates for weight-loss, green tea and its specific complement of flaviniods known as catechins is a relative newcomer. Recently, a lot of papers have been published exploring the utility of green tea as a viable weight-loss 'drug'. Some authors have even attempted to portray the beverage as nothing less than a panacea for the gastrointestinal system [84], but most are much more cautious. The outcomes are, at best, mixed [85]. If we consider the field with light touch interpretations and criticisms for the time being, then there appears to be a consistent and significant weight-loss with people who are taking green tea supplements. However, this weight-loss does not appear to be as strong as any of the known pharmacological interventions.

Green tea is a composite of several substances. Those chemicals found within the preparation of the beverage purported to be responsible for weight-loss are called epigallocatechin gallate or EGCG for short. Confusion about the effects of green tea is also wrought from the fact that it contains caffeine; however, there have been some recent attempts to offer the pharmacological grade EGCG and/or decaffeinated alternatives [86].

Catechins are believed to interfere in the deactivation of noreadrenaline throughout the body. Specifically, these chemicals interfere with the enzyme that deactivates noreadrenaline. This enzyme is called catechol-O-methyltransferase (COMT); and noreadrenaline we came across in previous chapters. Noreadrenaline was the complicated neurotransmitter that both inhibited and increased food intake depending on which receptor was activated. Consequently, the inability to breakdown noreadrenaline leads to a longer duration of increased thermogenesis and the usage of energy in the system. The creation of COMT, like all proteins, is reliant on the individual's genetic make-up. There also appears to be large differences in the genetic variation of COMT and the subsequent quantity of it circulating the body. This genetic variation would indicate that the usefulness of green tea derivatives will be limited based on individual differences. It will affect different people to different degrees. These differential effects have culminated in one minor reported side-effect of consuming green tea. This effect was an increase in diastolic blood pressure [87]. This was a relatively small increase despite it being significant, unlike other traditional remedies, and green tea does not appear to have any significant problems associated with its use.

The dosage of green tea supplements varies considerably between papers and samples. Usually, the dose is broken down into four capsules for a total concentration of 150mg of the active ingredient EGCG. This dosage appears to have similar problems with rapid onset of tolerance. All of the weight-loss associated with green tea derivatives happens within the first few weeks and is moderated by habitual caffeine consumption. People who drink more caffeine appear to lose more weight on green tea. Another extremely important factor associated with the efficacy of green tea is ethnicity [88].

The vast majority of studies have focused on Asian samples. In Asian people the effect of green tea on inducing weight-loss appears to be much more effective than in other ethnic groups. Asians will lose almost twice as much weight on green tea as Caucasians. The average Caucasian weight-loss on green tea is very minimal to non-existent. Therefore, the use of green tea is limited to Asian ethnic groups. The explanation of this ethnicity effect is based on the genetic determinants of the COMT enzyme that appears to significantly differ between Asians and other groups. Only one in four Caucasians have the prerequisite genetic make-up to even infer enough weight-loss for the administration of green tea to be close to effective [89].

If we return to the work on green tea with a more critical eye, then we will quickly uncover that irrespective of the title of the paper, many investigations were actually on overweight rather than obese people. As green tea has similar tolerance, saturation and interactive effects with caffeine, it is not beyond the bounds of possibility that the reported decrease in weight is optimistic. Data from larger individuals will probably show minimal effects compounded further by ethnicity. In effect, larger Caucasians will likely exhibit minute changes in body weight following a course of green tea supplements. Moreover, there are indications that long-term use will have minimal effects even in Asian populations [90].

On the Internet, green tea supplements are omnipresent starting from about £12 for 30 capsules. Often they come mixed with other ingredients including caffeine and Hoodia. Despite the fact that green tea is probably the best of the traditional herbal remedies (in terms of potential side-effects rather than efficacy), the scientific explanations of it by vendors is very poor. There are of course the usual drivel related to "fat burning" and "draining of toxins", but most do not understand how it is believed to work. Ironically, most vendors mention EGCG in relation to cell health or as an antioxidant for the sale of the product for other purposes. There are some affiliates and vendors who are up with the science and do mention the correct action of green tea, but these are in the minority.

The use of green tea as a credible candidate for treating obesity is sound. However, its efficacy is quite low and it languishes far below that of other pharmaceutical interventions. Perhaps with pharmaceutical exploitation, refinement of the pharmacological action of green tea can be undertaken to fully 'weaponise' its derivatives. Currently, green tea is the best known candidate of all the traditional herbal remedies. Personally, I do not believe that the use of green tea for weight loss purposes will ever be realised. The long-term efficacy is effectively non-existent. There may be some longevity in the use of green tea as a weight-maintenance tool, but it is unlikely to reach the heady heights of the previous pharmaceuticals. We will return to this maintenance hypothesis later.

CREDIBLE VERSUS NON-CREDIBLE

Phentermine, Orlistat, Hoodia (P57), caffeine and green tea (EGCG) are currently our main credible drugs for the purposes of weight-loss. They are 'credible' in the loosest possible sense of the word. Though they currently stand alone, they are not truly so. Pharmaceutical companies are continuously involved in the research and development of obesity drugs. Most attempt to interfere with the neurotransmitters and hormones involved with appetite regulation.

As each year passes, more and more refinement and accuracy of specific receptor agonism (activating) or antagonism (blocking) of different appetite targets occurs. The vast majority do not make it beyond initial investigations. The more refined the drug target becomes the more it is recognised that the system is interactive. Harping all the way back to the first chapter, it seems that our assumptions about pharmacotherapy do not hold. Thus, an impasse is reached. Regulatory agencies are reluctant to allow combined therapies for the treatment of non-life threatening conditions such as obesity. The more we delve into the biochemistry of appetite the more it would appear that this combined approach is necessary. This leads to the development of less specific drugs. It then transpires that the less specific drugs have serious side-effects leading to regulatory intervention and withdrawal. If lessons learned from Rimonabant are anything to go by, the life-expectancy of a new diet drug is very short-lived. This leaves us with an ever decreasing circle of viable targets and acceptable drugs. Currently, we only have the five in this chapter, of which only one is advocated by the European regulatory agencies.

Even the credible list has varying levels of credibility. Caffeine for example really should not be in this chapter at all. It scraps in just about, but as we will conclude later when we talk about efficacy of pharmacological interventions, caffeine really is not a viable or acceptable option. Hoodia has been tried and developed in private by two large companies and then rejected. Its future application is in doubt. If hearsay is anything to go by, even if Hoodia made it to market it will soon wonder off into the realms of chapter five and abdication as a viable pharmacotherapy. Phentermine is promising, but it is also highly addictive, short-lived with significant tolerance issues. Green tea looks as if it might have promise, but only for a highly select group of people with a specific genetic composition that may be undermined by habitual lifestyle choices and diet. Finally we have Orlistat. Orlistat is interesting candidate as it is the only one that does not attempt to interfere with appetite. However, it is seriously undermined by its potential to cause social embarrassment. One public 'accident' or a 'near miss' will mean the individual will discontinue their course. It would seem if the regulatory agents do not 'get' the drug, social implications/repercussions will. Credibility in the obesity-related pharmaceutical world really is a fine line. Very few drugs successfully walk it.

With the conclusion of the credible candidates, we get to attack the charlatans, the pretenders, and those substances that have no scientific merit whatsoever. Few have been tested under scientific conditions. Those that have, have been found wanting. Most of those compounds found in the next chapter are those that derive their merit based on some other form of biased interpretation. Some of it is simply made up, or tenuously inferred. In the next chapter, we shall hunt these down and slay them.

Chapter 7

OF THE PRETENDERS TO THE THRONE: SELLING DREAMS?

At the end of the last chapter you were told we would hunt. To get through this with some semblance of sanity, for there are a lot of claims out there, we are going to strafe a few down immediately. In alphabetical order, the following have seriously dubious scientific merit for the basis of their claims: Chitosan; Chromium picolinate; Garcinia cambogia; Guar gum; Plantago psyllium; Phenethylamine; Pyruvate; and Yerba Maté [90]. Although it varies between the various substances in terms of the scale of rejection, it is accepted throughout the credible scientific community that these products do not work. Any claims that they do are based on very tenuous or very specific studies. When all the data is evened out they come out as seriously doubtful. A good proportion of diet 'drugs' contain at least one of these ingredients and claim that they have an effect to aid weight-loss. Any company that makes such a claim does not currently have the backing of the scientific community.

Now that we have shot a few of these targets down, satisfying our lust to discredit, the rest of this chapter will be devoted to surgically dissecting some of the other substances claimed to aid weight loss. It is important to note that this list grows daily and physiologists, pharmacologists and psychologists cannot test all of them fast enough. The Internet, with the power of instant publication without justification means that someone need only make a nebulous claim before it permeates the world, hits the headlines and starts to become "the next great thing". Ironically, none of these fads have ever come close to being any good. To state it is the next best thing simply states that it is the next fad people have been sucked in to. Credibility is important in this process. "Scientists have found" is not a defense for its inclusion. 'Scientist' is a generic term denoted by the method of investigation not the expertise and field of study. A social scientist may have investigated that a certain chemical has a reported effect on a group of people in a far flung place. This is all good science, but it is far from being any good, specific or ready for application in weight-loss. Until such time as the path of appropriate testing has started by a plethora of experts from different fields, such comments are nothing more than speculation. It is a statement of potential, not a right to cart-blanch sprinkle it into a pre-existing product and sell it as a successful, scientifically valid, diet 'drug'. In short, we need to know which scientists, when, where and how did they find. Not that they just found. The minute any argument is started, defended or advertised under the 'brand' of "scientists have found" one should immediately start looking for the evidence. It will always be 'interesting'.

First substance under the microscope will be bitter orange extracts. It is not first for any particular reason other than it is very common in weight-loss supplements. Due to its common use it invariably attracts attention.

BITTER ORANGES

With the banning of ephedra came the surge in products claiming to be an ephedra substitute. For no particular reason, the one that emerged victorious was bitter orange. The reason for its success was probably due to economic reasons rather than anything else. It is in plentiful supply and will not overly affect the profit margin of a company wishing to add it to their products. A large proportion of diet 'drugs' add bitter orange to their products under a variety of terms. Some simply list it as a natural flavouring, but stake a claim to its supposed effects anyway. The names that the substance can be found under are green orange, kijitsu, neroli oil, Seville orange and sour orange. They are all one and the same thing and start from about £11 for thirty capsules on the Internet. Competitors to the bitter orange market, who themselves have dubious credibility, often discredit and scaremonger about the possible effects of bitter orange saying that they have serious side-effects. This tactic actually plays into the hands of the vendor of the product. If a 'drug' has a serious side-effect then it is often perceived to have serious effects by a lay person. Desperate people will then happily take the risk of serious side-effects if the effects are good. However, this scaremongering tactic is a useful strategy to switch people disillusioned by one product onto an equally useless product – exchanging one placebo for another. Therefore, the scaremongering itself is not an attempt to induce fear but to steal custom. It will also likely have an effect on the naïve first-time buyer too.

Scaremongering about the use of bitter orange comes from its supposed ephedra like qualities. The many affiliate websites and vendors will simply state the same side-effects of ephedra and attribute them to bitter orange. However, bitter orange does not contain ephedra; it contains Synephrine (also known as Oxidrine) and Octopamine. Very little is known about the effects of Octopamine. The vast majority of scientific investigations of Synephrine have been on its detection. Basically, science is more-or-less still at the stage of finding it. Moreover not all Synephrine is the same. There are different types or the substance with vastly different pharmacokinetic effects. Currently, what we know is that Synephrine exists in at least two natural forms designated as p- and m- dietary supplements contain the p- version. Some researchers state that some supplements contained the m- version, but the most accurate method thus far devised for detecting the m- form disputes this claim [92]. The whole argument around the efficacy of bitter orange is that it has thermogenic effects in the same manner as ephedra [93], however, there is a significant difference between the beneficial effects of the two forms of Synephrine. I am sure you have guessed it by now, but the one in the diet supplements is the p- form which is much weaker than the m- version [94]. It would appear that diet 'drug' companies do not understand that chemicals that share the same name do not necessarily have the same effects.

In terms of weight loss, the effects of bitter orange have been measured and found to have no significant effect. The amount of weight-loss that has been observed is in the region of 0.4kg compared to placebo after 6 weeks. At present, the vast majority of credible scientists do not accept bitter orange as a creditable candidate for treating obesity. In addition to its poor weight-loss record, there have been some side-effects reported by those taking bitter orange, which somewhat vindicates the scaremongers. It has been shown that Synephrine does increase blood pressure and cardiovascular problems in humans [96]. Initial toxicology tests on the p- form of Synephrine do however suggest it to be safe. Taking all of this information into account and looking at how these products are advertised on the Internet, if the company makes the claim it is 'safe' then invariably it contains the p- form. This has been shown to not be an effective weight-loss aid. If they do not make the claim it is 'safe' then it may contain the m- form but is likely to have little efficacy and importantly, there is a risk of cardiovascular problems. It would appear just because it does not help weight-loss does not mean that it still will not harm people. Although many credible scientists question the efficacy of bitter orange few question the need for safety tests to be carried as soon as possible.

Bitter orange may have won the battle to replace ephedra, but it failed in its ability to actually work. Currently, the users of bitter orange for the purposes of weight-loss are caught in a conundrum – take the supposed effective form and suffer side effects or take the non-effective form. Effective in this case is used in the loosest possible way. Bitter orange would appear to have many of the problems of ephedra without the associated positives. Not only are the makers of this product selling dreams, they may be selling nightmares.

HUMAN CHORIONIC GONADOTROPIN

Kevin Trudeau, an American author, has managed to more-or-less singlehandedly resurrect the public's desire to use this 'drug' despite it being rejected over thirty years ago [97]. Controversy has surrounded this hormone and there is serious money to be made from it – if the amount of spin off books and internet presence it claims is considered a basis. Somehow successive generations have been continually convinced that the injection of pregnancy hormones will help them lose weight. At what point each individual is convinced that this will help them is a mystery. Perhaps the key component is the nature and type of individual that sells human chorionic gonadotropin (HCG) or perhaps it is the manner in which it is sold.

It would appear that those that peddle HCG share one similar characteristic. They point their finger outward towards the institutions and pharmaceutical companies telling people that these are evil and trying to keep you fat to make money, while at the same time charging exorbitant fees for a product that has been shown time and time again not to work. Moreover, any critic of these people is an agent of the pharmaceutical industry. Last time I checked, there was not a Secret Police listed in the departments of pharmaceutical companies. In truth, they do not need to debunk these people. Credible scientists will do it for them. The finger, it seems, never points inwards. The fact that these products still exist and are still sold over the Internet without some form of government intervention is another mystery. The only evil that can be seen in this whole sorry situation is the fact that it has not stopped sooner.

Personally, I believe, the public's continued belief in HCG is born out of the fact humans like a good story. Often the truth is benign and uninteresting even when the factors in the story are intriguing. People simply listen more when everything is portrayed as illicit activities or power abuse. It would appear people enjoy the story more than the truth and they want to hear that it is all easy and will go away quickly. They want their lives to be interesting, just like the soap operas on television. They want to hear that there is a cover-up and that it is not their fault, it was a conspiracy against them. Step in the salesperson. Scratch the surface of the fiction and the wider factors do not make sense. Obesity is absorbing a terrible amount of resources. Everyone wants the 'cure'. If we had a cure, it would be offered immediately and without delay. Simply put, more money is 'lost' treating obesity than is made from it.

The establishment and credible scientists are so convinced that the HCG does not work that it is one of very few products that have actually been legally forced to be sold under a disclaimer that it does not work. This disclaimer, as you can imagine, does not appear on affiliate and vendor websites. What does appear on the affiliate and vendor websites is the same old rhetoric that appeared in the media in the 1950's. Then the man was Dr A. T. W. Simeons. We would be remiss in suggesting that Dr Simeons and Kevin Trudeau are one and the same type of person, and it is a shame that the two became intertwined. Simeons actually did not claim that the administration of HCG directly caused weight loss. This came from the 500 calories a day diet – any diet below 1200 calories has subsequently been rejected as a viable calorie restriction regime. Instead the original claim was the HCG suppressed appetite and improved mood. This suppression meant that the individual could remain on the very restricted diet without the uncomfortable side-effects. Along with the restricted calorie intake, the hunger claims have also been rejected [98].

The story of HCG is not a story of pharmacology or biology – well it was, but that ended years ago – it is a story of sociology. The past and continuing use of HCG would make a great topic for a PhD in the art of selling misinformation. People are hooked into it on the promise of pounds just dropping off. The principal mechanism of how this works is called starvation. People have been doing it for centuries, just not out of choice. It is starvation with some added extras to dress it up as scientific, but does not involve scientific reasoning at all. Often the prescription of the HCG diet comes with some additional supplements and homeopathic remedies. This gives us an indication of where the whole rigmarole lies. It would be fascinating to know how Dr Simeons would have responded if he had seen the outcome of his 'discovery'. Exploring the career of the man would suggest he would be horrified. He genuinely thought he had found the cure for obesity and did not live long enough to realise he was not even close. Dr Simeons was a well educated man and the whole HCG debacle was not the only aspect of his career. He had some success in the field of malaria too. The profile of the man suggests that he was a bit of a maverick, but not a 'loose cannon'. It is his blessing and our curse that he died before seeing what happened.

A new HCG type diet 'drug' appears to be rearing from the side-lines. This one is called Dehydroepiandrosterone (DHEA). Although in much earlier stages of development than HCG, DHEA has a similar, albeit a slightly better, research profile. DHEA is a hormone released from the adrenal gland and has been linked to a variety of functions. For our interests, some authors have attempted to link DHEA to fat metabolism [99], which invariably means a whole host of diet 'drugs' have appeared on the market claiming to contain this hormone. Depending on concentration, DHEA is relatively cheap compared to its other 'drug' kin. Prices start at about £6 for thirty capsules. Preliminary investigations with rats indicate that the effect of DHEA is promising, but it only works in the animals that prefer high fat diets and are also offered high fat foods. In humans the effects of DHEA are not promising at all [100]. To achieve anything like a loss of fat tissue, a dose of about 1600mg is required per day for lean people and much higher than that in obese people [101]. That would be over five times what the Internet vendors tell people to take. Scientific advocates are hanging on to DHEA to get the vast vestiges of research out of it until it is finally concluded it is not a viable target to pursue for clinical trials. It is not disputed that DHEA has an effect on appetite centres in the brain in some indirect manner, but it is likely to be very indirect indeed. Once HCG has finally fallen from grace, DHEA will likely take its place. There are simply too many animal papers showing effects on fat intake for diet 'drug' vendors to over-interpret and plenty of human ones for them to definitely ignore. There is enough conjecture for them to push this through and make it look credible to potential buyers. One potential problem with its use though is that it is controlled under the Misuse of Drugs Act in the UK as a class C drug and is also regulated as a medicinal product by the MHRA. Therefore, Internet vendors should not be selling this product without a license nor the buyer obtaining it without prescription.

FUCUS

Fucus is an alga and is also the genus classification sharing the name of at least three species found around the shores of many northern hemisphere oceans and seas. These are Fucus spiralis, Fucus vesiculosus and Fucus serratus. Diet 'drugs' do not state which of these are actually in their supplements. This is important as this depends on its registration rights as a traditional herbal remedy. It must be assumed that the derivative of Fucus in diet 'drugs' is in fact Fucus vesiculosus (F-V), as all of the others do not have the correct constituents to register it as a traditional herbal remedy. F-V does also have the known laxative side-effect that is listed as a possible complication of taking 'drugs' containing it [102].

F-V manages to scrape by under the rules of a traditional herbal remedy because it contains iodine. Iodine is the true active ingredient and harps back to the distant pharmaceutical interventions into obesity. It is a traditional herbal remedy because people used to be prescribed iodine in the past. It certainly does not have the same history as other substances such as Hoodia. Our distant ancestors did not come down from their caves to eat F-V seaweed to stop them from feeling hungry. They did however, pick it, burn it, and sprinkle it on their fields to aid crop growth.

The use of iodine as an anti-obesity agent was stopped after serious thyroid effects following completion of the treatment [103]. Obesity has been associated with thyroid function and, in some people, the release of thyroid stimulating hormone. A lack of iodine in the diet has been postulated to lead to a need to increase Leptin (the hormone realised from fat tissue and thus the need to increase fat mass) for the thyroid to compensate for this loss [104]. This has led some authors to hypothesize that increasing the intake of iodine should rectify thyroid function and lead to weight loss [105]. Another proposed method of action of iodine is to increase thermogenesis via interacting with brown adipose tissue. Brown adipose tissue is responsible for generating body heat. It has been known for a long time that insufficient iodine leads to problems with an underactive thyroid. This, in turn, affects the metabolism. Although brown adipose tissue is present in new born children, it is diminished, but not totally absent, in adult humans [106]. The net effect of iodine administration therefore increases thermogenesis leading to increased energy expenditure. The iodine dose required to successfully increase thermogenesis is around 0.8mg[1]. 600mg of Fucus (the max strength of all of the products containing this substance) contains roughly 0.2-0.3mg of iodine. Furthermore, the recommended daily allowance of iodine is 0.15mg [107]. Thus, there is a dosage problem with the effective use of Fucus for weight-loss.

There are a lot of studies on the effects of iodine in the public domain. Despite this, detailed searches in all of the relevant scientific search engines do not reveal any clinical trials on the efficacy of iodine as a treatment for obesity. Based on the theoretical postulations of how iodine is supposed to function to aid weight loss, we know that the utility of Leptin is extremely poor except in those individuals with a genetic disorder. Very few people world-wide have been diagnosed with this disorder despite persistent testing on Leptin levels in obese populations. Following the second proposed mechanism of action – thermogenesis – to its natural conclusion means that the current dosage of iodine found in F-V is more than the recommended daily amount, but is a factor of four times two small to have the desired effect. Even if the appropriate dose was administered, it would likely have little positive impact on thermogenesis because adults do not have enough brown adipose tissue for it to work on. If they even attempt to increase the dose, it will likely have negative side-effects.

In the UK, Fucus is sold under a specific brand name costing around £3.6 for the strongest dose of 600mg for thirty tablets. In the rest of the world it is sold under the generic name of Bladderwrack or Kelp tablets. To avoid this costly expense, a consumer could just buy iodine at a fraction of the price and get the same effect with a much more controlled dose. All in all, Fucus is not a viable diet 'drug'. More research may uncover a hitherto unknown action of Fucus in the future. For now, and based on our understanding of its nutritional content, Fucus has no place in the arsenal of a psychopharmacologist interested in weight-loss and should have no place on the kitchen shelf of those trying to lose weight. Iodine does, of course, have other essential benefits, just none for weight-loss.

CHO YUNG TEA

Let me get one thing straight from the start; Cho Yung Tea is not novel. It is not supported by any evidence and is not in any way special. Well, it is supported by evidence through its action of green tea that was considered in the last chapter, but there is nothing special about this specifically. It is riding on the coat tails of the popular beliefs about Chinese ancient mysticism and traditional herbal remedies. In short, if you are any other ethnicity other than oriental Asian then there is a very low chance that it will work and a minuscule chance that you will lose a clinically significant amount of weight. Cho Yung Tea is nothing more than a brand name for a blended tea. It would be no different than if Twinnings or any other tea based company made claims that their green tea blend caused weight loss. The 'blend' contains no other known active ingredients. The rest of the stuff in it is nothing more than alternative therapy 'fluff'. It has no basis in evidence other than its own contrived specifically accredited legal criteria that we discussed earlier in this book. Remember, it is not necessary for them to provide proof for their claims as long as they adhere to the legal requirements of a traditional herbal therapy or homeopathic intervention.

---

[1] Same citation as in note 129.

The three reasons to take Cho Yung Tea for weight-loss purposes, as advertised by the vendors, are that it is 1) supported by the Ministry of Health in China. A detailed search on the official Chinese Government website does not support this claim and even some of their own affiliate sites also suggest the claim is unsubstantiated. 2) That they only use high quality Chinese herbal ingredients. So does most tea blend companies – either Chinese or Indian, it is one of their primary exports. 3) You only need to drink two cups a day. Clearly, these people do not, or have not, read the research on green tea. If they had then they would know that this is not enough to elicit a worthwhile effect.

The other ingredients in the tea allegedly and in no particular order: stop you from rusting (yes rusting. They claim that the Oolong tea in the blend prevents oxidation. If they mean this by the strict chemical terms they might want to say it stops atoms from binding and the loss of electrons from the body, but in short they claim that if you drink their tea you will not rust)[2]; promote digestive activity (mild laxative effect); aid digestion (nebulus comment probably associated with vitamin or mineral content); expels toxins (no evidence for this at all, it is another stock comment made by all alternative therapies); and boosts the immune system (another stock comment probably derived from the vitamin and mineral content).

The reason that this has been given its own section rather than as a foot note in the green tea section is because of its pervasive aggressive affiliate marketing scheme and reported scams across the Internet. It would appear that the company offers free two week trials, but then charges people even if they return the product. Furthermore, they explicitly state that their product is backed by scientific research (actually, it is the same ones cited in the green tea section). They take quotes out of context and do not report the actual amount of weight lost. Green tea is, after all, associated with weight loss, just not that much. The exact claim that the company makes about 'what the experts say' is very carefully constructed. They say that their tea has 'health' rather than 'weight-loss' benefits. For those really interested, you can download their 'clinical trial' undertaken by the Fujian Center for Disease Control. This was a sponsored study and not a clinical trial in the true sense of the word. It also is not peer reviewed (the English language is shaky at best and it is not written in an appropriate scientific style) and is not published in a scientific journal. There was no blinding, no controls or measurement of what the participants were doing in excess of taking their product. Even with all these biases in their data, they still only managed to lose 1.5kg in five weeks. Over that period of time they could have legitimately lost, gained, relost and regained that amount of weight on diet manipulation alone. This is not strong evidence at all. However, it does 'look right'. The fact that it is there at all is probably enough to placate the lay person. Even more worrying is that all this information is advertised as clinical proof. No scientist would ever say they have proved something. They will only say that they have evidence for it and/or it has been proved wrong. The joys of science means nothing is proved only ever disproved. The minute I see such comments, I instantly become suspicious and so should everyone else. Writing 'proved' is the remit of the salesperson not the scientist.

The cost of Cho Yung tea is £56.50 for two weeks. At two cups a day that constitutes 28 servings. Recently, there has been a cut in price with 30 teabags only setting the buyer back £40. You can buy forty bags of green tea for £1.79. If you really want to go fancy, you can

---

[2] Dr Ben Goldacre points out a similar error elsewhere in other alternative therapy doctrines in his Book 'Bad Science'. Diet pills do not appear to be immune from this pervasive mistake within the industry. I too have never heard of anyone rusting.

get the Harrods Green tea for £4 for the same amount. If you wish to, you can buy all of the ingredients in this product in much higher quantities for a fraction of the cost. It really is a high profit item and one that does not work through pharmacological means. If I was to be flippant I would say buy the £1.79 teabags and give the rest to an obesity research charity. You will get more value for money.

One last comment that often circulates around the Internet by affiliate websites is that Cho Yung tea works because it has not been disproved or that scientists are not interested in testing herbal remedies. This is why, they say, scientists cannot prove how it works. There could not be a statement further from the truth. The whole debacle with Hoodia should instantly dismiss any such comments. However, because the alternative therapists insist in painting scientists as mad professors creating things from 'Frankinstein like experiments', let us consider how drugs come to be. Firstly, pharmaceuticals are not unnaturally created. There are basically two processes in how to create a viable drug. Either, the natural chemical that has the desired effect is isolated from a natural source, this is the case for the vast majority of drugs, or the endogenous hormone/neurotransmitter is mapped and mimicked by an artificial compound. Most of the time scientists and pharmaceutical companies do not know how the 'system' works and it is a case of finding the food that has the effect and then isolating the chemicals in the plant and testing them one by one until the same effect as eating the food is observed. The test-tubes, solutions and various large pieces of equipment are only there to allow the pharmacologist to break down the complex organic material to isolate its various chemical constituents. They are not there to randomly throw together, make something explode, get a powder residue, and use it as a drug. The procedure is often to take the organic material and through a set, highly refined, process, isolate the compound that is the active ingredient to the drug. Basically, the pharmaceuticals will take the same material as the herbalists and alternative therapists and strip it back to give you the active ingredient in them. The herbalists will just give you the organic matter. Therefore, pharmaceuticals are extremely interested in herbal remedies and will test them to exhaustion, ploughing vast sums of money into their development. There is only one reason a pharmacologist would not be interested in a specific herbal remedy.

MULBERRY LEAF

Finally, we come to the last of the supposed weight loss ingredients. Mulberry leaves have a long association with diabetes as a traditional herbal remedy in some parts of the Far East. Some authors have anecdotally reported that alterations, specifically Westernisation, of the diet in the Far East have led to a sharp increase in diabetic conditions. Early evidence indicates that the consumption of mulberry leaf in the form of a tea-like solution suppresses the levels of glucose in the blood of a rat following a meal [108]. The argument for how mulberry leaves work is through inhibiting the action of enzymes in the intestines. The specific enzymes, called disaccharidase, are those responsible for breaking down sugars, specifically sucrose. In addition to the role of mulberry leaf in sugar metabolism, there are also some interesting interactions between mulberry leaf and signalling chemicals in fat tissue. In particular, it appears to improve factors related to the development of metabolic syndrome and eventually diabetes. Obviously, this would have some benefit for decreasing glucose peaks following a meal in those individuals with diabetic/metabolic syndrome x-related problems, which has been shown in rats and mice.

Mulberry leaf extract has some interesting applications in the potential treatment of diabetes, probably as an adjunct to current intervention rather than as a replacement, but it has not been associated with obesity or weight-loss anywhere within the credible scientific literature. The belief that mulberry leaf is a possible viable treatment for obesity is entirely concocted by 'alternative' therapists and completely misrepresented and misunderstood by them. There really is very little data about the effectiveness of mulberry leaf extract on humans.

The argument that mulberry leaf derivatives will aid weight loss stems solely from its ability to inhibit the absorption of sugar. Targeting carbohydrate absorption will have the obvious net effect of decreasing the amount of calories eaten; however, it is not an appropriate strategy for weight-loss. Limiting or deleting carbohydrates from the individuals diet has met with both limited success and unpleasant side-effects. In the case of mulberry leaf, it would appear that administration of one gram leads to a decrease in the peak of blood glucose following consuming 75g of sucrose in both lean and diabetic people. What is also interesting and very rarely, if ever, talked about is the fact that it also results in elevated levels of blood sugar after two hours. Therefore, it is highly debatable whether the removal of the glucose peak is in fact simply a delay in absorption. The addition of mulberry leaf may simply extend the absorption time rather than prohibiting the absorption of sugar. Advocates of mulberry leaf suggest that this increase is the release of fat into the blood and thus proves their claims. There is absolutely no evidence for this claim what-so-ever. The inferred data from human studies would suggest that it is the delay in absorption rather than the release of fat [109]. To be totally honest, this has not been directly tested and a good scientist would state this; a bad one would use it as proof of what they want to say in order to sell their product.

The most worrying component to all of this is that a lot of vendors of mulberry leaf for the purposes of weight loss suggest that it is safe and has no known side-effects. No safety data has been undertaken on the effects of taking mulberry leaf. Fifteen percent of people taking 1g of mulberry leaf reported bloating, gas and diarrhea [110]. Furthermore, these same pharmaceutical interventions showed that the subsequent decrease in the prevalence of diabetes was not observed; rather it delayed the onset of the disorder [111]. Taking this evidence together, it would suggest that the use of mulberry leaf is very limited for preventing diabetes and there is no evidence for its use as a weight-loss 'drug'.

Despite its abysmal scientific record, mulberry leaf is available to buy for weight loss. It sells for around £10 for thirty tablets. The recommended dosage is roughly 1g before each meal, which is similar to the required dose to support the observed effects. Ironically, one of the reported unique selling points is that the product has not been tested on animals. In terms of the specific product, that is accurate – it has not been tested at all. If we consider mulberry leaf extract, which is the primary ingredient, then this, like all of the other drugs and 'drugs' in this book, has been tested on animals. Indeed, testing the product on animals is necessary for it to be considered safe to sell to the public. It may not be necessary to test a specific brand, but that brand cannot claim that the derivation/active ingredient of the product or its supposed effects is not derived from tests on animals. If they believe that they can, then they are selling nothing more than a food supplement in a concentration that is similar to the food itself. In that situation, buy and eat the food. It will be cheaper and you will get other benefits from it such as fibre/roughage.

With the conclusion of mulberry leaf, comes the end of the weight-loss drugs available on the market that has enough credible information to totally discount them as viable weight-loss 'drugs'. However, it does not conclude all of the important aspects to the field. Firstly, we have yet to consider the homeopathic remedies. These will need to be considered to fulfill our evaluation of the weight-loss 'drugs' on the market. We have also not explored the efficacy of all of the drugs, so we still must do this too. Before, we move onto all of this though, it is important to consider the content of the weight-loss supplements. The very manner in which these tablets are constructed offers some interesting insights into how they manage to survive and make statements such as the "best weight-loss blend ever".

DOUBLE, DOUBLE, TOIL AND TROUBLE

The title of this section is a little flippant, but it portrays the point that needs to be made. The 'alternative' therapy market is hell bent on portraying the pharmaceutical industry as mad evil scientists who want to do nothing more than rip the public off by withholding better treatments. Invariably, these 'better' treatments just so happen to be their treatments. Without exception, these treatments are traditional herbal remedies and have been around for many years, often, but not always, predating the pharmaceutical industry. Most of these have been directly tested and found to be ineffective or less effective than other biological targets. Some traditional herbal remedies have even attempted to emulate the pharmaceutical industry rather than actually predate it. This is evidenced in many areas and extends from the need for the MHRA to designate only fifteen years to be the cutoff point prior to the amnesty that is about to set what is, and is not, considered a traditional herbal remedy. In general, the pharmaceutical market deals with the 'alternative' therapists by ignoring them or in some cases buying out these companies and selling the products themselves. As we have already discussed, the pharmaceutical and 'alternative' therapy practitioners take different routes to creating their pharmacological intervention. 'Alternative' therapists simply sell the plant to the buyer (albeit in various simple preparations), while the pharmaceutical refine the plant to find its active ingredient and then sell this. This in itself is not a problem and in the majority of cases is not a cause for concern. However, there is another as yet not discussed difference between the two. Many of the weight-loss 'drugs' are composite substances made up of several 'active' ingredients. Some will throw many ingredients together in an attempt to have multiple modes of action. The most common is caffeine with Hoodia Gorfondii, but others also discussed in this book are also frequently added. It is the product equivalent of "well it has been shown to work in mice doing something vaguely related to weight-loss, throw it in with the others and say it's a new even stronger formula".

There is a reason that the pharmaceutical, medical and regulatory bodies are reluctant to allow a combined pharmacotherapy. This reason is that drugs tend to interact with one another to have additional, usually undesirable, effects. Each drug, when taken in isolation, usually has a select set of side-effects beyond the intended effect undermining the reason the drug was prescribed. A constant balance between cost and benefit is maintained to ensure that the outcome of taking the drug is more advantageous than not taking it. In the case of obesity, the balance is firmly tipped in favour of very limited set of side-effects. In the diet pills industry, this problem is not considered. Scientific investigations into the effect of a single drug are still in their infancy. Some have progressed further than others and this is usually denoted by the frequency and necessity of the illness the drug is supposed to treat. Very little is known about the effects of interactions between substances. Most of this information is limited to case studies reported by accident and emergency practitioners. There is an obvious ethical issue of studying the negative effects of combined pharmacotherapy meaning that it is not possible to explicitly test interactions between drugs. A recent case of herbal remedies having unexpected side-effects was Hydroxycut. In a press release from the FDA in the US on the 8th May 2009 (also released by the MHRA), Hydroxycut was reported to have serious and potentially fatal side-effects. Specifically, the pill was associated with liver damage/failure. It is still not known how the combination of herbs in Hydroxycut led to the liver damage. The primary active weight-loss ingredient was caffeine. It is not suggested that caffeine led to liver damage just that it is likely that a combination of substances in the specific quantities in the product led to the associated liver problems. Hydroxycut stands as a specific recent case highlighting the dangers of combined herbal remedies, as well as our naivety of how substances interact within living tissue.

Another difference between the two industries is the need to make specific statements about 'healthy lifestyle' choices. The ubiquitous statement across the Internet is that these 'drugs' *may* work alongside a healthy diet. At what point is the health diet the 'active' ingredient rather than the 'drug' itself is left up to the potential buyer to decide. Pharmaceutical interventions do not have to come with this caveat. The reason for this is because they met the necessary regulatory defined criteria for efficacy as a weight-loss drug (e.g. 5% weight-loss). As we have seen within this book so far, the effectiveness of these alternative pharmacologically active substances is dubious at best. Without exception, the 'healthy lifestyle' is not to live healthily; it is a calorie controlled diet alongside increased activity. Both limiting food intake and increasing activity will lead to weight loss. It is somewhat paradoxical that the current perception by society, as inferred through the language used by affiliate advertisers and diet 'drug' vendors, that a healthy life style is synonymous with calorie restriction. Restriction of calories below that used on a weekly basis would not constitute a healthy lifestyle. If taken to the extreme, this imbalance between energy in and energy out of the system would result in death. Energy maintenance would be considered as a healthy lifestyle. If the buyer simply matched their energy intake with their energy demands in tandem with taking diet 'drugs', the individual is unlikely to lose weight. If they do lose weight, then the pharmacological action would indicate that it would take an awfully long time to reach anything like a 'healthy' BMI from a starting weight status of obesity. This is probably known by the vendors and explains why they add the *may* work rather than *will* work as part of a healthy lifestyle. Even if the drug had been shown to have a definite, if minute, weight-loss effect, the addition of 'may' would not be legally required in any such statement. It simply works.

It is important that potential consumers of 'alternative' diet 'drugs' consider two significant differences between pharmaceuticals and herbal remedies. Both mixing in multiple 'active' substances and making 'may work' statements suggests that even the vendors do not consider their products to be particularly effective. It would be negligent to state that all weight-loss remedies offer combined products, but many do. This combined approach refers especially to products sold under a branded name. Selling composite substances does not just denote a lack of confidence, but it also represents a significant risk. Until such time as composite products are deemed safe, they really should not be sold. Just because a specific substance in isolation is deemed to be safe does not necessarily mean that the same dosage is equally safe when given with other biologically active ingredients. It would appear that an increased interest by the regulatory agencies is starting to occur exploring the interactive properties within multi-ingredient traditional herbal remedies; unfortunately, this is thanks to some specific cases of fatality. This may lead to increased difficulty in registering herbal remedies with the regulatory agencies following the amnesty of these products. What will follow in the coming years is an increased scrutiny for herbal companies and a reliance on products that have already been developed. This will likely lead to zealously defended statements about the traditional products and increased tension between the scientific community and the advocates for these remedies.

WEIGHT-LOSS WATER?

For those who spend any time on the Internet perusing diet 'drugs', it will not take long before they receive a pop-up or a 'buddle' offer that includes homeopathic remedies to complement their 'drug' of choice. This offer is made despite the fact that many homeopathic practitioners report that their interventions will not work when mixed with other forms of intervention (except calorie restriction and exercise). Moreover, there appears to be a significant disparity between how to treat obesity amongst homeopathic practitioners. Some sources state that there are numerous remedies for obesity and they have to be individually prescribed depending in the symptoms of the patient. Individually prescribed treatments suggest that there is room for interpretation. With pharmaceutical interventions, there are competitive alternatives to most drugs for many conditions except for obesity; however, the vast majority of alterations to the prescription are based on dose rather than type. When there is an alteration to a prescribed drug, it is usually substituted for a drug that has a similar action on the same target region, but functions in a different way (e.g. a different type of serotonin-related drug etc…). For the homeopathic practitioner, it would appear that the same rules do not apply. They will give multiple remedies tailored to the individual while pharmaceuticals give just one.

Remember from chapter two, homeopathic practitioners have the ability to offer their services in a similar manner to a pharmacist, but they are not allowed to make therapeutic claims. Instead, they are only allowed to state that they have a 'remedy' and that specific ingredients are associated with that remedy. As we have used the Internet throughout this book to investigate the claims made by affiliates and vendors, it is only fair that we stay with this medium.

To exemplify how homeopathic practitioners remain within the law, explore any website by searching for "homeopathic remedies for obesity". You will find numerous sites. You will also find that instead of making therapeutic statements, homeopaths will simply list an ingredient, then state its effects (in pharmacological doses) and then will give a description of a typical person that it would be applicable for. The two statements of 'effect' and 'applicable' are not intrinsically linked. It does not say that that ingredient will rectify the problem only that it "may help" or "is suited for". Therefore, with the inability to make a therapeutic claim, the construction of their material is extremely important. It is reliant on the reader inferring action rather than actually being told that it will directly lead to recovery or weight-loss. It is best to read any such material with a critical eye and ensure that no assumptions by the reader are made from one sentence to the next.

Another important component to remember is that safety is assumed. This assumption is based on the dilution of the product (according to the MHRA). Homeopaths are allowed to sell restricted substances such as DHEA within their remedies. They are even allowed to write on their products that they contain these substances just so long as they remain within their extremely dilute state where none or a miniscule amount of the original substance is left in the commercial product. Dr Ben Goldacre takes his readers through the dilution principle of homeopathy and interested readers are referred to this source. To provide an abridged version, the typical homeopathic dilution is well below the legally assumed level of 1×10^{24}. Most are at a dilution of 1×10^{60}. Any dilution of 1×10^{24} is unlikely to have any of the original 'active ingredients' in it. If you put just one drop of active substance into any lake, sea or ocean you will have a solution that is much stronger than any homeopathic remedy. If you put one drop in a bucket of water, the odds are good that if you filled up your vial from that bucket that you will not get any of the active ingredients in it. Ironically, it is more likely that you will get some of the active ingredient in standard tap water than in a homeopathic remedy. With so many people now taking pharmaceuticals and expelling them into the sewage system, a fraction of these will make it back into the water supply following water treatment. The amount would be very trace indeed almost imperceptible and immeasurable, but probably at a much higher dose than a homeopathic remedy. This is probably what the MHRA mean by assumed safety.

Considering these important factors prior to discussing the treatment of homeopathic remedies allows the reader to infer the pharmacological activity of the product. One molecule will effectively bind to one receptor before being deactivated, if it is not deactivated in the stomach, blood, or finds itself diffused into a different non-target region. Activating one receptor is not enough to activate a single cell let alone a whole pathway full of them. Therefore, the homeopathic remedy has no pharmacological action whatsoever. It simply cannot. It is well beyond the realms of our universal understanding of physics that such a product could have a pharmacological effect. It yet may have a psychobiological effect, but that is an entirely different story. In the homeopathic world, it would appear that everyone else needs to 'prove' that homeopathic substances do not work, while at the same time everyone else must provide evidence that theirs do. It most certainly is not a fair game. But it is a safe one.

Homeopathy is based on the work of Dr Hahnemann (1755-1843), who offered three main liturgies underpinning the profession. These are that: 1) Like cures like (in medical terms this would be a form of immunisation but given before or after contracting the illness but with one vital flaw – it does not contain any active ingredients). For homeopaths "like cures like" is derived from the reported symptoms in their proving procedures. If the consumption of a particular substance leads to a specific symptom in a healthy individual, then the consumption of this substance will treat the symptom in a sick person. Again, in scientific terms this would be the same logic as giving stimulants to children with Attention Deficit Hyperactivity Disorder. Now, the homeopath is also a naturopath, so they would suggest that the stimulant would not be pharmaceutical because they are in their words "unnatural". Their logic would however dictate giving a stimulant to these children.

The like cures like leads to the next homeopathic principle of "the Law of Infinitesimals". When pharmacologists identify a substance that has an effect they will effectively refine or condense the said product to get the active ingredient. They will isolate the active ingredient, name it, uncover its chemical structure and then obtain it in commercial quantities. Homeopaths, in contrast, will dilute it. Thus, the pharmacologists will suggest that increasing a dose will have an effect, while the homeopaths will suggest that giving a smaller dose through an increased dilution will have a larger effect. The flippant argument to this would be to take a natural substance like caffeine and suggest that decaffeinated drinks are more dangerous than caffeinated ones. Decaffeinated drinks once contained caffeine, but it has now been removed in a similar manner as the active ingredient was once in the homeopathic remedy and has now been diluted out. Remember, up to 10g of caffeine is lethal and as you go down in dose, it has less of a biological effect on the body. It is called an overdose, not an underdose, for a reason. Many homeopaths, but not all, would disagree with the use of caffeine as an example, because many of them believe it is an inherently bad substance. Everything in excess, including water, is bad for any individual, but most things are acceptable in moderation. This moderation principle is how people come to tolerate their environment. The small amounts of any ingested substance will have progressively weaker effects. Dilution to increase potency conflicts with every known physical, biological, chemical, phytological (herbalist) and pharmacological phenomenon.

The final, and probably most pertinent factor, is that the treatment must be based and indeed tailored on the individual. This is in direct contrast to the assumption made by all medical professionals working in the biological domain. There assumption is that everyone is effectively biologically similar and that a substance will have a universal effect. If it works on one person, then, apart from some slight genetic variations, it will work on every person. The only other group that also advocates some individuality in the treatment, beyond dosage, are psychologists. Psychologists know about the power of tailoring therapy. It provides perceived specificity to the client and increases their consumable resource[3] investment and vested interest. This motivates them to adhere to the programme and increase its perceived value. Outcomes of the treatment can derive simply from this personal investment. Some therapies, like the Interpersonal therapies (called IPTs for short), are born out of attempts to provide 'control' psychological treatments for patients. These therapies have benefit, but it is the applicability of the psychological intervention that is important. It is no different to the fact that nearly all people involved in a clinical trial for weight-loss lose weight. Even people on placebo treatments will lose weight irrespective of the fact that they are not active drugs. The power of belief is important in any intervention. It is for that reason that all drugs must be tested using blinded placebo-controlled randomised trials. This effectively ensures that this 'belief' is removed from the action of the drug. Homeopaths actively criticise these trials and the British Homeopathic Association (BHA) suggest that these will not work for their interventions. Instead they advocate open label trials where the participants on the placebo

---

[3] Consumable resources are those denoted as anything that is finite in amount but valued by the individual. This value means that the individual is reluctant to part with the resource unless they gain some perceived benefit that is equal to, or in excess of, the value of the resource. Primarily, I have only come across this theory when related to stress through the work of people like Hobfoll (1989) with his conversation of resources model. Obvious global examples of valued resources are time, money, energy and knowledge. According to Hobfoll all resources, including those that are individually valued, can be categorised under the terms of: object, condition, personal and energy groupings.

treatment know and are repeatedly told that they are getting nothing. One would question the vested interest of a participant who knows that they are getting nothing. In science, such studies are called evaluations rather than trials. These 'open trials' are important for finding out 'true' side-effects of the active drug, but they are not useful for working out efficacy. Open-label trials are integral to uncovering safety issues, but only that, nothing more. Homeopaths state that all of their products have no known side-effects, so performing evaluative research is a pointless endeavour. No matter how much they believe in the outcomes of the evaluation or to what they attribute the findings to, it has no basis in the evidence. And to nail this point home, no other health professional groups under the regulatory law can do this. Moreover, psychologists are able to and have provided clinical trials for their interventions. If they can where no 'active' ingredient is given, then so can the homeopath. Simply complete the consultation as it would ordinarily be done, but give a different solution to the participants in a double blind manner. That would be a placebo-controlled trial. There is no methodological reason why this could not be done. Homeopaths actively group their patients in 'types' and the treatments for them are based on this plus their symptoms. Some psychological disorders also have similar aetiologies. For the psychologists, they simply wait until they have enough people to group together before running the trial. Even if the groupings run into thousands then it could still theoretically be done with international co-operation. Geneticists undertake this scale of co-operation all the time.

Uncovering homeopathic remedies is a difficult process. One individual not party to the field may only find a tiny amount of information about a tiny proportion of possible interventions. According to the BHA, this should be a much easier process. They state that 44% homeopathic clinical trials indicate a positive effect, 8% a negative effect and 48% are inconclusive.

Of those substances reported to be effective homeopathic remedies for weight-loss, the most frequently found are: ammonium muriaticum; antimonium crudum; argentum nitricum; calcarea arsenicum; calcarea carbonica; capsicum; coffea cruda; ferrum metallicum; fucus; graphites; ignatia; kali bichromicum; lac defloratum; lycopodium; phosphorus; phytollaca; pulsatilla; sepia; senega; staphysagria; and thyroidinum. Without exception, none of these have any scientific evidence to back their claims. In the absence of any scientific evidence, it is impossible to understand either the mechanism of how they are supposed to work or understand the action they are supposed to have. Frequently, these homeopathic remedies are associated with terms such as improving digestion, 'elimination' and metabolism. Improving digestion would actually increase weight rather than decrease it. In fact, many pharmaceutical companies and herbal remedies attempt to interfere with digestion to have their weight-loss effect (e.g. Orlistat). The claims about elimination are either referring to some form of 'detoxification' or increasing the transit time through the intestines (i.e. laxative effect). Finally, 'improving metabolism' probably refers to increasing metabolism. This would be a similar action to many other diet 'drug' products through the use of caffeine; we also find that coffea cruda is on the homeopathic target list too. Whatever is the believed reason for offering a specific product to a client, without evidence, it is all supposition. Supposition is not a luxury afforded to any other groups of medical, health or allied health professionals. Clinical experimentation in the absence of evidence is only reserved for the extreme, life-threatening cases where all of the other accepted treatments have been exhausted and have failed. Homeopathic practitioners constantly vocalise about persecution from other scientific and health professionals. This is not an accurate representation. Perceived attacks on homeopathic medicine are not an attempt at eradication or persecution of the specific field of study. It is an attempt to instill a set of universal rules that all health-related practitioners must adhere to. That is, what they are doing to the patient has precedence and evidence for efficacy, especially related to expectations of the level of effective outcome. Without this information, it is considered experimentation and requires the express informed consent of the patient complete with a detailed discussion with the health-professional about realistic expectations. In other health-related fields, if the practice does not have evidence then it must come with the caveat that it is an experiment, requires ethical approval from a peer-reviewed panel and is unlikely to be effective. I am of the opinion that homeopaths are lucky that they do not have to state similar expectations to all of their patients.

In terms of homeopathic predispositions for weight-loss, the total amount of endorsement through open discussion offered by the BHA only links calcarea carbonica and graphites with obesity as well as several "personality types". These personality types bear no resemblance to psychological characterisation of personality or evidence on which they are based. The specific personality types associated with obesity are the "wild cat [112]" and "calc carb [113]" people. We shall come back to these later. In fact, the BHA website talks more about barriers to treatment than it does about actual treatment for obesity. These barriers are, unsurprisingly, not eating appropriately, taking other medications, severe disease, poor lifestyle and psychological problems [114]. More surprisingly and in conflict to everyone else, homeopaths suggest drinking too much coffee (and thus too much caffeine) leads to problems with weight-loss. On a quick side note, the consumption of large amounts of caffeine has been the mainstay of herbal remedies for obesity for a long time. Here, the BHA suggests it undermines their treatment. It would seem that the 'alternative' therapists need to sit down and resolve this issue. Herbalists push for caffeine, while some homeopaths suggest it is a problem.

The only published evidence for successful homeopathic interventions for obesity is a single study [115]. The study by Werk & Galland is widely cited and has also been submitted to the British Government's Science and Technology Committee on the 22nd February 2010 as 'proof' that homeopathic remedies work. Rather worryingly, this is not a homeopathic study. As part of the homeopathic proving process, they consume the target substance prior to any dilution, report its effects and then dilute it for treatment purposes. The study by Werk & Galland was not a homeopathic remedy. The secret is in the title that was submitted to government: '*Comparative controlled trial on the effect of the homeopathic botanical medicinal product Helianthus tuberosus D1 as an adjuvant in the treatment of obesity*'. For those confused by this, the devil is again in the detail. The statement is that the product is a "homeopathic botanical medicinal product" not a "homeopathic remedy". The product has been prepared under similar procedures of homeopathic remedies, but it has not been diluted enough. This is shown in the "D1" designation. D1 is a dilution of 1×10^1 (i.e. 1 part active ingredient to 10 parts dilution). This would be classed as an herbal remedy at this dilution. Just because it has homeopathic in the title does not mean it is one. It just means it has been prepared under the auspices of homeopathy.

To wonder from the point a little, this title presented to government does not appear on the published article. I asked the British Library to search for it for me. You can ask them to do this in return for five pounds. They could not find this. Under the same reference in the same journal, they returned the article '*Helianthus tuberosus-therapy in overweight: long-term stabilisation of weight-loss*' or more accurately '*Helianthus-thuberosus-Therapie bei übergewicht: Gewichtsreduktion langfristig stabilisieren*' it was written in German. One would hope that the Government and the MHRA recognise this and act accordingly.

Through their unique perspective on dilution improves strength of the intervention, I am certain that homeopathic organisations will continue to cite the work of Werk & Galland as evidence but will offer it in massively dilute (i.e. >1x 10^{24}) preparations. They will have to dilute the substance, in this case Helianthus tuberosus (Jerusalem artichoke), beyond the level set out by the MHRA as acceptable for homeopathic remedies. If they do not then they will have to register them as an herbal remedy and they will not be allowed to diagnose or alter dosage (i.e. violate their individuality principle). Alternatively, they may register the product as a medicinal product and will not be allowed to use it at all without a medical license and an acceptable endorsement for efficacy (e.g. it will need a placebo-controlled clinical trial). Finally, they could legitimately suggest that Jerusalem artichoke is food product and register the intervention as a food supplement. Here, they would still not be allowed to alter dosage based on diagnosis and they could not make claims without clinical trials. In short, I believe, there is no acceptable evidence for efficacy of homeopathy for weight-loss purposes.

The periodical in which the Werk & Galland article appears is not without its controversy. *Therapie Woche* (Therapy Weekly) published articles for the German tobacco industry denying the serious side effects of smoking [116]. Furthermore, it is more akin to a magazine than a traditional scientific periodical. It is the German equivalent of *New Scientist*. This 'equivalency' is not in terms of quality; rather it is in terms of target audience. *New Scientist* is targeted to the interested member of the public and is not considered the place to publish research articles. The work itself is not published in the scientific style contains no rationale, contains limited information about how the study was carried out (what it does contain suggests that the participants were not obese. In fact the authors actively excluded anyone with a BMI above 35) and told those who took part that they were taking a pharmaceutical. Finally, the statistical analysis was inappropriate with the authors performing t-tests on data with multiple levels. Any second year undergraduate science student could tell them that they needed to perform an analysis of variance on this type of data. Performing repeated t-tests on data such as this massively increases the likelihood for positive results. Finally, within the discussion the authors repeatedly report the data in such a way to improve the outlook of their findings. For the experimental group they report those that achieved a BMI below 25 (in this case 47%) and then offered those that did not achieve this weight status on the placebo (72%). What would be more accurate to present would be that that 47% achieved a BMI lower than 25 in the experimental group and 28% did in the placebo. This type of presentation is more accurate. Moreover, since the experimental group had a 0.1 BMI advantage and much lower within-group weight variation, in terms of standard deviation, over the control group at the start of the study, these conclusions are questionable at best. Obviously 0.1 BMI point is very small, but if we compared 25.1 as the cutoff point then how many more people from the placebo group would have made the cut off for health weight? I guess we will never know. Furthermore, having a larger variation in control group has the potential to offer fewer people that will make the cut off BMI criteria for weight loss.

If we play along with accepting it as evidence for weight-loss through homeopathy and evaluate it based on outcomes and methodology, then this study falls from grace even further. On face value, the efficacy of homeopathy was a net loss of 2.5kg over three months compared to their placebo. The value of the loss is heavily biased towards positive outcomes. In all clinical trials for efficacy, best practice dictates a "last point carried forward" approach.

This is where, in the absence of follow up data on drop outs then it is assumed that the last measurement was reflective of the substance's overall efficacy. Basically, the participant left the trial, and once the product goes to market, it can expect similar dropout rates. Therefore, the overall efficacy of the drug on the population includes both those who complete and those that dropout. This was not the practice employed in the current study. Instead, dropouts were not considered. If those individuals' weights were factored into the overall weight-loss then the outcome may have been very different. In Werk & Garrand study, one hundred and sixty-six overweight participants took part and sixty-four dropped out before completing. Most participants that dropped out were from the placebo condition – forty versus twenty-four. When significant difference occurs between conditions this indicates that the study was not adequately blinded despite it saying that it was. Therefore, without appropriate blinding, the study does not measure efficacy, it measures safety.

The use of Jerusalem artichoke as a weight-loss tool does not appear anywhere within the literature except in this study. The most entertaining fact for the critics of homeopathic remedies is the simple truth that there is scientific data for artichoke as an anti-cholesterol agent [117]. Some authors have even suggested that it should be tested as an anti-obesity drug, as it is used in Brazil for a very long time as a traditional herbal remedy for weight-loss [118]. The leaves, in particular, are associated with its active effects of cholesterol metabolism in the liver. This may sound confusing, but we have not finished our story yet. This data relates, of course, to the globe artichoke (Cynara scolymus) not the Jerusalem artichoke (Helianthus tuberosus). For those people who have ever hung out in a greengrocer will know that these are two different plants. The homeopathic practitioners could save face through suggesting that Jerusalem artichokes contain inulin, which may help with intestinal flora function [119] aiding digestion. In fairness to the authors, they do suggest a role for inulin in their discussion. However, without a rationale at the beginning of the study concerning relative merits of inulin means that we will also not know whether the use of the Jerusalem artichoke was intentional or a mistake. To further discredit the inulin argument, when the refined substance is tested through a clinical trial it did show it had cardiovascular protective factors through decreasing LDL cholesterol [120]; but, the use of inulin has not been associated, by any credible source that I am aware of, with weight-loss. Therefore, the use of inulin is only associated with complications of being overweight or obese rather than weight-loss. Moreover, for homeopathic practitioners to make this claim will require them to refine inulin from the plant and dilute this. This would marginally conflict with their naturopathic perspectives and does not explain why Jerusalem artichokes were chosen above more local and cheaper alternatives with comparable levels of inulin. For example, the UK has a ready source of inulin in the form of dandelions. These are a weed in gardens everywhere and would not require commercial ventures to obtain the required amounts of inulin unlike the Jerusalem artichoke would.

I promised that I would return to the two personality types that the BHA associate with obesity mentioned earlier in this section. So here we go. Taking the "black jaguar" case first, the BHA describes these people as being:

> "[wild cat personality's are]...big with a loud voice and can be overpowering, taking over the consultation...They are often very successful and rise to the top in their profession... They tend to be outgoing, upbeat and energetic with a warm and affectionate nature. They are strong, self-assured and with a good opinion of themselves. They tend to be ambitious and

independent. They are self-reliant and often leave home early to get on in the world... They tend to be dare-devils, jumping from high places and climbing trees."

In the world of homeopathy, the description of personalities is a much more fluidic examination than in psychology. Psychologists often deconstruct personality variables and define people as having a personality trait if they score higher than the population norm on a psychometric test (usually a questionnaire). These questionnaires are specific to each potential personality attribute and following a detail examination of the individual (usually taking a very long time and people who have been for a full psychometric evaluation can attest to this). The homeopath does not appear to have the same rigorous methodological testing. It is all based on the homeopaths observation of the individual and a sort of pseudo-content analysis[4] of their conversation. It is an interpretation and imposing of perceived observed behaviour or conversational content extrapolating a series of preconceived ideas. Or in layman's terms, it is seeing what was expected to be seen. Psychologists have recognised the folly of such interpretations and are generally reluctant to 'group' people. Of course, there are some sub-fields and sub-disciplines in psychology that have the predilection for doing this, but on the whole, this is not common practice. Instead, psychologists will measure personality variables and place people on a continuum of these variables to get a wider picture of the individual before them. If we psychologically deconstruct the "wild cat personality" as stated in the quote above, then we would see that this is the description of a type A impulsive extrovert. The type A component comes from sentences one, two, four, five and six and this is a very accurate description of how these individuals tend to come across in a therapeutic setting. Sentence three gives us the extrovert component and the last sentence refers to impulsivity. There is no need in the psychological world to attribute any mysticism or animal patterns to their behaviour. If we were totally honest, then this description would be similar to the "red with purple over tone personality types" that are based loosely on Jungian theory. Needless-to-say, these colour personality groupings that often circulate popular media are not a Jungian creation, they seem to have appeared later as a way of 'spiritualising' or may be allowing easier access to psychodynamic theory for the lay person. Jung would have called this person an extroverted thinking sensation type. Modern day psychologists would probably just call them type A impulsive extroverts, but they would not stop there. The modern psychologist would go further by measuring other personality variables too.

Obesity has been reported to anecdotally respond to "wild cat" treatment by a homeopath in the BHA journal. At no point is this homeopathic personality type been inherently linked to weight-gain or loss. For that we would have to turn to our other group – the "Calc Carb" People.

In the BHA documentation available to the public, the description of the Calc Carb people provides clear insight into the development of homeopathic remedies. It is a symbolic rather than scientific endeavour. The continued reluctance of homeopaths to be considered spiritual healers does not match with how they go about explaining their 'measured'

---

[4] Content analysis is a form of qualitative analysis. It is extremely rigorous form of testing and is an accepted psychological analytic technique by most behavioural analysts. There are some psychologists who still resist qualitative methods as a valuable investigative tool, but these are getting less vocal as each year passes and the next generation of psychologists takes their place. Importantly, the use of these methods is not instead of the more quantitative psychometric methods. They are used as an additional strategy to answer different questions, not done in isolation or instead of other forms of investigations into personality.

phenomenon. Their personality types and remedies are based almost completely on the symbolic representation of the product rather than its pharmacological action. Perhaps if homeopaths just accepted this spiritual label, the continued attacks from the scientific establishment would cease. Instead, homeopaths continue to attempt to prove the scientific merit of their intervention and yet refuse to accept the most rigorous scientific testing as being best practice for their interventions. However, I have wondered off course slightly. Let us continue with the deconstruction of the Calc Carb people to further reiterate this symbolic representation.

> "Calc carb is the fundamental representative not only of the molluscs but also of all life forms derived from or influenced by the sea, including those mammals which returned to the sea and developed fish-like attributes. The obese human image is their constitutional counterpart."

Calc Carb (or oyster) people are based on their outward appearance more than their behaviour. The running theme is the predilection for associating blond hair and blue eyes with obesity. The rest of the description comes from a mix of symbolic comparison of human behaviour to animals or anthropomorphising animals and description of a human with excess fat or depression. Two quotes to reinforce this point from the BHA website are:

> "...the classic picture of the Calc carb woman: often blonde and blue-eyed; a great fat woman without breath, strength or energy; without firmness, colour or health; fair, fat and flabby with a hand that feels like an oyster, cold, clammy and boneless; and damp, cold, clammy feet. These types, male or female, are generally indolent, inert and sedentary, lacking initiative; like the oyster ever waiting for life to come to them; content and complacent, lethargic and unambitious, not easily aroused or stirred and immovably stubborn."
>
> "The Calc carb infant is often a floppy baby – soft, fat and flabby, with a big head and a distended abdomen; fair-haired, fair-skinned and blue-eyed; bloated and dimpled rather than of solid, hard fat."

It would appear that the homeopathic description of their personality type with a predilection for obesity is a person who presents with obesity – a somewhat circular argument. There also appears to be different types of calc carb people with different "reasons" for why they have gained weight and for a full understanding of the homeopathic description interested readers are referred to the BHA website.

Psychological explanations of obesity have been many and have been found wanting. The psychological variables associated with obesity are understood more by the social discrimination that obese people suffer and the difficult environmental situations they encounter rather than an inherent personality characteristic that predisposes them to adiposity. The longest-standing theory for obesity was externality where the individual was believed to derive feelings of hunger from environmental cues for food rather than physiological ones. However, this was later changed to be a behavioural variable that explains most people's eating rather than being specific to characterising one group. From a psychological perspective there is no known personality characteristic that will lead directly to obesity. This is further evidenced by the fact that obesity is fast becoming, and has become, the normal weight-status in certain parts of the world. It is a phenomenon best understood from an environmental, policy and food selection perspective than a psychological or genetic explanation.

Homeopathy is a lost art. It is not lost because it is was once good and was for some reason lost to human understanding through a disaster of some sort, rather it is lost because it does not know what it is. It would appear to be a mix of spirituality and psychology that borrows some of the historical authority of the medical/pharmaceutical fields while at the same time suggesting that these interventions are unnatural. Homeopathy is an art despite its attempts to portray itself as a scientifically 'proven' pursuit. It embraces the parts of each field (spirituality, psychology and biology) that suits its purpose while attacking, rejecting and claiming persecution from those that do not. In the case of obesity, when homeopathy claims to be evidence based to all those who query it, the organisational bodies troop out the same study time and time again. When we scratch the surface of this evidence it is extremely shaky and is certainly not a homeopathic remedy or a well conducted, or at least explained, clinical trial. It was a traditional herbal remedy prepared with homeopathic flair. In terms of scientific understanding of the chemistry, the use of Jerusalem artichoke may yet show evidence for treating some of the co-morbidities of obesity, but the evidence against its role as an aid to weight-loss is mounting. The globe artichoke on the other hand has precedence as a Brazilian traditional remedy and may prove to be effective as a weight-loss ingredient, but it is highly unlikely that it will. It too will probably result in benefits for the co-morbidities of excess weight rather than weight-loss. Homeopathy as a weight-loss intervention has very dubious evidence base to back its claims and as such finds itself in this chapter.

Consumer in Wonderland?

For a not so small fee you can buy a dream. The dream is to be thin, beautiful and popular. There is tenuous and questionable 'scientific' data to back the claim, but that does not matter. The consumer is desperate to be thin and will try anything. In my opinion, all products containing the ingredients detailed in this chapter should simply come in an empty bottle with the words "Drink Me" written on the side. Alice, I am sorry to say, there is no Wonderland. What works in literature seldom works in real life. May be it will exist one day, but that day is not today. Beware those that will sell the dream. Anecdotal evidence on the Internet has questionable credibility at best. Even if someone did actually exist and lost the weight they reported taking this product then they did this in the absence of any known pharmacological evidence.

People have too much confidence in pills. This confidence most likely stems from the association between feeling ill, taking a pain-killer, and then feeling better almost immediately. Most of these over-the-counter medicines do not treat the problem, they mask the symptoms. The infection or the tension is still there, the pill has just manipulated the biological basis of perceiving the pain. They did not cure you of your ailment. Even those potent drugs given to you by the doctor are either just a higher dose of those you can get over-the-counter or are 'helping' the system fight the infection. The onus is most definitely on the body to fight off most problems. It is for this reason that you have to continually take drugs to ensure that a specific dosage level is maintained in the system in order to not perceive the symptoms of the illness. Diet drugs, even the better ones, work on an efficacy level that is much lower than even over-the-counter drugs in other fields. Some, those endorsed by individuals and companies not a part of the NICE or MHRA government agencies, do not work at all according to the scientific literature. There is a reason that NICE only endorses the use of Orlistat and none of the others. That is because the cost/benefit ratio is at the right level; right in terms of efficacy rather than their purse strings. I am one hundred percent sure that if any of the herbal products worked then they would be adopted instantly and endorsed by the regulatory agencies. After all, they are vastly cheaper to produce than pharmaceuticals. The reason that they are allowed to continue to exist is that, on the whole, they do no harm. Hydroxycut is an example that the assumed harmlessness of these products is not always proven accurate within the test of time.

People desperately want a pill to cure everything. But it is not the pill they actually want. They want a quick solution to all of their problems. They want the dream sold to them by the vendors and affiliates. Failing that, they want to 'medicalise' the problem in an attempt to preserve the little amount of self-esteem they have left that has not been taken from them by the discriminatory society that they find themselves in. For those that are not overweight and are still taking diet drugs to achieve an ever decreasing weight, then the presence of, and desire for, the pill is a physical manifestation of psychopathology. This may be any one of a number of psychopathologies from simple depression to body dimorphic disorder or even a full blown eating disorder. Attribution of a specific psychopathological label will very much depend on the individual's fixation/preoccupation and current weight-status. For many, the desire to take these products stems from a desire to be thin not to lose weight. Medical professionals are trained to know the difference and give access to the drugs accordingly; although it really does not take a trained eye to 'know' this difference. For those who do not have this option than a raft of other diet 'drugs' are available. A product available through a more-or-less anonymous system does not discriminate between those that need the product and those that want it. This system deals in numbers. The numbers found on the little bits of paper that circulate society and most of us desire as a valued consumable resource.

Many people will be taking the current 'drug' because the other 'drugs' or pharmaceutical drugs did not work. Alternatively, they may have an ideological belief that will prohibit the use of pharmaceuticals. Such ideologies would include naturopathic beliefs, but it is not exclusive to them.

All is not bad with the substances offered in this chapter. They are providing a valuable service to the community. Because of the existence of those that want these products, we must be thankful that the products detailed in this chapter exist. Without them, people who want, rather than need, to lose weight would be able to obtain products that are effective treatments. Although, the surreptitious attempts to add pharmacological grade controlled substances to some weight-loss products does indicate that those that really want them will be able to eventually get them. Furthermore, we must be thankful for these products because they provide externalised belief that it is possible to lose weight for the consumer. No one wants to be considered gullible or having been ripped off, therefore, they will have a vested interest in ensuring the product succeeds. They will be determined to lose weight and will alter their behaviour accordingly – just as the companies that sell these 'drugs' tell them to do. Please do not misunderstand that these products have no effect, they might do. It is just that they are not an effective treatment in isolation. Taking these products may result in some minor increase in energy expenditure, but it is so small that it would have minimal impact without a concomitant lifestyle change. Their total observed effects are nothing more than a placebo. Just because they do not have a known biological effect does not mean that they do not have a psychological effect. However, all of the content in the last three chapter pales into insignificance against understanding the comparative success of these products. It is finally time we do this.

Chapter 8

OF SUCCESS AND FAILURE

And finally we come to it. We have arrived at the end of our whistle stop journey through the diet 'drug' industry and come to the comparison section. What works, how does it work and how does it compare. For some of the people reading this book, this section will give them a quick access to what works and what does not, for others it will be a guiding hand to offering advice. For everyone, it is probably the reason they picked this book up.

Let me say from the outset that this chapter is probably going to shock the reader and for those desperate to find out what 'works' may even be an anticlimax. It need not be. There are several interpretations about relative success and, unlike in other sections of this book, I will try and refrain from giving you mine. 'Try' being the operative word. You have heard this already and if you have changed your mind then that is fine and if you have not then that is fine too. As long as you heed the advice and questioned everything given to you on face value, then your mind is your own. After all, forewarned is forearmed. Let it be known now that the amount of weight loss attributed to every weight-loss ingredient in the drugs we have discussed is far lower than you may have thought.

MEASURING DIET DRUGS SUCCESS

Table 8.1 shows the average weight loss in placebo-controlled clinical trials (where possible) for each. It is obvious that there is a dominance of pharmaceutical drugs in the table. This is not because I am a 'lackey' or 'secret agent' for the drugs companies. Very soon you will be perturbed by the fact you ever thought it. The absence of this information is due to the limitations of the alternative therapies and 'drugs' to provide the necessary information or have run the essential studies. Pharmaceuticals are forced to run these studies prior to marketing their products so these appear more frequently in the table. There is another equally obvious difference for those people who have paid attention throughout this book. Drugs that target the brain have a larger effect than those that target the periphery. Those substances with known brain targets have an effective range of 5.0-2.4kg while peripheral-related 'drugs' range from 0.2-2.9kg. This offers significant evidence for why pharmaceutical companies repeatedly attempt to target the brain over the body for the purposes of weight-loss.

Table 8.1. Total amount of weight loss when on the 'drugs' in this book

Drug	Weight loss (kg) compared to placebo
Rimonabant	4.7[a]
Sibutramine	4.3[b]
Orlistat	2.9[c]
Fenfluramine	2.4[d]
Phentermine	3.6[e]
Topiramate	4.7[f]
Fluoxetine	5.0[g]
Caffeine	0[h]
Green Tea	1.3[i]
Human Chorionic Gonadotropin	0.2[j]
Homeopathy	2.5[k]

[a-c]Padwal, R. J. & Majundar, S. R. (2007) [121].

[d-e]Haddock et al., 2002 [122] (6-17 weeks).

[f]McElroy et al., 2007 (14/16 weeks) problem with this is that it was on binge eating disorder obese.

[g]Li et al., 2005 (52 weeks) [123]

[h]Unknown because it has rarely been given in isolation. No direct data available, however, most authors indicate a negligible effect (e.g. Westerterp-Plantenga, 2010) [124]

[i]Hursel et al., 2009 (12-24 weeks).

[j]Stein et al., 1976 (32 days). Only Asher & Harper (1973) [125] would dispute this claim whose work has yet to be replicated and has received significant methodological criticism.

[k]Werk et al., 1994 (12 weeks) problem with it not being a clinical trial or not carrying dropout rates forward.

The best possible outcome for taking a drug for at least 3 months is the loss of only 5 kg. In old money, that is 10.10 pounds. That is not even a stone. Therefore if you are obese, the most likely outcome is that you will still remain obese when on the drug alone. If you wish to look at in BMI terms, then I will use myself as an example. I am a thirty year old man with height of 172.7cm (5ft 8ins) and a weight of 70kg (11stone exactly). My BMI is 23.4. Remember any BMI between 19 and 25 is normal (depending on sex and age), anything above 25 and under 30 BMI is overweight, with above 30 being considered obese. If I took Fluoxetine and lost 5kg my BMI would drop to 21.7. That is a net BMI difference of 1.7. To be considered obese, then a man my age and height would have to weigh in excess of 90kg (14st 2lb). If such an individual took only the drug and did nothing else, they would still be on the high end of overweight.

For a woman the same age with a height of 165.1cm (5ft 5in) then to be considered obese they must have a weight higher than 82kg (12st 12lb). The same weight loss would constitute a 1.8 BMI drop. They too would still be on the upper end of overweight. If it is believed, as it is by many, that 'drugs' are the 'cure' for the global obesity pandemic then they have most definitely failed. They have not only failed, they have spectacularly failed. To actually be able to cure the obesity pandemic alone then a single intervention must result in a minimum net weight loss of 15kg for an individual with my height and 14kg for a 5ft 5 woman.

COMPARATIVE FAILURE

So the diet drugs have failed, spectacularly so. To understand just how spectacularly diet drugs fail we need to compare it to other forms of weight loss. Namely, simply eating less (known in the trade as low calorie diet – 1000-1800 calories per day), really restricting food intake (called the imaginative very low calorie diet - <800 per day), behavioural therapy, exercise and surgery. As you can imagine, for as much as the diet 'drug' industry vie for the attention of people wanting to lose weight, so there are other groups also using similar strategies. Some are more vocal than others, but all have more success at inducing weight-loss than diet drugs of all types.

Very low (VLCD) and low calorie diets (LCD) both have had a successful run over the last few decades with multiple authors setting up various tactics to help people consume less calories. Some, like Atkins, advocated the removal of carbohydrates from the diet, while others took a more holistic lifestyle approach. Most psychologists would advocate the change of a lifestyle rather than attempting to diet. This probably explains why those private enterprises that have withstood the test of time are those that also advocate such methods. Evidence from weight-loss studies exploring VLCD and LCD provide a stark reminder and example to anyone attempting more drastic calorie restriction measures to lose weight.

Data indicates that drastic weight-loss resulting from consuming less than eight hundred calories per day is initially promising with an average decrease of 16.1kg over a period of a couple to a few months. Compared to LCD, employing a VLCD constitutes a net loss of an extra 6.2kg. LCD results in a loss of 9.9kg over the same period. However, the longer that you leave the person, the more this extra weight-loss is evened out until after two years where they are roughly equal at a standard total loss of 6.3kg (VLCD) and 5.0kg (LCD) [126]. It would seem that destiny dictates that a proportion of the weight lost will be regained. Such long term data is not available from the diet drugs. In the vast majority of clinical trials, the treatment rarely lasts longer than six months. However, we can infer based on all other interventions that the minute that the pharmacological intervention is removed at least part of the weight lost will be regained. Over a similar period of time, it would appear that simply restricting food intake to a magnitude of roughly five hundred calories will have at least double the effect of even the best diet drug.

Exercise is commonly touted as a valuable and viable intervention for obesity and a valid method to lose weight. This is simply not true. I frequently have to debate this concept with both professionals [127] and lay people alike due to my vehement opposition to this apparently accepted doctrine. In fact, anyone who actually cares to look at the data will find that exercise is not, and never has been, a viable weight-loss strategy. Most health professionals advocate the use of exercise to improve the co-morbidities and general fitness of the individual rather than as a weight-loss intervention. Its use for weight-loss is purely a media creation. Ironically, those individuals who suggest that exercising obese and overweight people thin are those that get paid to offer such services. Personal trainers have a lot to answer for when it comes to perpetuating this particular myth.

The effectiveness of exercise for weight-loss purposes is difficult to measure as it has not been tested in isolation. Combining exercise with LCD results in an additional weight loss of between 0.7kg [128] and 2.2kg [129] compared to simply LCD alone. This magnitude of weight-loss is far below most people's expectations and would probably be disputed by those involved in the industry. The science is there for anyone to see, while evidence for the use of exercise for weight-loss is absent. Until such time as these individuals can offer a total of fifty-six peer-reviewed and published studies to alter this evidence, I am inclined to ignore exercise as a viable intervention method. Moreover, the amount of weight-loss observed through exercise suggests an efficacy level below that of even alternative therapies, let alone the pharmaceutical industry. Stalwart advocates of this form of intervention should bear this in mind when making their claims.

Against psychological interventions, diet drugs fare little better. Simply having contact with a psychological practitioner will result in an extra 50% weight loss (7.8kg) [130]. The more the psychologist moves towards a specific intervention, the less impressive the weight loss. For example, offering generic problem-solving therapy will result in a net loss of 6.7kg [131]. This perceived 'responsive' component to the psychological intervention offers some insight into the power of simply having someone there who will respond to the needs of the dieter. Perceived responsiveness may even be explained as a function of social-support where networks of people, both professional and peers, provide encouragement and praise for losing weight reinforce the dieters compulsion to continue. A comparison between contact with a psychologist and more 'official' problem-solving therapy offers a difference of 1.1kg in favour of the support, which is not far off the power of green tea. Whether the employment of a psychological therapist to provide this support for the additional loss of 7.8kg is worthwhile will be something that society will have to collectively decide. Employing such a person would probably be much cheaper than prescribing drugs to everyone.

Society may simply decide to endorse the surgical route. A recent report on the dramatic explosion in the uptake of bariatric surgery (popularly known as banding or stapling) has been met with poorly concealed horror by the media and wider population. The general belief appears to be related to the distain about the amount of money being spent on the NHS to treat obesity using rather drastic and ultimately irreversible, for the non-gastric banding, solutions. However, even combined, the use of LCD and diet drugs will not meet the magic 15kg weight-loss number for an obese person who has a BMI of 30 getting down to a BMI of 25 within a six month period. Moreover, these solutions are not guarantees, it is an average score based on a normal distribution.

We all know that pandering to the mean or even finding a person who is the mean is difficult. Therefore, the weight-loss denoted as 'mean weight-loss' is the expect outcome rather than the actual one. By the nature of the normal distribution, there will be a significant amount of the population that will not even reach the weight-loss of the mean. For these people, constant failure to lose weight turns them to engage in drastic solutions. After all, if you do not have a stomach or it has been banded to the point of being ineffectual then no matter what or how strong a person's motivation to eat is they simply cannot. Weight-loss in this situation is forced. In short, it is guaranteed. Such guarantees are strong pulls for those who are desperate enough. However, unlike other 'guarantees' offered by other industries, surgery can offer real ones.

There are variations in the amount of weight-loss observed between the various types of bariatric surgery[1] [132], but the weight-loss is so profound that it is measured in BMI point drop rather in kilograms. The average weight-loss following bariatric surgery is a drop of 15 BMI points. For a 5ft 8ins man that is 45kg. Even a morbidly obese individual (BMI>40) would fall inside the healthy BMI range following surgery [133]. The loss is so profound, and because the surgery is irreversible, it is not regained. Even after eight years those who elected to have surgery will still be 16.5% lighter while their peers who were just dieting will have likely gained 0.7kg [134]. This would suggest that electing to have surgery is not a frivolous activity with an idea of wasting tax payers' money. It is a weight-loss strategy of last resort when all else has failed.

The financial reason for it is to remove the burden of the evitable development of co-morbidities that accompany obesity. For example, a one shot surgical intervention is more cost effective than a lifetime of diabetic treatment. Indeed, recent cost saving projections suggests that offering surgery will save on average 75% of the annual costs of obesity. This is a somewhat rose-tinted view of the cost savings offered by a group of people with a vested interest in increasing obesity surgery [135], but it is beyond much doubt that surgical interventions would save rather than cost money in the medium- to long-term.

Comments from the general public that frequently circulate when such stories surface in the media are those relating to the assertion that obese people got themselves into their 'state' and the state should not have to pay to get them out of it. Such critics clearly do not understand the irony in such statements. Having a national health service free at the point of entry and need means that surgery for obesity is a legitimate treatment. After all, who would voluntarily and knowingly become obese in a society that vilify people of a high weight status. It is the environment and modern society that is responsible for the obesity pandemic not the individual's gluttony or sloth. Both gluttony and sloth requires intention that is why they are both deadly sins. Obesity is a natural and inevitable outcome of living in the current world today in the same way as famine and thinness was the same for our distant ancestors.

Everything about modern life is sedentary – we work sitting down processing data and we spend our free time with modern media such as television programming and computer games. Add to this mix our pre-programmed desire to consume food high in calories and the comparative cheapness of food containing higher energy value while at the same time offering little nutrient value. In such a scenario, it should come as little surprise that people put on weight. To deny obese people surgical interventions for weight-loss is morally no different from denying an impulsive person treatment when they have broken a bone or cancer treatment for individuals that engage in activities, including employment, that increase the prevalence of developing the illness. Effectively, it is little different than denying treatment for any ailment either now or in the future that resulted from the individual's decision-making.

Everyone has made a mistake at some point and everyone has sought medical advice because of it. Furthermore, obesity is not the outcome of a single journey but the destination

---

1 There are in fact four common types of bariatric surgery. They all do this through altering the stomach and duodenal regions of the upper digestive tract. The most popular techniques are laparoscopic adjustable gastric banding (LAGB), vertical banded gastroplasty (VBG), Roux-en-Y gastric bypass (RYGBP) and bilio-pancreatic diversion (BPD). The most common procedures used today are laparoscopic adjustable gastric banding and Roux-en-Y gastric bypass (Cummings et al., 2008). However, general guidelines state that the surgical approach and technique used should be tailored to the individual.

of many. Different people that are overweight achieve this status for very different reasons. Denying medical treatment under the guise that "the money is better spent elsewhere" is no different than any other form of discrimination. Perhaps if society did not vilify obesity so much, these people, if they wish to, may be able to galvanise enough confidence to lose weight in other ways. Alternatively, these people may be happy with their weight-status and just unhappy with how they are treated by society. It seems humans are still preoccupied on visual appearance to judge the value of others. Need we be reminded that many of the great thinkers and leaders of history were in fact of a higher weight-status? Until government policy intervenes to make the consumption of energy dense nutritionally poor food more costly, then no one can be punished for requiring treatment for a problem that is partly due to the product of modern environment. Obesity is not a hand-to-mouth process. It is much more complex than that.

WHEN TO USE WHAT AND WHY?

The first and most blatant criticism of the last section was that it made direct comparisons between various interventions. Most of these interventions have specific and unique targets to aid in weight-loss. Some do not even advocate the sole use of their intervention. Well, credible advocates would not. Thus direct comparisons are not as helpful as a 'horses for courses' or combined approach. When explored in combination, then the various interventions suggest a different pattern of effectiveness than one offered by direct comparison.

Taking exercise first (as it took a bit of a beating in the last section), it quickly becomes evident that engaging in activity is effective at stopping weight regain. For all its impotent effect on weight-loss, exercise ensures that the weight lost does not return after finishing a LCD. In this scenario, the comparably limited calorie expenditure from increasing exercise transforms from being an action of weight-loss to become an action of 'error of margin'. Increasing activity following reaching a target weight means that habitual over-consumption through eating energy-dense snacks and taking needlessly large portion sizes, which we are all pre-programmed to do, have progressively smaller effects on increasing positive energy balance and weight-gain. Simply increasing activity is much easier to do than vigilantly maintain a restrictive diet consuming a fixed amount of calories on a daily, weekly, monthly basis for the rest of their lives. In such situations, poor mood would surely follow. Maintaining this restrictive diet does not apply to surgical interventions; these physically maintain the small portion sizes through the absence of stomach tissue that is responsible for allowing the consumption of larger amounts of food. For those people without this enforced motivation, physical exercise is of paramount importance for weight-maintenance for both adults [136] and children [137].

Psychological interventions also appear to be effective at weight-maintenance than loss. In particular, the support offered by the therapist through telephone conversations or relapse awareness and prevention appear to be strong predictors in limiting weight regain following interventions [138]. Most of these interventions appear to be didactic lectures and the imparting of knowledge rather than actual psychological support or assessment. Undoubtedly, the role of the psychologist is to assess the individual and tailor the intervention to the client, thus increasing perceived applicability, is integral, but does not appear to be essential. For the best possible outcomes however, understanding the predisposing, precipitating, maintaining, and risk of relapse factors would increase successful weight loss.

For the most effective non-surgical solution to obesity would require a multidisciplinary approach to get the excess weight off and keep it off. LCD, along with some form of medicinal, non-invasive, MHRA regulated and NICE endorsed product (i.e. Orlistat – as it is the only one that fits these criteria) would help to start the process of losing weight. A word of caution must be offered at this point. This relates specifically to the guidelines for prescribing weight-loss drugs to people. Medics cannot prescribe weight-loss drugs without first checking the patient has attempted a concerted and appropriate effort to lose weight without pharmacological intervention.

All weight-loss drugs available on the NHS are proposed as an adjunct to, not instead of, all the other interventions. If the medic believes that the person is not appropriately engaging with other weight-loss strategies in addition to the drug then they are advised to terminate the prescription. The specific guidelines set out by the Royal College of Physicians suggests that pharmacotherapy for obesity should only be offered after the individual has failed to lose ten percent of their body weight over six months through LCD and exercise [139]. These guidelines predate the over-the-counter availability of Orlistat and so would likely need modification. In effect, the modern medic is offering a higher dose rather than allowing access to pharmacotherapy. However, similar timeframe expectations would be required prior to prescription.

The NICE guidelines for the use of weight-loss drugs extend on those offered by the Royal College of Physicians. NICE require that, prior to prescription of Orlistat, the obese individual should have lost 2.5kg through diet and exercise. This is because initial weight-loss and motivation predict the successful outcomes for pharmacotherapy. In short, the drug will only work if the individual is motivated to lose weight. It is an aid rather than having a potent direct action. Following prescription, NICE recommends a three and six month follow up where the therapy should only be continued if a steady rate of weight-loss is achieved. The prescription should be stopped if the person has not lost and additional ten percent of their body weight by six months [140]. In addition to motivation predicting efficacy, the implementation of a low fat diet prior to starting the course of Orlistat means that the potential side-effects will be limited. Obviously, if the individual is already consuming a low fat diet then the effects of Orlistat will be significantly diminished.

In addition to the limitations of prescribing Orlistat, other factors are also important. Social support and psychological guidance may further facilitate the process of weight-loss and keep the dieter motivated. Furthermore, as the dieter's weight-status decreases then a process of limiting weight gain must begin. When the person is able, physical activity should be integrated and progressively increased to an individually set and viable level that can be maintained as a part of a person's normal life. For additional support, some form of guidance should be offered to limit relapse into old habits of eating that led to the weight gain in the first place. It is important that this change is one that becomes part of the person's life from that moment on. This means that enjoyment and motivation to limit weight regain is integral to long-term success. If the alterations become a chore then they are unarguably pointless. This change to eating habits, exercise habits and social support is what is commonly referred to as altering lifestyle in contrast to the previous attempts to diet in order to lose weight. In an environment where it is easy to gain weight, it is abnormal, if not artificial, to maintain a stable weight.

Combining all of these interventions together and implementing them at the appropriate time during weight-loss means that the expected outcome would be a decrease of around 16.4kg over the course of a year; although it must be stated that combining all of these interventions together has never been tested. The value of 16.4 is extrapolated from the various numbers offered in the previous sections. It may be the case that some of these interventions tap into the same processes and thus overlap. Therefore, this weight-loss would constitute an upper rather than average weight loss. For an individual just within the obese range this would return them to just within the healthy weight category. Surgery would exceed this by a factor of three in a much shorter time frame.

Managing expectation is integral to success. Against better judgment to avoid undermining motivation to lose weight through denying people what they want to here, the loss of a significant amount of weight and keeping it off for a significant period of time requires an appropriate and achievable target. Setting target dates of weeks or months in the future will likely fail. It took the whole of an individual's life to achieve their current weight-status. Undoing this lifetime of weight-gain is neither quick nor an easy process. Resetting an appropriate lifestyle without setting target weights or goals will allow the individual to achieve a healthy weight over time and will have a greater success at staving off regain. However, such long-term and nebulous goals often end in failure too. People prefer quick fixes and will follow those people that offer them.

Alongside managing expectations, offering a viable lifestyle is equally important. Perceiving the changes to the individual's life as permanent rather than transient and dependent on achieving a specific weight is important to both weight-loss and weight-maintenance. There is little point of instilling or viewing a lifestyle that is not liked. It will only make the person more miserable and they will not adhere to it. It may even push them further away from non-surgical solutions as they view them as punishment. It is important that the individual does not view weight-loss or weight-maintenance as a chore. If they do, it is doomed to fail.

WILL PEOPLE STICK TO IT?

It really does not matter about the efficacy of a specific intervention or combined intervention if people will not stick to it. The usual inference from those people that drop out refers to one of two possible outcomes. Either the intervention had too many adverse side-effects that the participants discontinued or that the participants believed that the intervention was not working and they left. This inference is rarely backed with any data, although in the more recent studies it is, and the attribution of one particular scenario over another very much depends on the type of intervention. The drop out from drug interventions is usually associated with side-effects and the behavioural link to questionable efficacy. Based on the clinical research, this would clearly not be the case. If the behavioural interventions are unequivocally better at inducing weight-loss, questioning the efficacy of the behavioural interventions that may also have the resultant effect of increasing adverse symptoms (such as psychological consequences and increased and prolonged feelings of hunger) without considering similar criticisms of diet drugs seems contradictory. With the population's overconfidence in the efficacy of pills, they are likely to be more tolerant of potential side-effects compared to behavioural interventions but concomitantly less tolerant at slower rates of weight-loss.

Managing expectations and ensuring people remain diligent at adhering to their intervention is important but it is a balancing act. Being too draconian or light touch will lead to the participant becoming resistant. People do not mind a little punishment but too much will have a negative effect on outcomes. Motivating the participant is the key to success irrespective of potential side-effects or efficacy rates. It is somewhat obvious to state that efficacy rates are related to keeping the individual in the programme; however, it may not be as obvious to say that maintaining the person's intensity on the programme will have a large impact on outcomes.

Comparing the various interventions offered in this book, there is a clear bias towards withdrawal from some, but not all, drug treatments. This type of evidence provides insights into the cost benefit statements by regulatory and clinical guidance agencies. People often complain when a drug is withdrawn by regulatory agencies. These are often the small proportion of people that tolerate the side-effects (or do not suffer from them) and also find the drug effective. However, in a system where cost of the intervention is important, high rates of withdrawal or a significant amount of people not taking the drugs in the prescribed dose means that it is ineffective. Moreover, in a litigious or overly cautious society, if one person suffers serious side-effects then the drug is withdrawn on safety grounds. Being overly cautious with weight-loss drugs is appropriate as serious side-effects will not only result in equally serious consequences for all involved, it may also undermine the quality of life of the person taking the substance.

Table 8.2. Withdrawal rates for different weight-loss interventions

Drug	% Withdraw
Rimonabant	16%
Sibutramine	48%
Orlistat	33%
Fenfluramine	37%
Phentermine	8%
Topiramate	27%
Fluoxetine	57%
Caffeine	Unknown
Green Tea	Unknown
Homeopathy	29%
Psychological Interventions	18%
Simple Dieting	16%

Based on the scientific literature, there appears to be a lot less withdrawal from psychology, LCD, phentermine and rimonabant interventions compared to fluoxetine, sibutramine, Orlistat and fenfluramine. All but one of the drugs with the worst withdrawal rates are now banned in the UK. Orlistat still remains because of its safety record and specificity to the intestinal tract. It certainly does not remain based on its efficacy, which is reported to be only an additional loss of 2.9kg. Furthermore, a third of people taking Orlistat will not complete the course. The low amount of weight lost and high instance of side-effects surrounding the inability to control bowel movements in some cases offers a somewhat negative picture of the only drug that is endorsed for use in the UK.

What is not considered on this table and somewhat saves the case for Orlistat, is the fact that dosage is not offered. The rates of withdrawal offered here are based on clinically prescribed levels of Orlistat and the other drugs rather than those available over-the-counter. The dose of over-the-counter Orlistat is half the strength of clinically prescribed levels. This lower dose will likely have fewer side-effects on average, but it may equally be less effective.

WHAT SCIENCE CANNOT ACCOUNT FOR?

Frequently science is portrayed as a pseudo-religion within the media. Scientists are often described as having blind faith 'in science' over other potential explanations. Needless-to-say, science is not a religion and does not require faith. It is a methodological philosophy and nothing more. Scientific investigation is a way of testing the world not explaining it. Of course the philosophers would argue the finer points of the interaction between testing the environment and viewing it, but science is not blindly followed without reason. The main difference is that scientific explanations are dependent on evidence from experimental data. Variables are manipulated and the outcomes measured. Theories are then formed on these outcomes and the effect of them. These theories last only as long as the experimental observed data matches their hypothesised outcomes. The minute that a theorised hypothesis is not met the theory is rejected in favour of a better explanation. In religion, doctrine is formed without evidence and acceptance or rejection is based on Faith. This necessary data dependent caveat to scientific theory is both its strength and its limitation.

Where possible in this book, I have used combined results from numerous studies available in the published domain. But all of these are limited by a variety of methodological factors, even down to the measurements themselves, and are not always representative of the complex real world. More-often-than-not, scientific data over-represents the effectiveness of the intervention. Compared to a person attempting to lose weight on their own, those individuals involved in studies are consistently monitored and measured for relative success by the researchers. This simple interaction may reinforce the desire to lose weight in a proportion of participants. Therefore, the outcomes or observations in quantitative studies of weight-loss are not always as representative as scientists are sometimes guilty of portraying. The simple act of observation will have an effect on the individual being observed.

Quantitative studies are also limited by the process of the hypothesis. In order to make a valid observation in a scientific experiment, it must first be hypothesized. Someone must first think up the importance of a specific factor and then rationalise how it is involved in the weight-loss intervention. Once they have done this they then need to find a valid way of measuring it and then find people to actually measure. The whole process is confined and defined by our perceptions. Thus, efficacy in this case may be driven by other factors yet unknown to us. At some point in the future, an investigative scientist may increase the efficacy of a given drug by considering, accounting for and including/excluding a specific factor from the intervention. For example, if people were fully prepared for the side-effects of Orlistat or are offered a solution that would save potential social humiliation through their inability to sufficiently control their bowel movements, they may be less likely to withdraw or would tolerate higher doses. The net effect would be decreased fat absorption and more weight-loss. These constitute the limitations of the research presented within this book and the arguments on which it is based.

The findings of the research in itself have limitations, but equally so does the practical application of it. Beyond the obvious "bedside manner" of the clinicians offering the interventions affecting people's perceptions and thus efficacy of a drug, sometimes clinicians simply ignore the guidance offered by the regulatory agents. There is evidence that the pharmaceutical interventions detailed in this book are not followed as they should be by medics that prescribe them. In the US, specialist obesity practitioners will frequently offer doses of phentermine in excess of the recommended dose and offer it in combination with L-5-hydroxytryptophan (5-HTP). This combination has never been tested. Clearly there is disparity between the practitioners and the scientific investigators. There are two possible explanations of disregarding regulatory guidance. The first would be that the regulatory bodies' dose is not as effective as the patient desires and so they place pressure on the practitioner to increase the dose to a mutually tolerable level. Alternatively, another explanation might be that the practitioners are 'experimenting' in the field and have moved ahead of the researchers in order to provide more effective healthcare. The anecdotal evidence would indicate that the behaviour of these practitioners is an attempt to emulate or recreate the phen-fen combination. Offering 5-HTP alongside phentermine would have a similar theoretical mode of action to phen-fen. Perhaps the explanation lies in the practitioners' belief that the withdrawal of this combination treatment was overly cautious and undermines their effective interventions. In the UK, this is all a moot point as neither drug is available for obesity treatment.

In contrast to ignoring guidelines on the prescription of pharmaceuticals, it also appears that around half of all rheumatologist and internist practitioners surveyed regularly prescribe placebo treatments to patients [141]. In some instances, and when all else fails, some medics will resort to placebo interventions in a similar manner to alternative therapists. Most of the 'placebos' prescribed by medics are over-the-counter analgesics or vitamin supplements; rather than sugar pills or saline injections. Other placebo treatments offered by medics are prescriptions for antibiotics and sedatives. Clearly, this is an accepted practical application by many medical professionals. In short, there is accepted value, biological repercussions and clinical aspirations for administering a placebo.

The point to this section is to state that the information offered here is based on informed expert opinion through interpretation of the available data derived from experimental investigations. This opinion is based on what is available now and may change in the future through either informed debate or new evidence. This may be considered as scientific hedging, and it is, but there are far too many examples of theoretical flaws exposed by new evidence. Rest assured, to overturn the information offered in this book would require a fundamental shift in new scientific knowledge. This opinion is all based on vast amounts of data conducted over the last sixty years.

Such a shift is not without precedent. After all, Newton's Laws were usurped by Einstein's theories only to be semi-replaced by quantum theory. Stranger things could easily happen in psychopharmacology of weight-loss. Therefore, there is still room for negotiation and personal interpretation. People may decide to accept this data as 'fact' and formulate their own opinion from it. Alternatively, they may reject it all in the hope that it will all be replaced by something else in the future.

The truest picture is probably a little bit of both. Pharmaceutical interventions are quite crude. In the future, they are likely to be much more elegant, direct and multi-faceted. What is certainly not the case though, is that herbal or alternative interventions are the 'hidden' scientific answer. Without exception, they are yet cruder attempts at operating through similar principles to pharmaceuticals. Herbalism would be a backwards, not forwards, step. Our ancestors did not know more than we do today. They just had cruder forms of anecdotal observations passed down from one generation to the next. Acceptance of the effects of various herbs was done on faith and shrouded in mysticism.

In short, they just believed in them more. Ironically, this same conclusion could be drawn about us by our descendents when exploring a historical perspective of our current medicinal drugs. This would be especially relevant if the commentator is writing from a perspective of a more refined pharmacological understand and utilising more elegant pharmaceutical solutions. In summary, hindsight is a powerful thing.

THE POWER OF THE MIND

Faith may have little place in science, beyond the faith in current theory, but it does in health. These are two highly inter-related but altogether separate subjects. We train our aspiring medical and psychological practitioners hard in the doctrines of science over the course of their educational and practical training. For all, this will be duration of about nine years before being left to offer unsupervised interventions to the general public. They are taught the power of belief and have frequent continuing professional development courses throughout their careers to reinforce this initial education. Integral to this lesson is that biology and psychology are inseparable when dealing with the health of any individual. People with no good reason for surviving horrific injuries live while others with less severe presentations die. Succeeding in losing weight is more a state of mind than any pharmacological intervention that can be offered. This is evidenced in the scientific quantification of behavioural interventions for obesity far out scoring pharmacological, phytological, supplemental and alternative therapies for successful weight-loss. In short, if the patient does not 'believe' they will not stay the course. They will withdraw or they will undermine the pharmacological action through not taking the drug in the prescribed doses.

Psychologically opting into the treatment is individually determined. If a person inherently believes in the intervention then it will be more successful than if they do not. Some people opt into the faith based explanations of the world and actively opt out of the mainstream scientific society. Yet others manage to resolve the conflicting doctrines of science and faith to live with both as part of their lives. Both of these 'types' of people are less likely to seek help from professionals from a scientific background or will engage in dual interventions concurrently. For the more draconian amongst us, the response is usually "so what, their choice, leave them to it and do not provide support for them if they do not want it". However, I take a more pragmatic view than this. If these people recover then we, as good scientists, are honour bound to uncover the answers of how they got better and then incorporate it into the mainstream interventions to improve effectiveness.

The mind can quite literally act like a drug. If we assume that drugs are simply pharmacological attempts to increase or decrease specific biological processes either in the brain or the body, then this can also be done, to some degree, but not to the same magnitude, without the need for drugs. Health interventions work on marginal effects. Clinical trials on placebo treatments have found time and time again that there is value in offering a pseudo-psychological treatment through administration of placebos. In depression, placebo treatment has been shown to be effective to a magnitude of thirty percent while active pharmacological treatment works in fifty percent of cases. Even on the placebo-controlled trial, the placebo is stronger in relative terms to the active drug [142]. Depression is a significant co-morbidity and efficacy destroyer in weight-loss interventions. Anything that will limit or actively treat depression or negative self-belief will, by proxy, increase the amount of weight lost on any intervention. The perfect weight-loss solution will give a small amount of help to the biology through limiting crippling feelings of hunger and energy debt and, more importantly, give the person belief that they can achieve a long-term goal. The treatments will not only aid biology but it will also improve diligence, goal directed behaviour and long-term motivation to those who lack these attributes in sufficient quantities.

The reluctance for the medical establishment to actively engage with non-active treatments probably stems from the ethical complexities around deception. Prescribing placebo treatments to patients with serious complaints can result in excessive costs to the service, may provide false hope to the family and could, and indeed has, resulted in successful litigation against the practitioner involved. However, in the right situation, providing an appropriate placebo prescribed with confidence will likely result in favourable outcomes. Moreover, in individuals that are psychologically receptive to a placebo treatment, but biologically unable to receive pharmaceutical interventions, then giving them an additional thirty percent instead of a fifty percent improvement would be worthwhile. After all, when ill, humans seek emotional comfort as well as physical treatment. If they receive this comfort from the placebo intervention then it is difficult to deny them this reassurance. Moreover, this ethical concern about deceiving patients can quickly diminish if they are told they might be deceived. It would appear that the placebo effect is robust enough to withstand even being told that the intervention is based on deception [143].

In reading this section, it may unintentionally be interpreted that the use of alternative therapies or 'drugs' might be useful or that they are endorsed. This is not a true representation of the meaning behind this section. There is a significant difference between a medic and a private enterprise providing placebo treatments. The medic is prescribing placebo treatment for free and under the guise of wanting to help. The private enterprise is doing the same for the purposes of profit. Profit in itself is not a problem if the intervention offered is suitable, evidence-based, with an active and known mechanism of action. Selling placebos to people desperate to lose weight is not the appropriate climate or best-practice for offering an acceptable placebo intervention. Furthermore, anonymously selling placebos to people without meeting them or understanding their condition suggests disregard, exploitation and/or neglect.

Chapter 9

OF THE FUTURE AND FINAL THOUGHTS

People are spending vast sums of money on dieting drugs. Some are credible, others not even close. All do not work as well as most people would expect. What works for one person does not necessarily translate into working for the next. Belief in the product appears to determine the weight-loss outcome much more than any potential biological effect. Due to the average weight-loss of all interventions, apart from surgery, having limited short-term efficacy, anyone wanting to lose weight must be resigned to investing a significant period of time before they will achieve a healthy BMI and then must adopt a healthy lifestyle forever more to ensure that they do not gain all the weight they lost. It took a significant amount of time to achieve obesity and it is only appropriate that an equal, if not longer, amount of time will be required to get the excess weight off.

Why people start dieting in the first place is usually because of body dissatisfaction. Their fixation on a specific body part(s) will galvanise their motivation to engaging in, for what are for all intents and purposes, a highly restrictive lifestyle. This lifestyle really does not lend well to an individual's happiness. Ironically, the potential for changing the desired body part is limited and, when successful, often compromises other regions of the individual's silhouette that they are happy with. The reason for this dissatisfaction stems from several potential explanations and usually relates directly or indirectly to perceived social standing and/or the individual's value for mate selection.

For the feminists, dieting is a patriarchal-determined and imposed concept concerning the social value of women defined by the manner dieting practice and products are sold. Placing social importance on female's bodies in order to placate male sexual desires creates a pressured environment alongside unrealistic goals that are not healthy for their mind or their body. The reason why people adhere to these unrealistic goals stems primarily from social comparison and to control other people's impressions of us.

If one person attempts to diet, and that individual is considered of social importance, then others may end up emulating their efforts. From an initial starting point of one person dieting, the whole group may start and even implicitly include the act of dieting as an integral definition of being in their group. In this situation, dieting can quickly become normalised and internalised irrespective of the need to diet. For a comparatively few people, this social element is less important and they diet for another reason. For these people, dieting is pseudo-forced upon them by others. This 'force' comes from health professional advice following the individual suffering adverse health consequences from carrying excess weight. All of these insecurities and consequences related to weight provide diet 'drug' vendors with an easy way to manipulate/persuade people into buying their product. In a world where the professionals are advocating hard work and hardship to come, the privateers pitch on ease and limited/no side-effects. It is all-to-easy to be sucked into a sales pitch that plucks at the desires of those who demand weight loss.

The legality behind bringing a product to market for the purposes of weight-loss is necessarily complex. With one hand we want to use pharmacotherapy to help, but with the other we wish to control the same substances from being abused. Within this legal battleground there are different laws for different groups. It is not a level playing field. Medicines sold by or given through a medic have laws of efficacy through the clinical trials. Other groups have lobbied government continuously to ensure that this biological-related independent criterion to ensure that the substance works is not legally applied to them. Some have had more success under the law than others.

The homeopaths have had by far the most success with having their own regulatory rules for getting their product to market. Until recently, all but the scientific community were happy with this arrangement because homeopathic remedies do not physically contain any active substances. However, change is afoot and more restrictions are likely to be imposed on the practitioners of this method. Although the level of change is not yet determined, the fact that the homeopathic governing body has been requested to submit evidence to the UK government for their claims about weight-loss suggests regulatory backlash to come – at least for weight-loss claims. This is especially the case when their evidence is based on a single study, which was not a homeopathic remedy and not published under the same name in the documentation submitted to government means that much more careful scrutiny of the practices of this profession is advised.

The lesson to be learnt here is that when unique exceptions are made about specific products, practitioners will not always adhere to them. Medics do not always adhere to the guidelines set out by regulatory bodies (although there is no evidence of illegality), so offering further 'wriggle' room to other groups means that it costs to regulate and increases the likelihood of lawbreaking in private, if not public, consultations. One law for all substances ingested for purposes other than nutrition irrespective of the preparation method would result in fewer problems and would be much easier to regulate. The public would surely welcome the necessity of having to prove beyond reasonable doubt that the product is effective before they part with their money for it.

Attempts to control food intake is not a new pursuit. There has been a long history of substances that have fallen from grace for numerous reasons. These include dangerous side-effects, ineffectiveness and poor cost/benefit ratios. Some of the substances with the more potent effects yet serious side-effects resurface from time-to-time as surreptitious additions to other weight-loss products, usually those registered as traditional herbal remedies. This has ostensibly led to the need for the introduction of tighter regulation.

However, this introduction of new regulation is also because some of the traditional herbal remedies have also been found to have serious side-effects themselves from time-to-time. The majority of the drugs found in the history books are there because they had serious unwanted effects. Recent psychopharmacological attempts to interfere in appetite for the purposes of losing weight have actually been less successful than those of the past. However, this weaker effect comes with increases in relative safety of taking the product.

Notably the two most credible candidates are Phentermine and Orlistat. These are both pharmaceutical drugs. Also in the credible candidate bracket are: Hoodia Gorfonii, because it has yet to be publically scrutinised; caffeine, because it is used as the principle agent that allows companies to legally sell a product as a dieting aid; and green tea. Some of the 'other' non-pharmacological substances have been found to be particularly ineffective. Many more substances sold in the open market as viable weight-loss aids have not been tested, very dubiously tested, not peer reviewed or found to be complete failures.

These are those that are the pretenders to the field. Products containing these substances alone and claiming them to have significant weight-loss properties are no better than placebo. Such products containing specific ingredients in isolation are rare because the industry standard is to offer tablets or capsules containing multiple substances. Packing multiple substances with extremely limited potential impact does not improve outcome. In the world of pharmacology two kilograms plus two kilograms does not equal four kilograms. This is doubly important for those drugs that have the 'psycho-' suffix. Drugs interact, have unexpected side-effects, and mutually undermine one another. Equally, they can combine to have a stronger effect and even fatal consequences that in isolation are harmless. Without expressly testing these interactions, it is not possible to know the exact resolution of what two plus two is, because in different situations with different drugs given to different people have different outcomes. This simple pharmacological understanding appears to beyond some businesses.

And then there is homeopathy. I think the future will have a lot to say about the use of this intervention. History already has. However, medicine, law and government policy are at best only partial scientific endeavours. There appears to be some temperance amongst the proponents of this spiritual endeavour to sell it as such. The beginning of homeopathy as a really good form of placebo is emerging rather than these continual attempts to forcibly (re)marry it to science. Homeopathy was derived from an old scientific hypothesis that was rejected based on evidence and experimentation. Pharmacological and traditional sciences has taken homeopathy as a suitor and found it wanting in all respects. Only psychology is left to hear its pleas. To survive into the long-term future, homeopathy must accept the hand of psychology. There are some steadfast diehard advocates of homeopathy as a standalone intervention that continually whinge about the applicability of the clinical trial. They attempt to question it, find holes in it and attempt to offer alternatives that are loosely based on it but allow them to test their interventions without the need for blinding themselves. In short, the clinical trial is the only effective way to test efficacy. There are other really important scientific methods that must be carried out, but the trial is the necessary final point of scientific understanding, and the legal criteria for proving beyond reasonable doubt that the product offered works.

The fact that alternative interventions exist and are relatively popular with people suggests that modern medicine is not fulfilling all of the health needs of their patients. In a system that lacks the resources to adequately provide for the psychological needs of the individual, pushes this need into the unregulated privateer domain. This does not mean that these less than credible interventions should be provided by the state. That would be a rather simplistic interpretation of the 'efficacy' of alternative therapy. What is needed is that the current health provision must move away from fixation on biological dysfunction towards a more global representation of the individual.

Medics operating like conveyor belt mechanics paying lip service to the mental health of their patients mean that they are actually actively disengaging from the strongest tool within their healing arsenal for aiding weight-loss. Before the 'energy' healers jump on this statement with glee, there is no place for these interventions in a system rightly reliant on evidence-based practice. What we need is effective interaction between medical professionals and those responsible for the mental health of the patients. Combined psychobiological interventions are required. This is not the current system with medics, health and allied health professionals operating autonomously and under the manner of a pseudo-militaristic hierarchy where medics rule health services.

In cases of serious biological dysfunction this hierarchical arrangement may work, but the more chronic (long-lasting) the condition the exponentially increased need for providing psychological support is necessary for effective outcomes. Each group have a valid role within the health of the nation and, according to the data for weight-loss interventions, pharmacological interventions should be one of the smallest parts of the overall therapy. Instead, the current system for weight-loss is to ask if the person has been dieting, offer them Orlistat and then eventually refer them for surgery. Publically funded therapeutic decisions and interventions for obesity are far too biological dependent.

The role of psychology in the service is limited to looking for psychopathology (i.e. depression and binge eating disorder) and treating the findings than providing viable behavioural interventions. The beneficial psychological interventions are left to the private sector to perform often without qualified psychologists being involved. Continuing along this biological dependent path where drugs are the predominant intervention plays into the hands of those that hunt the fridges of healthcare professions. It gives them legitimacy and allows them to galvanise following. From this base, they can petition governments and alter law. What the 'people' want the 'people' get, especially when they are more vocal.

Ignoring these alternative groups or attacking them based on scientific inefficacy has not, and will continue not to, work. There must be something within this intervention beyond efficacy that appeals to people. If we uncover what this really is then it can be incorporated into the appropriate medical and health provision. Dealing with this need will effectively eliminate their market base. Their voice will diminish and eventually disappear to be replaced by another private enterprise that fulfils another 'gap' in health provision. Instead of marginalising these interventions we should learn from their successes. After all, they have survived without the need for government funding. The obvious question would be – would medical or pharmaceutical industries be as successful without a guaranteed subsidised revenue stream. The answer would be probably, but they would not have been as successful and would be heavily reliant on pandering to those with the disposable income to afford it. Certainly research and development would cease to exist overnight and become the sole pursuit of academics and higher education institutions.

The success or failure of a particular drug or intervention will not be judged based on its economic impact; rather it will be judged by history. Our decedents will tell us who was right and wrong and we will not know the outcome ourselves. At this time, only our morality can guide us. I cannot speak for others, but personally I would not want to be judged for pumping people full of crude substances in an attempt for them to lose weight to meet social ideals. I would not want my conscience marred by the fact that I caused someone to needlessly have a psychotic episode, organ failure, heart attack or stroke. Furthermore, I would not like to look at my bank account and see its numbers tainted by the misery of others or the knowledge that I had sold them an inferior, no better than placebo, product. Not everyone has similar morals guiding their actions. People cannot be judged for this. Humans are naturally opportunistic. It is one of the defining features of our evolutionary success and a behaviour that is imbedded within all aspects of society from the economy to social organisation and right through to our biological make-up. Denying our nature forces us into a situation of attempting to regulate against ourselves. This will not lend well to long-term success. Instead, we must be more optimistic of why things exist. To instantly assume wrongdoings within groups that have survived the turbulent world of the economy needlessly vilify them, marginalises them and ultimately undermines potential positive developments in mainstream health provision. There is too much adherence to rhetoric by all professions. A 'horses-for-courses' route based on rigorous evidence-base derived from solid epistemological foundations understood from both quantitative and qualitative perspectives must be our best approach to avoid the judgment of our decedents. Alongside this investigation, all parties must be equally open to criticism and development. Denying the efficacies of others eventually denies the efficacy of all.

We have been specific to weight-loss drugs in this book; however, similar lessons can be learned from other 'additional' proposed therapeutic interventions offered by individuals over the Internet or outside the healthcare professions. There is a whole raft of people trading nutritional supplements and tea blends over the Internet for a variety of real and ambiguous ailments. The majority of these have little or no credible evidence to support their claims. The lesson for the lay person to learn here is to watch out for those that make the "may" claims. If strong legally acceptable evidence is available for a specific intervention for any ailment this "may" will not be required.

Society, through its policy makers, has decided that interventions with a proven track record need to be delivered by a relevant professional. These people are often registered under a specific regulatory body who will investigate claims of impropriety. When found guilty of wrongdoings, rogue individuals will be banned from practice. Those individuals trading under ambiguous, unregulated or unrecognised occupations without a definite career pathway starting from a strong, credible and internationally recognised educational background within a recognised educational institution should be avoided at all costs. Discerning the difference between the credible and less than credible individual can be difficult as they often use highly related terms that are not protected by a profession and so are unregulated[1]. The attempts by non-accredited individuals to convince the general public that they are credible will naturally be manipulative. They will make accusations about the 'establishment' in an attempt to galvanise support amongst those people that the 'establishment' has failed. In countries where healthcare is free at the point of need, we must immediately question those people that charge for services reputed to aid health. Those that can avoid this obvious criticism are those that are trained in occupations that are available for free by healthcare institutions but have waiting lists that are too long to receive treatment in a timely manner. This would be a funding, rather than credibility, issue.

Amongst all of the individuals discussed in this book, the ones we should really feel sorry for are those designated as our defenders in this trade. The MHRA, and the global equivalents, have the unenviable task of attempting to regulate an arena fraught with difficulties. They must not only regulate the contents of the substances themselves, but they must also attempt to regulate what people say about them. At the click of a mouse, anyone anywhere in the world may make and remove statements from the Internet. At the rate that websites are updated and created, it is simply not possible to police it all. The jurisdiction of the MHRA ends at the borders of its country and has some influence within the European

---

1 Examples of these are psychologist (regulated) vs therapist or dietition (regulated) vs nutritionist.

Union. Moreover, it is not as if there are police officers available to wonder the Internet to find the less reputable affiliates. Our defenders are often civil servants that are those forgotten by society apart from to be bundled in with the red tape bureaucratic arguments of politicians and the media. They do not wear uniforms, are not visible to the public and as such are not known to the average person. The remit of these organisations is to regulate the use of Medicines using the laws available to them to control thousands of substances. Only one tiny aspect of their remit is weight-loss products.

It is therefore by necessity a conservative organisation. That is, it does not support the Conservative party, rather it will let the world get on with itself until harm is done, new products are made available or distributor licenses are requested. Only then it will intervene. It is a light-touch regulatory organisation, as long as you adhere to its rules. It leaves the creation of policy to the EU and FDA and the enforcement of other laws (Trade Descriptions Act, Food Standards Act etc...) to other organisations. To help these agencies function, it is important that recognised wrongdoings are reported under their whistle blowers scheme. They will investigate and regulate where necessary.

The Internet is here to stay, it cannot be uninvented and international law does not extend to the sale of substances for weight-loss purposes. Affiliates will not disappear as long as there is money to be made, and vendors will remain as long as there is a significant desire by the large pharmacies and pharmaceuticals to trade through this virtual environment. Therefore, what will the future look like?

It is always difficult to predict what the future will look like or what the best scenario would be; yet it is always the first question asked of me by family, friends or in a professional setting. The answer I always give is I do not know. When pushed I will give what I would like to see rather than dealing in definite predictions. First and foremost, it would be great if people were given the information that they require without attempts to control their thinking in order to sell them a product that they likely do not need. Rubbishing the claims of the 'establishment' to sell a 'secret' that does not exist is really not a conducive environment to aiding weight-loss. In fact it may undermine it. Simply stating that taking a pill will cure all ills when it comes to weight-loss denies the person the motivation necessary to succeed. Weight-loss attempts made following previous failures all increase subsequent failed attempts and will deny the dieter the potential to achieve their target goals. Unrealistic statements in either timeframe or efficacy are really unhelpful to those desperately wanting help. Furthermore, convincing people of falsehoods in order to make money is not victimless. Detachment from the person is not a defense against using them to make money. A distinct lack of empathy is evident throughout this field. In a better world, credible individuals would confront those who are not and educate the masses to a level that they can avoid being manipulated. Furthermore, people involved in all aspects of the process must have more empathy with one another to create a truly multi-disciplinary approach. Curtailing the activities through forcibly intervening with those making unfounded statements about products is not a viable option. This would also have the undesired effect of curtailing dissenters, who are integral to development of novel interventions. The key difference between dissenters and those that manipulate is the subtle difference between saying that something does not work and saying that something will. To say it does not work (i.e. the dissenters) suggests there is room for convincing them, just that the current evidence has not achieved a preconceived individually determined level to convince them of the efficacy of the intervention in question. Those that manipulate suggest that something does work until proven that it does not. In science, unfounded statements to say it does not work (i.e. the null hypothesis) is allowed, unfounded statements towards saying it does (i.e. the experimental hypothesis) is most certainly not acceptable.

The perfect diet drug has yet to be discovered. As we come to understand more about appetite regulation, increased credence is given to multi-component combined pharmacotherapy. The efficacy of the drugs currently available suggests a large divide between drugs that target the peripheral body and those that act on the brain. Despite the higher potential for side-effects, targeting the brain is going to have a larger effect on hunger and fullness than interfering with the digestive system. There is also a general reluctance by the regulatory bodies to allow combined therapies. The only reason for this is the significant increased risk of serious side-effects. The answers to the efficacy question and the potential for side-effects are tied up in answering the same question. This is the delivery method. No matter how accurate and specific we make the drug, it is all for naught if it does not reach its destination. Oral administration of a drug significantly and instantly limits is potential effect. The resultant need to be able to cross the intestinal wall, travel in the blood, cross the blood brain barrier and finally reach its destination without being deactivated along the way is far too limiting. Side-effects stem from the drug getting into regions it was not intended, which is inevitable if the drug must travel the circulatory system. Efficacy is related to both the drug not getting to its intended destination in sufficient quantities and not lasting for a sufficient duration of time to ensure the individual does not have the desire to eat. Therefore, it is not our understanding of the chemical drug that is important; rather it is the delivery method that requires attention. Large leaps can be made in drug efficacy if a novel and accurate drug delivery solution is devised. As an intermediary, preferentially targeting peripheral sites such as enzymes in the gut may allow a better understanding of the limitations of targeting the central nervous system. Injecting substances directly into the brain is not an option, and for those people who have ever had a lumber puncture, neither are injections directly into the spinal column. They are simply too painful and unacceptable dangerous for weight-loss. The solution for novel drug delivery probably will not come from researchers interested in psychopharmacology. It is much more likely to be discovered within the realms of oncology. The need to directly and specifically target cancerous cells without harming healthy cells is integral to this treatment and more funds will be diverted into research for oncology problems than will ever be for obesity.

In the short- to medium-term, the solution to the weight-loss is not going to be a pharmacological one. For the highest and fastest efficacy, surgical solutions are the only viable option. It is expected that requests for surgical interventions will increase exponentially in the next few years. Reversible solutions would be best-practice, but the specific surgical solution will depend on the individual's circumstances. Concomitant to the increase in surgical requests to treat obesity, equal amount of requests for plastic surgery will be necessary. Rapid weight-loss will result in problems with excess skin. The relationship between speed of weight-loss and requests for plastic surgery is likely to be proportional. In effect, dissatisfaction with weight will quickly become dissatisfaction over aesthetic appearance. Surgical solutions will beget more surgical solutions.

For those that can, the only true solution to obesity is to galvanise enough personal resources to slowly but surely chip away at the fat stores. To change their lives forever and live a life free from excess. Some will consider that this is simply not worth it and will continue along their path to future weight gain. It is not the responsibility of anyone to interfere or force people along a path they do not want to travel. They will not be successful and we will end up with a group of people marginalised and resenting society. Living with excess weight and the co-morbidities that may eventually manifest will probably provide all the motivation that is necessary to alter behaviour. People are motivated by nothing more than their own mortality. However, this healthy lifestyle rhetoric has been blurred by privateers selling dreams. While the population awaits credible scientists to come up with a 'cure' for obesity, they are effectively being robbed of the ability to help themselves by those less than credible individuals that tell society they have already got it. Without legal requirements to substantiate the efficacy of a product prior to coming to market, this practice will continue indefinitely. We publish league tables on much harder subjects to quantify such as schools and universities, but we do not on subjects as easy as weight-loss pills. The difference between the two is that one is commercially funded while the other receives funds from the public purse. The closest we get to league tables for pharmaceuticals are NICE guidelines. Publishing tables for efficacy of a variety of products based on independent data would effectively destroy the affiliate markets overnight. However, interfering with commercial activities will inevitably result in the legal quagmire of claim and counter claim for all eternity. It would also affect the profits of a variety of large multi-national companies. This is something governments are always reluctant to do.

The only real matter of certainty in all of this supposition is that governments hold the keys. They hold them all. Whether they are willing to use them is another matter. When it comes to direct action on obesity, governments prefer to spend money on adverts, leaflets and letters to parents than offering anything meaningful. Sending letters to parents of obese children is about as unhelpful as can be in the current environment. Children have no place to go and are offered little in terms of interventions for excess weight. Notifying a parent that their child is overweight is unhelpful without actively helping them with the child. It simply creates anxiety in the parent and further stigmatises the child. With one hand government withdraw time dedicated to physical education on the curriculum while with the other blame parents for their child's activity rates and weight-status. Irrespective of whether people believe in the 'nanny state' or not, the fact-of-the-matter is that the government have more time with our children than their parents do. In that time they provide little in terms of healthy living, have been until recently filling our children with cheap nutritionally poor food and limiting their physical activity at every turn. Government have also taken the line that everyone must work placing little credit on people that actually want to raise their own children. Pushing everyone into work means that they get home late, are tired when they are and perceive having little time to prepare nutritionally wholesome food. This would explain the rise in convenience meals. Perhaps the government would like to send a letter to the Children's Secretary's and Education Secretary's home too. Clearly they are failing in their role. A child's education and comparative poverty are important, but they pale into insignificance if they do not have the health to enjoy changes to their prospects or living standards. Notifying people about problems without providing viable solutions is not tolerated in any other domain. Responsibility for a child firmly lies with the parent, responsibility for the population rests with social policy and government. If the population is getting fat then devolving responsibility to the individual is not appropriate – clearly there is something wrong with society.

In my opinion, sending letters to parents and pushing healthy lifestyle education material down their throats is simply the wrong stick. The stick should not just be waved at the population for being fat; rather it should be waved at the companies that provide nutritionally poor foods. Tax them and tax their products. Add levies to foods that are sold in portions beyond what would be considered acceptable as part of a healthy diet. Offering food information about acceptable quantities of a given product that is far below the portion size that they are either sold or habitually eaten in is not conducive to helping people maintain their current weight-status. There was a time when supermarkets placed chocolate, biscuits and crisps all on the same aisle now they have exploded to take over a significant proportion of the store. Light-touch or voluntary regulation is not a viable solution. If a stick needs to be welded then it must be at both the companies' and the public's pockets. Make luxuries just that. Not the necessities that they have become. Make nutritionally poor calories expensive again. Alternatively write off the current generation as it stands and move on with those that can be 'saved' through light-touch regulation. Move on to prevention, as it appears cure is not an option without policy intervention.

Prevention is fundamental to solving the obesity pandemic. All attempts to intervene have been met with spiraling rises in the prevalence rates of obesity; although currently rates appear to be somewhat leveling off. Preventing obesity is almost as difficult as treating it. The only difference is that the individual being educated is not currently obese and is generally young and impressionable enough to internalise the edicts of preventing weight gain. Soon it will be uncovered that education without some form of environmental manipulation is folly. Humans are simply hardwired from birth to prefer foods high in fat and sugar and foods that they invest little time in collecting. In a world where convenience food high in fat and sugar is immediately and ubiquitously available and sold in ever increasing portion sizes, education to resist is not going to work. It simply goes against our inherent nature.

In terms of the diet drugs market, the harmonisation of laws everyone must adhere to is most welcome. Ensuring everyone adheres to the same criteria prior to being allowed to sell the product limits the potential for abuse. Personally, I would like this to go further and ensure that emphasis is placed equally on efficacy as well as safety prior to market. Either clinical trials are the appropriate efficacy measure or they are not. Everyone wanting to sell a product with the express desire to use it for weight-loss purposes should be forced to show effective double-blind placebo-controlled clinical trials. Not everyone is 'playing with a straight bat' and they clearly cannot be trusted to regulate themselves. Irrespective of the philosophical derivation, manufacture process or belief structure surrounding the pill, it is not appropriate that there are different regulatory rules for different groups based on nothing more than the wishes of a capitalist venture. Efficacy and evidence about introducing a substance into a biological milieu are not privy to prior belief structures. Either the substance is found to work or it does not. There is no may be or room for beliefs when people are charging for these services. Making profit through excellence is not a problem in a capitalist society; profiteering on nothing more than a placebo has to be. If nothing else, the government should alter policy to reflect the need for clinical trials for all substances and precedence given to meta-analytic review evidence on quality trials where possible. Furthermore, this must be done in public with full transparency. It should not be allowed that a company privately holds the very data that provides the only evidence that their product works. Trials for efficacy do not encroach on copyright or intellectual property of the chemical in question. With this regulation in place, it would be possible to effectively regulate the diet pill industry sorting out those that work from those that do not, as well as dealing with people that make unfounded claims from those that do not. Once discovered, those people that make such unfounded claims must face the full force of the regulatory body's powers.

The future is uncertain. Advances are required in all areas of diet drugs to ensure that a viable and effective solution is developed. Currently, the field is littered with products that are based on little more than 'cherry-picked' evidence devoid of quality efficacy data. Providing this data in the absence of legislation to do so is the remit of higher education research laboratories, but in order to do this we require funding. In the current climate, this is not going to be forthcoming. Until evidence is available to the contrary, individuals after diet pills must cloak themselves in the assumption that until credible independent evidence is offered the substance does not work. They must view everything with a critical eye and fortify themselves with 'good science'. They must question everything and accept nothing. They must go into every transaction with eyes wide open. If the product does not meet the claims made, they must report it, request a refund and complain about the affiliate who told them the information. After all, they have made a lot of money and should have to earn it. If the buyer has any questions about the product, they must be asked of the affiliate and the vendor. If either refers them to another then they must be reported and complaints upheld. Accepting anything that these individuals say at face value and the information that they offer must be stringently investigated for accuracy. If vendors offer free money back trials and the buyer is charged then the company must be investigated and guidance about the outcomes of the investigation made publically available. If there is only one thing that is taken from this book, then this is the power for change is with the individual. It is not at the bottom of a pill jar or the end of a surgeon's knife. The questions, the answers and the most viable solution to losing weight are inside each individual's head. It is not anywhere else. Once the individual has resolved this conundrum, they will find a sense of purpose and solace in the recognition that they can successfully alter their lifestyle, that they can, if they wish to, lose weight. The judge, jury and sentencing should not be undertaken by society. The social cognition towards people who are overweight is wrong, discriminatory and robs the individual from their ability to help themselves. Successful weight loss is not a matter of professional pride; it is a necessity for the individual's health. Treating the individual has to be the main objective. To do that we must understand the individual, accept the individual and guide them towards a potentially healthier future

REFERENCES

[1]   Blanck, H. M., Khan, L. K. & Serdula, M. K. (2001). Use of nonprescription weight loss products. Results of a multistate survey. *JAMA, 286,* 930-935.

[2]   Birch, L. L. & Fisher, J. O. (1998). Development of eating behaviors among children and adolescents. *Pediatrics, 101*, 539-549.

[3]   Goldacre, B. (2009). *Bad Science.* London: Fourth Estate.

[4]   Jarry, J. L., Polivy, J., Herman, C. P., Arrowood A. J. & Pliner, P. (2006). Restrained and Unrestrained Eaters' Attributions of Success and Failure to Body Weight and Perception of Social Consensus: The Special Case of Romantic Success. *Journal of Social & Clinical Psychology, 25,* 885-905.

[5]   Grogen, S. (1999). *Body Image: Understanding Body Dissatisfaction in Men, Women and Children.* London: Routledge.

[6]   Rodin, J., Silberstein, L. R., & Striegel-Moore, R. (1985). Women and weight: A normative discontent. In T. B. Sonderegger (Eds). *Nebraska Symposium on Motivation: Vol 32. Psychology & Gender* (pp. 267-307). Lincoln: University of Nebraska.

[7]   O'Dea, J. A. & Abraham, S. (2002). Eating and exercise disorders in young college men. *Journal of American College Health, 50,* 273-278.

[8]   Stice, E. (2002). Risk and maintenance factors for eating pathology: A meta-analytic review. *Psychological Bulletin, 128,* 825−848. Stark-Wroblewski, K., Yanico, B. J. & Lupe, S. (2005). Acculturation, internalization of western appearance norms, and eating pathology among Japanese and Chinese international study women. *Psychology of Women Quarterly, 29,* 38−46. Unikel, C., Aguilar, J. & Gomez-Peresmitre, G. (2005). Predictors of eating behaviors in a sample of Mexican women. *Eating and Weight Disorders, 10,* 33−39.

[9]   Cossrow, N. H., Jeffrey, R. W. & McGuire, M. T. (2001). Weight stigmatization: A focus group study. *Journal of Nutrition Education, 33*, 208–214. Hebl, M. R. & Mannix, L. M. (2003). The weight of obesity in evaluating others: a mere proximity effect. *Personality and Social Psychology Bulletin, 29*, 28–38. Wade, T. J. & DiMaria, C. (2003). Weight halo effects: Individual differences in perceived life success as a function of women's race and weight. *Sex Roles, 48*, 461–465.

[10]   Finer, N. (2006). Medical consequences of obesity. *Medicine, 34*, 510-514.

[11]   Puhl, R. & Brownell, K. D. (2001). Bias, discrimination, and obesity. *Obesity Research, 9*, 788-805.

[12]   Johnson, K. L. & Tassinary, L. G. (2005). Perceiving sex directly and indirectly: meaning in motion and morphology. *Psychological Science, 16,* 890-897. Bak-Sosnowska, M. & Zahorska-Markiewicz. B. (2010). The relation between the adequacy of visual body mass estimation and weight reduction in overweight people (body percept and weight reduction). *Archives of Psychiatry & Psychotherapy, 1,* 31-36.

[13]   Wertheim, E. H., Paxton, S. J., Schutz, H. K. & Muir, S. L. (1997). Why do adolescent girls watch their weight? An interview study examining sociocultural pressures to be thin. *Journal of Psychosomatic Research, 42,* 345-355. Hutchinson, D. M. & Rapee, R. M. (2007). Do friends share similar body image and eating problems? The role of social networks and peer influences in early adolescence. *Behaviour Research & Therapy, 45,* 1557-1577. Mack, D. E., Strong, H. A., Howalski, K. C. & Crocker, P. R. E. (2007). Does friendship matter? An examination of social physique anxiety in adolescence. *Journal of Applied Social Psychology, 37,* 1248-1264.

[14]   Dovey, T. M. (2010). *Eating Behaviour.* Glasgow: McGraw Hill.

[15]   Homan, K. (2010). Athletic-ideal and thin-ideal internalization as prospective predictors of body dissatisfaction, dieting, and compulsive exercise. *Body Image, 7,* 240–245

[16]   Ogden, J. & Taylor, C. (2000). Body size evaluation and body dissatisfaction within couples. *International Journal of Health Psychology, 5,* 25-32.

[17]   Ghaderi, A., & Scott, B. (2001). Prevalence, incidence and prospective risk factors for eating disorders. *Acta Psychiatrica Scandinavica, 104,* 122–130. Hutchinson, D.M. & Rapee, R.M. (2007). Do friends share similar body image and eating problems? The role of social networks and peer influences in early adolescence. *Behaviour Research and Therapy, 45,* 1557-1577. Stice, E. (1998). Modeling of eating pathology and social reinforcement of the thin-ideal predict onset of bulimic symptoms. *Behaviour Research and Therapy, 36,* 931–944. Stice, E., Burton, E. M. & Shaw, H. (2004). Prospective relations between bulimic pathology, depression, and substance abuse: Unpacking comorbidity in adolescent girls. *Journal of Consulting and Clinical Psychology, 72,* 62–71.

[18]   Peterson et al., (2006). *Body Image, 3,* 237–246; Myers & Crowther (2007). *Body Image, 4,* 296–308; Swami et al (2008). *Body Image, 5,* 224–229

[19]   Oates, M. E. & Slotterback, C. S. (2004). Prejudgments of those who eat a "healthy" versus an "unhealthy" food for breakfast. *Current Psychology, 23,* 267-277.

[20]   Chaiken, S. & Pliner, P. (1987). Women, but not men, are what they eat: the effect of meal size and gender on perceived femininity and masculinity. *Personality & Social Psychology Bulletin, 13,* 166-176. Basow, S. A. & Kobrynowicz, D. (1993). What is she eating? The effects of meal size on impressions of female eater. *Sex Roles, 28,* 335-344.

[21]   Vartanian, L. R., Herman, C. P. & Polivy, J. (2007). Consumption stereotypes and impression management: how you are what you eat. *Appetite, 48,* 265-277.

[22]   Roth, D.A., Herman, C.P., Polivy, J. & Pliner, P. (2001). Self-presentational conflict in social eating situations: a normative perspective. *Appetite, 36,* 165-171.

[23]   Nisbett, R. E. & Storms, M.D. (1974). Cognitive and social determinants of food intake. In London, H. & Nisbett, R. E. *Thought and Feeling: Cognitive Alterations of Feeling States.* Chicago: Aldine.

[24] Crow, S., Eisenberg, M. E., Story, M., & Neumark-Sztainer, D. (2006). Psychosocial and behavioral correlates of dieting among overweight and non-overweight adolescents. *Journal of Adolescent Health, 38*, 569-574.

[25] Lowe, M. R., Annunziato, R. A., Markowitz, J. T., Didie, E., Bellace, D. L., Riddell, L., Maille, C., McKinney, S. & Stice, E. (2006). Multiple types of dieting prospectively predict weight gain during the freshman year of college. *Appetite, 47,* 83-90. Neumark-Sztainer, D., Wall, M., Haines, J., Story, M. & Eisenberg, M. E. (2007). Why does dieting predict weight gain in adolescents? Findings from project EAT-II: A 5-year longitudinal study. *Journal of the American Dietetic Association, 107,* 448-455.

[26] McLean, J. A. & Barr, S. I. (2003). Cognitive dietary restraint with eating behaviors, lifestyle practice, personality, personality characteristics and menstrual irregularity in college women. *Appetite, 40(2),* 185-192.

[27] Pudel, V. & Westenhoefer, J. (1992). Dietary and behavioural principles in the treatment of obesity. *International Monitor on Eating Patterns and Weight Control, 1,* 2-7. Smith, C. F., Williamson, D. A., Bray, G. A. & Ryan, D. H. (1999). Flexible vs. rigid dieting strategies: relationship with adverse behavioral outcomes. *Appetite, 32,* 295-305. Westenhoefer, J. (1991). Dietary restraint and disinhibition: Is restraint a homogenous construct? *Appetite, 16,* 45–55.

[28] Wansink, B. (2007). *Mindless Eating*. London: Bantam Press

[29] Dalley, S. E. & Buunk, A. P. (2009). "Thinspiration" vs. "fear of fat". Using prototypes to predict frequent weight-loss dieting in females. *Appetite, 52,* 217–221.

[30] Dewsbury, C. & Uusher, J. M. (1994). Restraint and perception of body-weight among British adults. *Journal of Social Psychology, 134,* 609-619. Gendall, K. A., Joyce, P. R., Sullivan, P. F., Sullivan, P. F. & Bulik, C. M. (1998). Personality and dimensions of dietary restraint. *International Journal of Eating Disorders, 24,* 371-379. Geschwind, N., Roefs, A., Lattimore, P., Fett, A-K. & Jansen, A. (2008). Dietary restraint moderates the effects of food exposure on women's body and weight satisfaction. *Appetite, 51,* 735-738. Herman, C. P. Polivy, J., Pliner, P., Threlkeld, J., & Munic, D. (1978). Distractibility in dieters and nondieters: An alternative view of "externality." *Journal of Personality and Social Psychology, 36,* 536-548.

[31] Carter, D., Cole, J., Gor, R., Parker, S., Taylor, C. & Edwards, A. (2007). *A Guide to what is a Medicinal Product*. MHRA Guidance Note No. 8.

[32] Taylor, J. (2001). Recommendations on the control and monitoring of storage and transportation temperatures of medicinal products. *The Pharmaceutical Journal, 267,* 128-131.

[33] Blundell, J.E. (1977) Is there a role for serotonin (5-hydroxy-tryptamine) in feeding? *International Journal of Obesity, 1,* 15-42. Blundell, J.E., Lawton, C.L., & Halford, J.C.G. (1995). Serotonin, eating behaviour, and fat intake. *Obesity Research, 3,* 471-47 Dube, M.G., Sahu, A., Phelps, C.P., Kalra, P.S & Kalra, S.P. (1992). Effect of D-fenfluramine on neuropeptide Y concentration and release in the paraventricular nucleus of food-deprived rats. *Brain Research Bulletin, 29,* 865-869 Halford, J. C. G., Cooper, G. D., Dovey, T. M., Iishi, Y., Rodgers, J. & Blundell, J. E. (2003). The psychopharmacology of appetite: targets for potential anti-obesity agents. *Current Medicinal Chemistry: Central Nervous System Agents, 3,* 283-310. Halford, J. C. G., Boyland, E. J., Blundell, J. E., Kirkham, T. C. & Harrold, J. E.

(2010). Pharmacological management of human appetite expression. *Nature Reviews Endocrinology, 6*, 255-269.

[34]   Kissileff, H.R., Pi-Sunyer, F.X., Thornton, J. & Smith, G.P. (1981). C-terminal octapeptide of cholecystokinin decreases food intake in man. *American Journal of Clinical Nutrition, 34*, 154-160. Muurahainen, N., Kissileff, H.R., Derogatis, A.J. & Pi-Sunyer, F. X. (1988). Effects of cholecystokinin-octapeptide (CCK-8) on food intake and gastric emptying in man. *Physiology & Behavior, 44*, 645-649. Muurahainen, N., Kissileff, H.R., Lachaussee, J. & Pi-Sunyer, F. X. (1991). The effect of a soup preload on the reduction of food intake by cholecystokinin in man. *American Journal of Physiology, 29*, R672-R680. Geary, N., Kissileff, H.R., Pi-Sunyer, F.X. & Hinton, V. (1992). Individual, but not simultaneous, glucagon and cholecystokinin infusions inhibit feeding in men. *American Journal of Physiology, 31*, R975-R980. Melton, P.M., Kissileff, H.R. & Pi-Sunyer, F.X. (1992). (CCK-8) affects gastric pressure and ratings of hunger and fullness in women. *American Journal of Physiology, 32*, R452-R456. Neary, M.T. & Batterham, R.L. (2009). Gut hormones: implications for the treatment of obesity. Pharmacological Therapy, 124, 44-56. Roses, A.D. (2009). Stimulation of cholecystokinin-A receptors with Gl181771X: A failed clinical trial that did not test the pharmacogenetic hypothesis for reduction of food intake. Clinical Pharmacology & Therapeutics, 85, 362-365.

[35]   Verdich, C., Flint, A., Gutzwiller, J.P., Näsland, E., Beglinger, C., Hellström, P.M., Long, S.J., Morgan, L.M., Holst, J.J. & Astrup, A. (2001). A meta-analysis of the effect of glucagon-like peptide-1 (7-36) amide on ad libitum energy intake in humans. *Journal of Clinical Endocrinology & Metabolism, 86*, 4382-4389. Gutzwiller J.P., Goke B., Drewe J., Hildebrand P., Ketterer S., Handschin D., Winterhalder R., Conen D. and Beldlinger, C. (1999). Glucagon-like peptide-1: a potent regulator of food intake in humans. *Gut, 44*, 81-86. Näslund, E., Barkelin, B., King, N., Gutniak, M., Blundell, J.E., Holst, J.J., Rössner, S. & Hellström, P.M. (1999b). Energy intake and appetite are suppressed by glucagon like peptide 1 (GLP-1) in obese men. *International Journal of Obesity, 23*, 304-311 Näslund E., King N., Mansten S., Adner N., Holst J.J., Gutniak M. (2004). Prandial subcutaneous injections of glucagon-like peptide-1 cause weight loss in obese human subjects. *British Journal of Nutrition, 91*, 439-446.

[36]   Buse, J.B., Rosenstock, J., Sesti, G., Schmidt, W.E., Montanya, E., Brett, J.H., Zychma, M. & Blonde, L. (2009). Liraglutide once a day versus exenatide twice a day for type 2 diabetes: a 26-week randomised, parallel-group, multinational, open-label trial (LEAD-6). *Lancet, 374*, 39-47

[37]   Batterham, R.L., Cowley, M.A., Small, C.J., Herzog, H., Cohen, M.A., Dakin, C.L., Wren, A.M., Brynes, A. E., Low, M. J., Ghatei, M. J., Cone, R.D. & Bloom, S.R. (2002). Gut hormone PYY(3-36) physiologically inhibits food intake. *Nature, 418*, 650-654.
Neary, N.M., Small, C.J., Druce, M.R., Park, A.J., Ellis, SM., Semjonous, N.M., Dakin, C.L., Filipsson, K., Wang, F., Kent, A.S., frost, G.S., Ghatei, M.A. & Bloom, S.R. (2005). Peptide YY3-36 and glucagon-like peptide-17-36 inhibit food intake additively. *Endocrinology, 146*, 5120-5127. Alvarez, B.M., Borque, M., Martinez-Sarmiento, J., Aparicio, E., Hernandez, C., Cabrerizo, L., (2002). Peptide YY secretion in morbidly obese patients before and after vertical banded gastroplasty. *Obesity Surgery, 12*, 324-327. Batterham, R.L., Cohen, M.A., Ellis, S.M., Le Roux, C.W., Withers, D.J., Frost,

G.S., Ghatei, M.A. & Bloom, S.R. (2003). Inhibition of food intake in obese subjects by peptide YY3-36. *New England Journal of Medicine, 349,* 941-948. Sloth, B., Holst, J.J., Flint, A., Gregersen, N.T. & Astrup, A. (2007). Effects of PYY_{1-36} and PYY_{3-36} on appetite, energy intake, energy expenditure, glucose and fat metabolism in obese and lean subjects. *American Journal of Physiology, Endocrinology & Metabolism, 292,* E1062-E1068. Degen, L., Oesch, S., Casanova, M., Graf, S., Ketterer, S., Drewe, J. & Beglinger, C. (2005). Effect of PYY3-36 on food intake in humans. *Gastroenterology, 129,* 1430-1436. Park, A., Sileno, A., Brandt, G., Quay, S. & Bloom, S. Nasal peptide YY3-36: Phase 1 dose ranging and safety study in healthy subjects. (2004). *International Journal of Obesity & Related Metabolic Disorders, 28,* S222.

[38]   Huda, M.S.B., Dovey, T., Wong, S.P., English, P.J., halford, J., Mcculloch, P., Cleator, J., martin, B., Cashen, J., hayden, K., Wilding, J.P.H. & Pinkey, J. (2009). Ghrelin restores 'lean-type' hunger and energy expenditure profiles in morbidly obese subjects but has no effect on postgastrectomy subjects. *International Journal of Obesity, 33,* 317-325. Wren, A.M., Seal, L.J., Cohen, M.A., Brynes, A.E., Frost, G.S., Murphy, K.G., Dhillo, W.S., Ghatei, M.A. & Bloom, S.R. (2001). Ghrelin enhances appetite and increases food intake in humans. *Journal of Clinical Endocrinology & Metabolism, 86,* 5992-5995.

[39]   Yamada, T., Hattori, K. & Ishimoto, (2001). Purification and characterization of two α-amylase inhibitors from seeds of tepary bean (*Phaseolus acutifolius* A. Gray). *Phytochemistry, 58,* 59-66. M.Harthoorn, L. F. (2008). Salivary α-amylase: a measure associated with satiety and subsequent food intake in humans. *International Diary Journal, 18,* 879-883.

[40]   Birari. R. B. & Bhutani, K. K. (2007). Pancreatic lipase inhibitors from natural sources: unexplored potential. *Drug Discovery Today, 12,* 879-889.

[41]   Halford, J. C. G., Cooper, G. D., Dovey, T. M., Iishi, Y., Rodgers, J. & Blundell, J. E. (2003). The psychopharmacology of appetite: targets for potential anti-obesity agents. *Current Medicinal Chemistry: Central Nervous System Agents, 3,* 283-310. Wang, G-J., Volkow, N. D., Logan, J., Pappas, N. R., Wong, C. T., Zhu, W., Netusil, N. & Fowler, J. S. (2001). Brain dopamine and obesity. *Lancet, 357,* 354-357. Meier, A. H., Cincotta, A. H. & Lovell, W. C. (1992). Timed bromocriptine administration reduces body fat stores in obese subjects and hyperglycemia in type II diabetics. *Experientia, 48,* 248-253.

[42]   Harrold J. A. & Halford, J. C. G. (2006). The hypothalamus and obesity. *Recent Patents on CNS drug Discovery, 1,* 305-214. Fernstrom, J. D. & Choi, S. (2008). The development of tolerance to drugs that suppress food intake. *Pharmacology & Therapeutics, 117,* 105-122.

[43]   Ricca, V., Castellini, G., Mannucci, E., Monami, M., Ravaldi, C., Amedei, S. G., Lo Sauro, C., Rotella, C. M. & Faravelli, C. (2009). Amphetamine derivatives and obesity. *Appetite, 52,* 405-409.

[44]   Shekelle, P. G., Hardy, M. L., Morton, S. C., Maglione, M., Mojica, W. A., Suttorp, M. J., Rhodes, S. L., Jungvig, L. & Gagné, J. (2003). Efficacy and safety of ephedra and ephedrine for weight loss and athletic performance: a meta-analysis. *Journal of the American Medical Association, 289,* 1537-1545.

[45]   Hendricks EJ, Rothman RB, Greenway FL. (2009). How physician obesity specialists use drugs to treat obesity. *Obesity, 17,* 1730-1735.

[46] Weintraub, M. Plus various co-authors on different studies. (1992). Long-term weight control studies I-VII (weeks ranging from 0 to 210). *Clinical Pharmacology and Therapeutics, 51*, 586–641.

[47] Bryant, S. M., Lozada, C. & Wahl, M. (2005). A Chinese Herbal Weight Loss Product Adulterated With Fenfluramine. *Annals of Emergency Medicine, 46, 208.*

[48] Ward, A. S., Comer, S. D., Haney, M., Fischman, M. W. & Foltin, R. W. (1999). Fluoxetine-maintained obese humans: effect on food intake and body weight. *Physiology & Behavior, 66,* 815-821.

[49] Corwin, J., Connelly, S., Paz, S., Schwartz, M. & wirth, J. A. (1995*).* Chart review of rate of weight gain in eating disorder patients treated with tricyclic antidepressants or Fluoxetine. *Progress in Neuro-Psychopharmacology & Biological Psychiatry, 19*, 223-228.

[50] Halford, J. C. G., Boyland, E. J., Dovey, T. M., Huda, M. S. B., Dourish, C. T., Dawson, G. R. & Wilding, J. P. H. (2010). A double-blind, placebo-controlled crossover study to quantify the effects of sibutramine on energy intake and energy expenditure in obese subjects during a test meal using a Universal Eating Monitor (UEM) method. *Journal of Psychopharmacology, 24(1)*, 99-109. Birch, L. L., Fisher, J. O., & Davison, K. K. (2003). Learning to overeat: Maternal use of restrictive feeding practices promotes girls' eating in the absence of hunger. *The American Journal of Clinical Nutrition, 78*, 215–220. Tanofsky-Kraff, M., Ranzenhofer, L. M., Yanovski, S. Z., Schvey, N. A., Faith, M., Gustafson, J. Yanovski, J. A. (2008). Psychometric properties of a new questionnaire to assess eating in the absence of hunger in children and adolescents *Appetite, 51,* 148-155. Eating the absence of hunger derives from externality theory of obesity first introduced by Shachter et al., 1968.

[51] Westenberg, H. G. M., Gerritsen, T. W., Meijer, B. A. & van Praag, H. M. (1982). Kinetics of l-5-hydroxytryptophan in health subjects. *Psychiatry Research, 7,* 373-385. Magnussen, I. & Nielsen-Kudsk, F. (1980). Bioavailability and related pharmacokinetics in man of orally administered l-5-Hydroxytryptophan in steady state. *Acta Pharmacologica et Toxicologica, 46,* 257-262.

[52] Turner, E. H., Loftis, J. M. & Blackwell, A. D. (2006). Serotonin la carte: supplementation with serotonin precursor 5-Hydroxytryptophan. *Pharmacology & Therapeutics, 109*, 325-338.

[53] Nisijima, K., Yoshino, T. & Ishiguro, T. (2000). Risperidone counteracts lethality in an animal model of the serotonin syndrome. *Psychopharmacology*, 150, 9-14.

[54] Venhuis, B.J., Vredenbregt, M.V., Kaun, N., Maurin, J.K., Fijałek, Z. & de Kaste, D. (2010). The identification of rimonabant polymorphs, sibutramine and analogues of both in counterfeit Acomplia bought on the Internet. *Journal of Pharmaceutical and Biomedical Analysis, In Press* doi:10.1016/j.jpba.2010.07.043

[55] Silverstone, T (1972). The anorectic effect of long-acting preparation of phentermine (Duromine). *Psychopharmacologia, 25*, 315-320. Weintraub, M Plus various co-authors on different studies. (1992). Long-term weight control studies I-VII (weeks ranging from 0 to 210). *Clinical Pharmacology and Therapeutics, 51*, 586–641. Truant, A. P. Olon, L. P. Cobb, S. Phentermine resin as an adjunct in medical weight reduction: a controlled, randomised, double-blind prospective study. *Current Therapeutic Research & Clinical Experiment, 14*, 726-738. Li, Z., Hong, K., Yop, I., Huerta, S., Bowerman, S., walker, J., Wang, H., Elashoff, R., Go, V. L. W. & Heber, D.

(2003). Body weight loss with phentermine alone versus phentermine and fenfluramine with very-low-calorie diet in an outpatient obesity management programme: a retrospective study. *Current Therapeutic Research, 64,* 447-460.

[56] Su, Y. C., Doran, S., Willert, G., Chapman, I. M., Jones, K. L. & Smout, A. J. P. M. (2002). Effects of exogenous corticotropin-releasing factor on antropyloroduodenal motility and appetite in humans. *American Journal of Gastroenterology, 97,* 49-57.

[57] Leibowitz, S. F. (1978). Paraventricular nucleus: A primary site mediating adrenergic stimulation of feeding and drinking. *Pharmacology, Biochemistry & Behavior, 8,* 163-175.

[58] Smathers, S. A., Wilson, J. G. & Nigro, M. A. (2003). Topiramate effectiveness in Prader-Willi syndrome. *Pediatric Neurology, 28,* 130-133. McElroy, S. L., Hudson, J. I., Capece, J. A., Beyers, K., Fisher, A. C. & Rosenthal N. R. (2007). Topiramate for the treatment of binge eating disorder associated with obesity: A placebo-controlled study. *Biological Psychiatry, 61,* 1039-1048. Arbaizar, B., Gómez-Acebo, I. & Llorca J. (2008). Efficacy of topiramate in bulimia nervosa and binge-eating disorder: a systematic review. *General Hospital Psychiatry, 30,* 471-475.

[59] Richard, D., Ferland J., Lalonde, J., Samson, P. & Deshaies, Y. (2000). Influence of topiramate in the regulation of energy balance. *Nutrition, 16,* 961-966.

[60] McElroy, S. L., Hudson, J. I., Capece, J. A., Beyers, K., Fisher, A. C. & Rosenthal, N. R. (2007). Topiramate for the treatment of binge eating disorder associated with obesity: a placebo-controlled study. *Biological Psychiatry, 61,* 1039-1048.

[61] Björntip, P & Rosmond, R. (2000). Obesity and cortisol. *Nutrition, 16,* 924-936.

[62] Jhanwar-Uniyal, M., Roland, C. & Leibowitz, S. (1986). Diunal rhythm of α2-noradrenergic receptors in the paraventricular nucleus and other brain areas: relation to circulating corticosterone and feeding behaviour. *Life Sciences, 38,* 473-482.

[63] Hauptman, J. B., Jeunet, F. S. & Hartmann, D. (1992). Initial studies in humans with the novel gastrointestinal lipase inhibitor Ro18.0467 (tetrahydrolipastatin). *American Journal of Clinical Nutrition, 55,* 309S-313S.

[64] Harp, J. B. (1998). An assessment of the efficacy and safety of Orlistat for the long-term management of obesity. *The Journal of Nutritional Biochemistry, 9,* 516-521. Melia, A.T., Koss-Twardy, S.G., and Zhi, J. (1996). The effect of orlistat, an inhibitor of dietary fat absorption, on the absorption of vitamins A and E in healthy volunteers. *Journal of Clinical Pharmacology, 36,* 647–653. Zhi, J., Melia, A.T., Koss-Twardy, S.G., Arora, S., and Patel, I.H. (1996). The effect of orlistat, an inhibitor of dietary fat absorption, on the pharmacokinetics of beta-carotene in healthy volunteers. *Journal of Clinical Pharmacology. 36,* 152–159. James, W.P.T., Avenell, A., and Whitehead, J. (1997). A one-year trial to assess the value of orlistat in the management of obesity. *International Journal of Obesity, 21,* S24–S30.

[65] Chanoine, J. P., Hampl, S., Jensen, C., Boldrin, M. & Hauptman, J. (2005). Effect of Orlistat on weight and body composition in obese adolescents: a randomized controlled trail. *JAMA, 293,* 2873-2883. Forrester, M. B. (2007). Pattern of Orlistat exposures in children aged 5 years or less. *The Journal of Emergency Medicine, 37,* 396-399.

[66] MHRA. (2010). *Drug Safety Update, 3(7),* (February)

[67] McCarty , M. F. (2005). Nutraceutical resources for diabetes prevention – an update. *Medical Hypotheses, 64,* 151-158.

[68]   Shimura, S., Tsuzuki, W., Kobayashi, S. & Suzuki, T. (1992). Inhibitory effect on lipase activity of extracts from medicinal herbs. *Bioscience, Biotechnology and Biochemistry, 56,* 1478-1479. Tsutomu Hatano, T., Yamashita, A., Hashimoto, T., Ito, H., Kubo, N., Yoshiyama, M., Shimura, S., Itoh, Y., Okuda, T. & Yoshida, T. (1997). Flavan dimers with lipase inhibitory activity from *Cassia nomame. Phytochemistry, 46,* 893-900.

[69]   Sharma, N., Sharma, V. K. & Seo, S-Y. (2005). Screening of some medicinal plants for anti-lipase activity. *Journal of Ethnopharmacology, 97,* 453-456.

[70]   Lee, R. A. & Balick, M. J. (2007). Indigenous use of hoodia gordonii and appetite suppression. *Ethnomedicine, 3,* 404-406.

[71]   Madgula, V. L., Avula, B., Pawar, R. S., Shukla, Y. J., Khan, I. A., Walker, L. A. & Khan, S. I. (2010). Characterization of in vitro pharmacokinetic properties of hoodigogenin A from Hoodia gordonii. *Planta Medicinal, 76,* 62-9.

[72]   Van Heerden, F. R., Vleggaar, R., Horak, R. M., Learmonth, R. A., Maharaj, V. & Whittal, R. D. (2002). Whittal, pharmaceutical compositions having appetite-suppressant activity, *Patent Application, PCT/GB98/01100.* Pawar, R. S., Shukla, Y. J., Khan, S. I., Avula, B. & Khan, I. A. (2007). New oxypregnane glycosides from appetite suppressant herbal supplement Hoodia gordonii. *Steriods, 72,* 524-534. Abrahamse, S. L., Povey, K. J. & Rees, D. D. (2004). Appetite suppressant compositions, US *Patent Application, US 2007/0207227.*

[73]   Avula, B., Wang, Y-H., Pawar, R. S., Shkla, Y. J., Schaneberg, B. & Khan, I. A. (2006). Determination of the appetite suppressant P57 in Hoodia gordonii plant extracts and dietary supplements by liquid chromatography/electrospray ionization mass spectrometry (LC-MSD-TOF) and LC-UV methods. *Journal of AOAC International, 89,* 606-611.

[74]   Haller, C. A., Benowitz, N. L. (2000). Adverse cardiovascular and central nervous system events associated with dietary supplements containing ephedra alkaloids. *New England Journal of Medicine, 343,* 1833-1838.

[75]   Gartside, P. S. & Glueck, C. J. (1993). Relationship of dietary intake to hospital admission for coronary heart and vascular disease: the NHANES II national probability study. *Journal of American College of Nutrition, 12,* 676-684. Stamler, J., Caggiula, A., Grandits, G. A., Kjelsberg, M., Cutler, J. A. (1996). Relationship to blood pressure of combinations of dietary macronutrients. Findings of the Multiple Risk Factor Intervention Trial (MRFIT). *Circulation, 94,* 2417-2423.

[76]   Barone, J. J. & Roberts, H. R. (1996). Caffeine consumption. *Food and Chemical Toxicology, 34(1),* 119-129.

[77]   Nehlig, A. (1999). Are we dependent upon coffee and caffeine? A review on human and animal data. *Neuroscience and Biobehavioral Reviews, 23,* 563-576.

[78]   Robertson, D., Wade, D., Workman, R. Woosley, R. L. & Oates, J. A. (1981). Tolerance to the humoral and hemodynamic effects of caffeine in man. *Journal of Clinical Investigation, 67,* 1111-1117.

[79]   Tremblay, A., Masson, E., Leduc, S., Houde, A. & Despres, J. P. (1988). Caffeine reduces spontaneous energy intake in men but not women. *Nutrition Research, 8,* 553-558. Yoshioka, M., Doucet, E., Drapeau, V., Dionne, I. & Tremblay, A. (2001). Combined effects of red pepper and caffeine consumption on 24 h energy balance in subjects given free access to foods. *British Journal of Nutrition, 85,* 203-211.

Oberman, Z., Herzberg, M., Jaskolka, H., Harell, A., Hoerer, E. & Laurian, L. (1975). Changes in plasma cortisol, glucose and free fatty acids after caffeine ingestion in obese women. *Israeli Journal of Medicinal Science, 11*, 33-36.

[80]   Westerterp-Plantenga, M. S. (2010). Green tea catechins, caffeine and body weight regulation. *Physiology & Behavior, 100*, 42-46.

[81]   Pasman, W. J., Westerterp-Plantenga, M. S. & Saris, W. H. (1997). The effectiveness of long-term supplementation of carbohydrate, chromium, fibre and caffeine on weight maintenance. *International Journal of Obesity & Related Metabolic Disorders, 21*, 1143-1151.

Bracco, D., Ferrarra, J. M., Arnaud, M. J., Jequier, E. & Schutz, Y. (1995). Effects of caffeine on energy metabolism, heart rate, and methylxanthine metabolism in lean and obese women. *American Journal of Physiology, 269*, E671-E678.

[82]   Dulloo, A. G., Geissler, C. A., Horton, T., Collins, A. & Miller, D. S. (1989). Normal caffeine consumption: influence on thermogenesis and daily energy expenditure in lean and post-obese human volunteers. *American Journal of Clinical Nutrition, 49*, 44-50.

[83]   Acheson, K. J., Zahorska-Markiewicz, B., Pittet, P., Anantharaman, K. & Jéquier, E. (1980). Caffeine and coffee: their influence on metabolic rate and substrate utilization in normal weight and obese individuals. *American Journal of Clinical Nutrition, 33*, 989-97.

[84]   Koo, M. W. L. & Cho, C. H. (2004). Pharmacological effects of green tea on the gastrointestinal system. *European Journal of Pharmacology, 500*, 177-185.

[85]   Diepvens, K., Kovacs, E. M. R., Nijs, I. M. T., Vogels, N. & Westerterp-Plantenga, M. S. (2005). Effect of green tea on resting energy expenditure and substrate oxidation during weight loss in overweight females. *British Journal of Nutrition, 94*, 1026-1034.

Auvichayapat, P., Prapochanung, M., Tunkamnerdthai, O., Sripanidkulchai, B-O., Auvicayapat, N., Thinkhamrop, B., Kunhasura, S., Wongpratoom, S., Sinawat, S. & Hongprapas, P. (2008). Effectiveness of green tea on weight reduction in obese Thais: A randomised, controlled trial. *Physiology & Behaviour, 93*, 486-491.

[86]   Richard, D., Kefi, K., Barbe, U., Poli, A., Bausero, P. & Visioli, F. (2009). Weight and plasma lipid control by decaffeinated green tea. *Pharmacological Research, 59*, 351-354.

[87]   Berube-Parent, S., Pelletier, C., Dore, J. & Tremblay, A. (2005). Effects of encapsulated green tea and guarana extracts containing a mixture of epigallocatechin-3-gallate and caffeine on 24h energy expenditure and fat oxidation in men. *British Journal of Nutrition, 94*, 432-436.

[88]   Hursel, R., Viechtbauer, W. & Westerterp-Plantenga, M. S. (2009). The effects of green tea on weight-loss and weight maintenance: a meta-analysis. *International Journal of Obesity, 33*, 956-961.

[89]   Palmatier, M. A., Kang, A. M., Kidd, K. K. (1999). Global variation in the frequencies of functionally different catechol-O-methyltransferase alleles. *Biological Psychiatry, 46*, 557-567.

[90]   Tsai, T. H., Hsu, C. H., Kao, Y. H., Tseng, T. Y., Hwang, K. C. Chou, P. (2008). Effect of green tea extract on obese women: a randomized, double-blind, placebo-controlled clinical trial. *Clinical Nutrition, 27*, 363-270.

[91]   Pittler, M. H. & Ernst, E. (2004). Dietary supplements for body-weight reduction: a systematic   review.   *American   Journal   of   Clinical   Nutrition,   79*,   529-536.

Dwyer, J. T., Allison, D. A. & Coates, P. M. (2005). Dietary supplements in weight reduction. *Journal of the American Dietetic Association, 105,* S80-S86.

[92] Santana, J., Sharpless, K. E. & Nelson, B. C. (2008). Determination of para-synephrine and meta-synephrine positional isomers in bitter orange-containing dietary supplements. *Food Chemistry, 109,* 675-682.

[93] Fugh-Berman, A. & Myers, A. (2004). Citrus aurantium, an ingredient of dietary supplements marketed for weight loss: current status of clinical and basic research. *Experimental Biology & Medicine, 229,* 698-704.

[94] Brown, C. M., McGrath, J. C., Midgley, J. M., Muir, A. G., O'Brien, J. W., Thonoor, C. M., Williams *C. M.* & Wilson, V. G. (1988). Activities of octopamine and synephrine stereoisomers on alpha-adrendoreceptors. *British Journal of Pharmacology, 93,* 417-429.

[95] Bent, S., Padula, A. & Neuhaus, J. (2004). Safety and efficacy of citrus aurantium for weight loss. American Journal of Cardiology, 94, 1359-1361. Dwyer, J. T., Allison, D. B. & Coates, P. M. (2005). Dietary supplements in weight reduction. Journal of the American Dietetic Association, 105, S80-S86.

[96] Haaz, S., Fontaine, K. R., Cutter, G., Limdi, N., Perumean-Chaney, S., & Allison, D. B. (2006). Citrus aurantium and synephrine alkaloids in the treatment of overweight and obesity: an update. *Obesity Reviews, 7,* 79–88. Bui, L. T., Nguyen, D. T., Ambrose, P. J., (2006). Blood pressure and heart rate effects following a single dose of bitter orange. *Annals of Pharmacotherapy, 40,* 53-57.

[97] Stein, M. R., Julis, R. E., Peck, C. C., Hinshaw, W., Sawicki, J. E. & Deller, J. J. (1976). Ineffectiveness of human chorionic gonadotropin in weight reduction: a double-blind study. *The American Journal of Clinical Nutrition, 29,* 940-948.

[98] Lijesen, G. K., Theeuwen, I., Assendelft, W. J. & Van Der Wal, G. (1995). The effect of human chorionic gonadotrophin (HCG) in the treatment of obesity by means of the Simeons therapy: a criteria-based meta-analysis. *British Journal of Clinical Pharmacology, 40,* 237-243. Bosch, B., Venter, I., Stewart, R. I. & Bertram, S. R. (1990). Human chorionic gonadotrophin and weight loss. A double-blind, placebo-controlled trial. *South African Medical Journal, 77,* 185-189.

[99] Pham, J., Porter, J., Svec, D., Eiswirth, C & Svec, F. (2000). The effect of dehydroepiandrosterone on Zucker rats selected for fat food preference. *Physiology & Behavior,*   70,   431-441. Haffner, S. M., Valdez, R. A., Stern, M. P., Katz, M. S. (1993). Obesity, body fat distribution and sex hormones in men. *International Journal of Obesity and Related Metabolic Disorders, 17,* 643-649.

[100] Clore, J. N. (1995). Dehydroepiandrosterone and body fat. *Obesity Research, 3,* 613S-616S.

[101] Nestler, J. E., Barlascini, C. O., Clore, J. N., Blackard, W. G. (1988). Dehydroepiandrosterone reduces serum low density lipoprotein levels and body fat but does not alter insulin sensitivity in normal men. *Journal of Clinical Endocrinology & Metabolism, 66,* 57-61. Usiskin, K. S., Butterworth, S., Clore, J. N., Arad, Y., Ginsberg, H. N., Blackard, W. G. & Nestler, J. E. (1990). Lack of effect of dehydroepiandrosterone in obese men. *International Journal of Obesity, 14,* 457-463. Welle, S., Jozefowicz, R. & Statt, M. (1990). Failure of dehydroepiandrosterone to influence energy and protein metabolism in humans. *Journal of Clinical Endocrinology*

& *Metabolism, 71*, 1259-1264. Vogiatzi, M. G., Boeck, M. A., Vlachopapadopoulou, E., el-Rashid, R. & New, M. I. (1996). Dehydroepiandrosterone in morbidly obese adolescents: effects on weight, body composition, lipids, and insulin resistance. *Metabolism – Clinical & Experimental, 45*, 1011-1015.

[102] http://www.adiosdiet.co.uk/_assets/pdf/adios_patient_information.pdf

[103] Moro, C. O. & Basile, G. (2000). Obesity and medicinal plants. *Fitoterapia, 71*, S73-S82.

[104] Cettour-Rose, P., Burger, A. G., Meier, C. A., Visser, T. J. & Rohner-Jeanrenaud, F. (2002). Central stimulatory effect of leptin on T3 production is mediated by brown adipose tissue type II deiodinase. *American Journal of Physiology, Endocrinology & Metabolism, 283*, E980-E987. Kok P, Roelfsema F, Frolich M, Meinders AE, Pijl H. (2005). Spontaneous diurnal thyrotropin secretion is enhanced in proportion to circulating leptin in obese premenopausal women. *Journal of Clinical Endocrinology & Metabolism, 90*, 6185-6191. Menendez, C., Baldelli, R., Camina, J. P., Escudero, B., Peino, R., Diegues, C. & Casanueva, F. F. (2003). TSH stimulates leptin secretion by a direct effect on adipocytes. *Journal of Endocrinology, 176*, 7-12.

[105] Verheesen, R. H. & Schweitzer, C. M. (2008). Iodine deficiency, more than cretinism and goiter. *Medical Hypotheses, 71*, 645-648.

[106] Woodward, J. A. & Saggerson, D. (1989). Effects of hypthyriodism and hyperthyroidism on GDP binding to brown-adipocyte mitochondria from rats. *Biochemistry, 263*, 341-345. Nedergaard, J., Bengtsson, T. & Cannon, B. (2007). Unexpected evidence for active brown adipose tissue in adult humans. *American Journal of Physiology, Endocrinology & Metabolism, 293*, E444-E452.

[107] Gunnarsdottir, I., Gustavsdottir, A. G. & Thorsdottir, I. (2009). Iodine intake and status in Iceland through a period of 60 years. *Food & Nutrition Research, 53*, 1-4.

[108] Miyahara, C., Miyazawa, M., Satoh, S., Sakai, A. & Mizusaki, S. (2004). Inhibition effects of mulberry leaf extract on postprandial hyperglycemia in normal rats. *Journal of Nutritional Sciences and Vitaminology, 50*, 161-164. Chen, F. J., Nakashima, N., Kimura, I., Kimura, M., Asano, N. & Koya, S. (1995). Potentiating effects on Pilocarpine-induced saliva secretion, by extracts and N-containing sugars derived from mulberry leaves, in streptozocin-induced diabetic mice. *Biological & Pharmaceutical Bulletin, 18*, 1676-1680. Yoshikuni, Y. (1988). α-Glucosidase activity and post-prandial hyperglycemia by moranoline and its N-alkyl derivatives. *Agricultural & Biological Chemistry, 52*, 121-128.

[109] Mudra, M., Ercan-Fang, N., Zhong, L., Furne, J. & Levitt, M. (2007). Influence of mulberry leaf extract on the blood glucose and breath hydrogen response to ingestion of 75g sucrose by type 2 diabetic and control subjects. *Diabetes Care, 30*, 1272-1274.

[110] Balfour, J. A., McTavish, D. (1993). Acarbose: an update of its pharmacology and therapeutic use in diabetes mellitus. *Drugs, 46*, 1025-1054.

[111] Chiasson, J. L., Gomis, R., Hanefeld, M., Josse, R. G., Karasik, A. & Laakso, M. (1998). The STOPNIDDM trial: an international study on the efficacy of an α-glucosidase inhibitor to prevent type 2 diabetes in a population with impaired glucose tolerance rationale, design, and preliminary screening data. *Diabetes Care, 21*, 1720–1725.

[112] Hardy, J. (2008). *A case of Black Jaguar*. http://www.britishhomeopathic.org/export /sites/bha_site/hh_article_bank/medicines_a_to_j/summer_2008.3_black_jaguar_case_s tudy.pdf

[113] Lilley, D. (2001). Masterclass: major archetypes of the material medica. http://www.britishhomeopathic.org/export/sites/bha_site/hh_article_bank/medicines_a_ to_j/spring_2001.4_calc_carb.pdf

[114] Kaplan, B. (2008). *Obstacles to cure*. http://www.britishhomeopathic.org/export /sites/bha_site/hh_article_bank/in_practice/ patient_centred_healthcare/winter2008_2009_obstacles_to_cure.pdf

[115] Werk, W. & Galland, F. (1994). Helianthus-thuberosus-Therapie bei übergewicht: Gewichtsreduktion langfristig stabilisieren. *Therapiewoche, 44*, 34-39.

[116] Hirschhorn, N. (2000). Shameful science: four decades of the German tobacco industry's hidden research on smoking and health. *British Medical Journal: Tobacco Control, 9*, 242-248.

[117] Dickel, M. L., Rates, S. M. K. & Ritter, M. R. (2007). Plants popularly used for losing weight purposes in Porto Alegre, South Brazil. *Journal of Ethnopharmacology, 109*, 60-71.

[118] Saénz Rodriguez, T., Garcia Giménez, D. & de la Puerta Vazquez, R. (2002). Choleretic activity and biliary elimination of lipids and bole acids induced by an artichoke leaf extract in rats. *Phytomedicine, 9*, 687-693. Beghardt, R. (2002). Inhibition of cholesterol biosynthesis in HepG2 cells by artichoke extracts is reinforced by glucosidase pretreatment. *Phytotherapy Research, 16*, 368-372.

[119] Bosscher, D., Breynaert, A., Pietersm L. & Hermans, N. (2009). Food-based strategies to modulate the composition of the intestinal microbiota and their associated health effects. *Journal of Physiology & Pharmacology, 60*, 5-11.

[120] de Luis, D. A., de la Fuente, B., Izaola, O., Conde, R., Gutiérrez, S., Morillo, M. & Teba Torres. y C. (2010). Ensayo clínico aleatorizado con una galleta enriquecida en inulina en el patrón de riesgo cardiovascular de pacientes obesos. *Nutrición Hospitalaria, 25*, 53-59.

[121] Padwal, R. J. & Majundar, S. R. (2007). Drug treatments for obesity: orlistat, sibutramine, and rimonabant. *Lancet, 369*, 71-77.

[122] Haddock, C. K., Poston, W. S. C., Dill, P. L., Foreyt, J. P. & Ericsson, M. (2002). Pharmacotherapy for obesity: a quantitative analysis of four decades of published randomized clinical trials. *International Journal of Obesity, 26*, 262-273

[123] Li A., Maglione, M., Tu, W., Mojica, W., Arterburn, D., Shugarman, L. R., Hilton, L., Suttorp, M., Soloman, V., Shekelle, P. G. & Morton, S. C. (2005). Meta-analysis: pharmacologic treatment of obesity. *Annals of Internal Medicine, 142*, 532-546.

[124] Westerterp-Plantenga, M. S. (2010). Green tea catechins, caffeine and body-weight regulation. *Physiology & Behavior, 100*, 42-46.

[125] Asher, W. L. & Harper, H. W. (1973). Effect of human chorionic gonadotropin on weight loss, hunger, and feelings of well-being. *The American Journal of Clinical Nutrition, 26*, 211-218.

[126] Tsai, A. G. & Wadden, T. A. (2006). The evolution of very-low-calorie diets: an update and meta-analysis. *Obesity, 14*, 1283-1293.

[127] Dovey, T. M. & Biddle, S. J. H. (2008). Understanding the psychology of eating, and not physical activity, is the key to solving the obesity crisis. *Sport & Exercise Psychology Review, 4(1),* 59-67.

[128] Shaw, K. A., Gennat, H. C., O'Rourke, P. & Del Mar, C. (2009). Exercise for overweight or obesity (Review). The Cochrane Collaboration: JohnWiley & Sons, Ltd

[129] Curioni, C. C. & Lourenço, P. M. (2005). Long-term weight loss after diet and exercise: a systematic review. *International Journal of Obesity, 29,* 1168-1174.

[130] Perri, M. G., McAllister, D. A., Gange, J. J., Jordan, R. C., McAdoo, G. & Nezu, A. M. (1988). Effects of four maintenance programs on the long-term management of obesity. *Journal of Consulting & Clinical Psychology, 56,* 529-534.

[131] Perri, M. G., Nezu, A. M., McKelvey, W. F., Shermer, R. L., Renjilian, D. A. & Viegener, B. J. (2001). Relapse prevention training and problem-solving therapy in the long-term management of obesity. *Journal of Consulting & Clinical Psychology, 69,* 722-726.

[132] Cummings, S., Apovian, C. M. & Khaodhiar, L. (2008). Obesity surgery: evidence for diabetes prevention/management. *Journal of the American Dietetic Association, 108,* S40-S44.

[133] Pontiroli, A. E. (2008). Surgical treatment of obesity: impact of diabetes and other comorbidities. *Nutrition, Metabolism & Cardiovascular Diseases, 18,* 1-6.

[134] Torgerson, J. S. & Sjöström, L. (2001). The Swedish Obese Subjects (SOS) study – rationale and results. *International Journal of Obesity, 25(Suppl 1),* S2–S4.

[135] Triggle, N. (2010). More obesity surgery 'could save millions of pounds. BBC News Website 08/09/2010.

[136] Pavlou K, Krey S & Steffee W (1989) Exercise as an adjunct to weight loss and maintenance in moderately obese subjects. *American Journal of Clinical Nutrition, 49,* 1115-1123

[137] Wardle, J., Brodersen, N. H. & Boniface, D. (2007). School-based physical activity and changes in adiposity. *International Journal of Obesity, 31,* 1464-1468.

[138] Turk, M. W., Yang, K., Hravnak, M., Sereika, S. M., Ewing, L. J. & Burke, L. E. (2009). Randomized clinical trials of weight-loss maintenance: a review. *Journal of Cardiovascular Nursing, 24,* 58-80.

[139] The Royal College of Physicians of London (1998). *Clinical Management of Overweight and Obese Patients with Particular Reference to the Use of Drugs.* A Report of the Royal College of Physicians, Publications Department: London, England (ISBN 1 86016 098 0).

[140] National Institute for Clinical Excellence (2001). *Guidance on the Use of Orlistat for the Treatment of Obesity in Adults.* NHS. Technology Appraisal Guidance No. 22, March 2001 (Ref 23358, www.nice.org.uk). National Institute for Clinical Excellence (2001). *Guidance on the Use of Sibutramine for the Treatment of Obesity in Adults.* NHS. Technology Appraisal Guidance No. 31, October 2001 (Ref N0034, www.nice.org.uk).

[141] Tilburt, J. C., Emanuel, E. J., Kaptchuk, T. J., Curlin, F. A. & Miller, F. G. (2008). Prescribing "placeo treatments": results of national survey of US interists and rheumatologists. *British Medical Journal, 337,* a1938 & a2435

[142] Walsh, B. T., Seidman, S. N., Sysko, R. & Gould, M. (2002). Placebo response in studies of major depression: variable, substantial, and growing. *Journal of the American*

Medical Association, 287, 1840-1847. Fournier, J. C., DeRubeis, R. J., Hollon, S. D., Dimidjian, S., Amsterdam, J. D., Shelton, R. C. & Fawcett, J. (2010). Antidepressant drug effects and depression severity: a patient-level meta-analysis. *Journal of the American Medical Association, 303,* 47-53.

[143] Martin, A. L. & Katz, J. (2010). Inclusion of authorized deception in the informed consent process does not affect the magnitude of the placebo effect for experimentally induced pain. *Pain, 149*, 208-215.

NOTES

The objective of this section is to provide the reader with some citations and additional thoughts on various subjects covered in this book. These are some of the original sources from which the opinions are derived. All of the opinions offered are based on my reading within the literature and so all of it can be derived. This section is by no means an exhaustive list. I was reluctant to offer all of the possible references as this would likely double the size of this book and thus increase the cost of it. To limit this section as much as possible, I have kept to offering a single citation where possible. For the really contentious or multifaceted comments, then additional citations are offered.

For those readers with some understanding of advanced graduate level chemistry, biology and/or pharmacology then there are several eminent authors that are writing on this topic. Many will keep to the scientific predilection of sticking to the 'evidence', rather than offering such uncouth opinions as found in this book. However, they will give a very detailed evaluation of both the mechanisms and the various substances that healthcare professionals and companies are currently testing for treating obesity. For those with the specialist knowledge, I would recommend:

Garfield, A. S. & Heisler, L. K. (2009). Pharmacological targeting of the serotonergic system for the treatement of obesity. *Journal of Physiology, 587,* 49-60. (*Free Access*)

Bult, M. J. F., van Dalen, T. & Muller, A. F. (2008). Surgical treatment of obesity. *European Journal of Endocrinology, 158,* 135-145. (*Free Access*)

Little, T. J., Horowitz, M. & Feinle-Bisset, C. (2007). Modulation by high-fat diets of gastrointestingal function and hormones associated with the regulation of energy intake: implications for the pathophysiology of obesity. *American Journal of Clinical Nutrition, 86,* 531-541. (*Free Access*)

Halford, J. C. G., Boyland, E. J., Blundell, J. E., Kirkham, T. C. & Harrold, J. E. (2010). Pharmacological management of human appetite expression. *Nature Reviews Endocrinology, 6,* 255-269.

For those without this specialist knowledge and would still like to know more then you can always read some of a plethora of wonderful (and not so wonderful) books out on the market. I will only give you the good ones here.

I would particularly recommend the following:

Dovey, T. M. (2010). *Eating Behaviour*. Glasgow: McGraw Hill

Gilman, S. L. (2010). *Obesity: The biography*. Oxford: Oxford University Press.

Grogen, S. (2008). *Body Image: Understanding body dissatisfaction in men, women and children*. London: Routledge.

Ogden, J. (2003). *The Psychology of Eating: From healthy disordered eating*. Oxford: Blackwell Publishing

Wansink, B. (2007). *Mindless Eating: Why we eat more than we think*. London: Bantam Books.

INDEX

'

'drugs', 28, 34, 35, 37, 42, 44, 45, 47, 49, 50, 61, 63, 75, 76, 79, 81, 82, 83, 85, 93, 97, 98, 99, 110, 113
'what-the-hell' effect, 19

"

"cut and paste content" websites, 8

#

5-ht₂c, 71
5-HT₂C, 71
5-HTP, 123
5-hydroxytryptophan, 71, 78, 123, 142

A

A placebo-controlled trial, 30
academic, 6, 39, 40, 43
active ingredient, 21, 47, 75, 76, 77, 83, 85, 86, 93, 96, 97, 98, 101, 102, 104
active site, xxi, 58
adenosine, 49, 84
Adenosine triphosphate, 49
advertise, xi, 23, 29, 34, 35, 39, 40
advertising, xxiii, 6, 7, 16, 22, 25, 27, 29, 33, 34, 35, 37, 43, 44, 45, 57
affiliate, x, xxiii, 34, 35, 36, 37, 38, 39, 40, 41, 42, 44, 49, 76, 81, 83, 90, 92, 95, 96, 99, 134, 136
affiliates, 33, 35, 36, 38, 40, 41, 49, 50, 53, 87, 100, 110, 132
affinity, xxii
Alpha Melanocyte-Stimulating Hormone (αMSH), 55
alternative therapies, 95, 113, 116, 124, 125

alternative therapists, viii, 96, 123
alternative therapy, 94, 95, 129
amphetamine, 57, 66, 67, 68, 74, 77
amphetamines, 65, 66, 67, 68, 69, 70, 76, 79, 84
Amphetamines, 65, 66
amylase, 63, 141
anorexia, 56, 70
appetite, xxiv, 16, 47, 49, 50, 51, 53, 54, 55, 57, 60, 62, 63, 65, 66, 67, 71, 73, 76, 77, 78, 79, 81, 82, 87, 88, 92, 93, 128, 133, 139, 140, 141, 143, 144, 151
appetite suppressants, 50, 53
Arcuate nucleus, 53
assumptions, x, xii, xiii, xiv, xvi, xvii, xviii, xix, xx, xxi, xxii, xxiii, xxiv, 1, 5, 8, 17, 21, 52, 73, 75, 78, 87, 101, 102, 136
attractiveness, 10, 16

B

behaviour, xi, xii, xiii, xiv, xv, xvi, xvii, xviii, xix, xx, xxi, xxii, 1, 2, 3, 4, 8, 11, 12, 13, 14, 17, 18, 19, 29, 49, 54, 56, 58, 66, 73, 107, 108, 110, 123, 125, 130, 134, 143
Behaviour, xiii, xv, 48, 138, 145, 152
behaviourism, xiii, xiv, xv
binge-eating, xv, 77, 143
biology, xv, xvii, xviii, xix, xx, 3, 45, 49, 52, 56, 58, 92, 109, 124, 125, 151
bitter orange, 90, 91, 146
blood, xxi, 47, 48, 52, 54, 59, 60, 71, 73, 78, 80, 82, 84, 86, 91, 96, 97, 101, 133, 144, 147
blood brain barrier, xxi, 133
BMI, 3, 12, 15, 23, 80, 99, 105, 114, 116, 117, 127
body dissatisfaction, 1, 3, 4, 5, 6, 13, 15, 18, 20, 127, 138, 152
body image, 3, 6, 7, 8, 9, 10, 11, 13, 14, 15, 17, 18, 19, 45, 138

brain, xvi, xvii, xviii, xix, xxi, 19, 47, 49, 51, 52, 53, 54, 55, 56, 57, 58, 59, 60, 61, 63, 65, 66, 67, 69, 70, 71, 72, 73, 79, 84, 93, 113, 125, 133, 143
brain cells, xvii, 52, 66
bulimia nervosa, xv, 10, 143
Burrhus Skinner, xv
buyer, xxiii, xxiv, 14, 15, 26, 28, 35, 37, 41, 42, 67, 68, 73, 80, 82, 90, 93, 95, 98, 99

C

caffeine, 47, 58, 68, 76, 81, 83, 84, 85, 86, 87, 98, 99, 102, 103, 104, 129, 144, 145, 148
calc carb, 108
Calc Carb, 107, 108
calcarea carbonica, 103, 104
calcium, 76
calorie, 16, 17, 18, 51, 68, 70, 92, 99, 100, 115, 118, 143, 148
calories, 16, 17, 18, 19, 22, 48, 50, 62, 85, 92, 97, 99, 115, 117, 118, 135
cancer, xxii, 117
Cannabinoids, 57
capitalism, ix, 7, 135
carbohydrate, 48, 62, 97, 145
cardiovascular disease, 14, 22
Carl Jung, xiv
CART, 55, 66
Cassia Nomame, 81
catechol-O-methyltransferase, 86, 145
celebrities, 14, 25, 27
cell, xviii, xix, xxi, xxii, 47, 52, 53, 56, 62, 66, 69, 70, 78, 87, 101
chemical messengers, xvii, xviii, xix
chemical receivers, xviii
chemistry, xv, xvii, 95, 109, 151
Children, 13, 134, 137
Children's Secretary, 134
China, 33, 67, 95
Chinese, 6, 68, 94, 95, 137, 142
Chitosan, 89
Cho Yung Tea, 94, 95
Cholecystokinin, 60, 61, 140
Chromium picolinate, 89
circulatory system, 60, 62, 66, 133
classism, 7
clinical trial, 29, 61, 82, 95, 102, 105, 106, 109, 129, 145
clinical trials, 27, 81, 82, 94, 103, 105, 113, 115, 128, 135, 148, 149
Clinical trials, 125
Cocaine and Amphetamine Regulated Transcript (CART), 55

coffee, 47, 84, 104, 144, 145
cognitive, xiii, xiv, xv, xvi, xvii, 4, 6, 8, 18, 19
cognitive neuropsychology, xvi
cognitive psychology, xvi
cognitive science, xvi
cognitive-affective, xiii
combined pharmacotherapy, 69, 98, 133
COMT, 86
consumers, 4, 12, 80, 84, 85, 99
convenience meals, 134
Copyright, Designs & Patents Act (1988), 38
Coricotropin Releasing Factor (CRF), 55
Cortisol, 77, 78
Cortisol blockers, 78
credible experts, viii
CRF, 55, 66, 77, 78
Critical thinking, ix

D

D_2 receptor, 66, 71
Definitions of abnormality dysfunction, 14
Dehydroepiandrosterone (DHEA), 92
deniability, xii, 17, 35, 117, 125, 132
Deniability, 35, 40
depression, 6, 15, 69, 72, 78, 108, 110, 125, 130, 138, 150
d-fenfluramine, 69, 70
DHEA, 92, 101
diabetes, xix, 14, 22, 59, 96, 97, 140, 143, 147, 149
diet, 12
diet drugs, ix, x, xiii, xxiii, xxiv, 5, 6, 11, 13, 14, 20, 22, 23, 25, 26, 39, 44, 52, 56, 57, 60, 61, 63, 70, 75, 76, 110, 115, 116, 120, 135, 136
dieting, vii, viii, ix, xi, xiii, xvi, xxii, xxiv, 1, 3, 4, 6, 7, 8, 11, 12, 14, 15, 16, 17, 18, 19, 20, 26, 43, 48, 50, 51, 63, 67, 73, 82, 117, 127, 129, 130, 138, 139
Dieting, xi, 1, 3, 17, 50, 139
Dieting, 121
digestive system, xxi, 48, 49, 59, 60, 133
disaccharidase, 96
discrimination, 1
distributor, 33, 42, 132
distributors, 26, 33
DNA, 53, 56
doctor, 27, 28, 29, 109
dopamine, 55, 65, 66, 71, 141
duodenum, 60, 61, 79

E

early subsistence farming, 16
eating behaviour, vii, viii, xv, 11, 13, 20, 47, 48, 50, 52, 53, 58, 61, 66, 73, 77, 78, 83, 85, 139
eating disorders, vii, xv, 18, 23, 37, 80, 138
Education Secretary, 134
efficacy, viii, ix, xii, xix, xxiv, 14, 15, 25, 27, 28, 30, 61, 63, 66, 67, 68, 70, 72, 73, 76, 77, 81, 82, 83, 85, 86, 87, 90, 91, 94, 98, 99, 103, 104, 105, 109, 116, 119, 120, 121, 122, 123, 125, 127, 128, 129, 131, 132, 133, 134, 135, 136, 143, 146, 147
EGCG, 86, 87
energy, 5, 7, 12, 18, 19, 20, 22, 48, 49, 50, 51, 54, 58, 59, 60, 62, 85, 86, 94, 99, 102, 108, 110, 117, 118, 125, 140, 141, 142, 143, 144, 145, 146, 151
energy balance, 49, 50, 51
enzymes, 50, 52, 62, 63, 79, 81, 96, 133
ephedra, 67, 68, 90, 91, 141, 144
ephedrine, 67, 68, 83, 141
Ephedrine, 68, 73
epigallocatechin gallate, 86
Episodic signals, 54
Ergoset, 66
Erik Erikson, xiv
EU, 25, 26, 44, 71, 132
evidence, viii, ix, xi, xii, xiv, xxii, xxiii, xxiv, 1, 6, 7, 10, 14, 21, 23, 24, 25, 27, 29, 30, 34, 37, 44, 49, 57, 61, 66, 68, 76, 77, 78, 83, 84, 85, 89, 94, 95, 96, 97, 101, 103, 104, 105, 109, 113, 116, 121, 122, 123, 125, 128, 129, 130, 131, 135, 136, 147, 149, 151
evolution, xix, 16, 17, 148
evolutionary, xv, 6, 16, 17, 18, 20, 130
Evolutionary theorists, 9
exercise, 11, 36, 50, 100, 115, 116, 118, 119, 134, 137, 138, 149
experiment, xiv, xvi, 104, 122

F

faith, 81, 122, 124
fat, xi, xx, 2, 4, 5, 12, 14, 18, 19, 23, 47, 48, 49, 50, 51, 60, 62, 63, 79, 80, 87, 91, 92, 93, 96, 97, 108, 119, 123, 133, 134, 135, 139, 141, 143, 145, 146, 151
Fat, 12
fat burners, 49
fat cells, 5, 47
FDA, 99, 132
feminine ideal, 12
feminism, 6, 7, 8, 127
Fenfluramine, 69, 70, 76, 121, 142

fixation, 1, 3, 4, 17, 18, 19, 110, 127
fluff, 76, 94
Fluoxetine, 70, 114, 121, 142
food, vii, xiii, 1, 11, 12, 13, 16, 17, 18, 19, 21, 26, 27, 28, 29, 30, 44, 48, 50, 54, 56, 57, 59, 60, 61, 62, 66, 68, 69, 70, 71, 72, 77, 78, 81, 84, 85, 86, 96, 97, 99, 105, 108, 115, 117, 118, 128, 132, 134, 135, 138, 139, 140, 141, 142, 146
Food (lot marking) Regulations (1996), 28
food restriction, 12
Food Safety Act (1990), 28, 29
food selection, 12, 109
freedom of expression, 36, 37, 41
Fucus, 94
fullness, xv, 18, 53, 55, 56, 60, 61, 62, 66, 70, 133, 140

G

GABA, 56
GABA$_A$, 77
Gamma-Aminobutyric Acid (GABA), 56
Garcinia cambogia, 89
Gender, 11, 137
general population, xx, xxiii, 12, 30, 34, 44
genes, xix, 9, 11, 16, 17, 56, 77, 86, 88, 94, 102, 109
George Miller, xvi
Ghrelin, 60, 61, 77, 141
glia, 52
globe artichoke, 106, 109
Glucagon Like Peptide 1, 60, 61
Glucagon Like Peptide 2, 60, 61
good science, xxiii, 89, 136
government, 36, 42, 82, 91, 104, 110, 118, 128, 129, 130, 134, 135
graphites, 103, 104
green tea, 85, 86, 87, 88, 94, 95, 96, 116, 129, 145, 148
Guar gum, 89

H

HCG, 91, 92, 146
health, viii, xxiv, 1, 2, 14, 15, 16, 18, 19, 20, 22, 23, 25, 27, 33, 34, 36, 37, 43, 73, 87, 95, 99, 103, 105, 108, 115, 124, 127, 129, 131, 134, 142, 148
health complications, 1
health professionals, viii, 2, 25, 27, 34, 103, 115, 130
Health-related, 14
healthy lifestyle, 22, 99, 127, 134
heart attacks, 59
herbalists, 24, 25, 27, 81, 96
homeopathic practitioner, 100

homeopathic provings, 27
homeopathic remedies, 21, 25, 27, 28, 29, 30, 44, 92, 98, 100, 101, 103, 104, 105, 106, 107, 128
homeopathic remedy, 21, 27, 34, 101, 102, 104, 109, 128
homeopaths, 25, 27, 100, 101, 102, 104, 107, 128
Homeopathy, 26, 101, 109, 121, 129
homology, xxii
Hoodia, 76, 81, 82, 83, 87, 88, 93, 96, 98, 128, 144
hormone, 47, 52, 59, 60, 61, 77, 78, 91, 92, 93, 96, 140
hormones, 51, 55, 59, 60, 61, 62, 87, 91, 140, 146, 151
Hormones, 5
Hosting Platforms, 43
Hosts, 43
human chorionic gonadotropin (HCG), 91
Human Rights Act (1998), 36
hunger, xiii, xv, 12, 18, 19, 53, 55, 56, 60, 61, 62, 63, 66, 70, 76, 77, 92, 108, 120, 125, 133, 140, 141, 142, 148
hungry, 47, 48, 51, 54, 60, 66, 73, 93
hunter-gatherer, 16
Hydroxycut, 99, 110
hypothalamus, 52, 53, 78, 141
hypothesis, xiv, xxiii, 75, 87, 122, 129

I

ideals, 2, 7, 9, 15, 16, 130
ileum, 60
impression management, 11, 12, 14, 48, 138
inferential statistics, 30
Insulin, xix
Internet, vii, ix, x, xi, xii, xxi, xxiii, xxiv, 3, 4, 5, 8, 14, 22, 23, 25, 26, 27, 28, 31, 33, 34, 35, 36, 38, 40, 41, 42, 43, 44, 45, 50, 61, 63, 67, 68, 71, 72, 73, 75, 76, 80, 85, 87, 89, 90, 91, 93, 95, 96, 99, 100, 109, 131, 132, 142
intestinal, xx, xxi, 60, 61, 62, 82, 106, 122, 133, 148
inulin, 106
iodine, 93, 94

J

jejunum, 60
Jerusalem artichoke, 105, 106, 109
John Watson, xv

K

Khalahari Cactus Diet, 81

L

Lateral Hypothalamic Area, 53
Law of Infinitesimals, 102
laxative, vii, 93, 95, 103
lay person, xx, 21, 39, 61, 65, 73, 90, 95, 107, 131
LCD, 115, 116, 118, 119, 122
legal, xii, xv, xxiii, xxiv, 8, 21, 22, 25, 29, 30, 34, 36, 37, 38, 41, 70, 76, 80, 84, 94, 128, 129, 134
legal highs, 22, 26
legislation, 20, 21, 22, 24, 25, 26, 27, 28, 67, 83, 136
Leptin, 47, 93, 94
liberalism, 7
like cures like, 101, 102
limitations, xxii, 113, 119, 123, 133
lipase, xx, 63, 68, 79, 80, 81, 141, 143, 144
liver, 14

M

macronutrients, 47, 48, 62, 73, 144
management company, 40, 41
manufacturer, 20, 28, 38, 40
mate selection, 6, 10, 11, 127
media, vii, xi, 1, 6, 9, 36, 39, 44, 48, 66, 80, 81, 92, 107, 115, 116, 117, 122
medical interventions, x, xii, 59
Medicinal and Herbal Regulation Agency (MHRA), viii
Medicinal Products, 25
Medicine Act (1968), 21, 22, 25, 28, 35, 42
medicines, 20, 21, 22, 23, 25, 29, 30, 34, 37, 42, 44, 57, 72, 109, 148
Medicines (Advertising) Regulations (1994), 34
Medicines Act (1968), xii, 21, 24, 25, 27
Medics, 43, 44, 47, 119, 123, 125, 128, 129, 130
melanocyte-stimulating hormone, 55
men, 1, 4, 6, 7, 8, 10, 13, 14, 15, 84, 137, 138, 140, 144, 145, 146, 152
meta-analysis, 68, 69, 75, 140, 141, 145, 146, 148, 150
metabolism, 50, 82, 83, 93, 96, 103, 106, 141, 145, 146
MHRA, 21, 22, 23, 24, 25, 27, 35, 40, 42, 43, 56, 69, 81, 82, 93, 98, 99, 101, 105, 110, 119, 131, 139, 143
modeling, 11, 13, 14
motivation, vii, viii, ix, x, xxiv, 1, 3, 7, 12, 14, 15, 19, 20, 48, 51, 66, 116, 118, 119, 120, 125, 127, 132, 134
mulberry leaf, 96, 97, 98, 147
mulberry leaves, 147

N

National Institute for Clinical Health and Excellence (NICE), 68
neuroanatomy, xviii
neuromyths, 57
Neuropeptide Y, 66
neurotransmitters, 51, 52, 54, 55, 62, 66, 73, 87
news, vii, 37, 39, 42
NHS, 116, 119, 129, 149
NICE, 68, 110, 119, 134
Noam Chomsky, xvi
noreadrenaline, 65, 66, 70, 77, 86
null hypothesis, xxiii
nutrients, vii, xxi, xxii, 60, 62

O

obese, xix, 1, 2, 3, 9, 10, 13, 14, 15, 19, 47, 61, 67, 68, 69, 70, 77, 84, 85, 86, 93, 94, 105, 106, 108, 114, 115, 116, 117, 119, 120, 134, 135, 140, 141, 142, 143, 145, 146, 147, 149
obesity discrimination, 1, 3, 15, 19, 108, 118, 137
obesogenic environment, 2, 11
Octopamine, 90
opiate, 48
opioid, 48, 60
Oxidrine, 90

P

P57, 82, 83, 87, 144
Paraventricular nucleus, 53, 77, 143
peer review, xxiii, 34, 37, 38
peer support, 51
peer-review, 104
Peptide YY, 60, 61, 140
peristalsis, vii
Petri dish, xxi
Pfizer, 82
pharmaceutical companies, 26, 43, 44, 61, 79, 91, 96, 103, 113
pharmaceutical industry, ix, 43, 67, 81, 82, 91, 98, 116
pharmacist, x, 27, 28, 67, 68, 80, 100
pharmacology, xv, xix, 45, 89, 92, 102, 129, 147, 151
pharmacy, 28, 68, 80
Phenethylamine, 89
phen-fen, 69, 70, 123
phenotypes, 16

Phentermine, 57, 68, 76, 77, 78, 79, 87, 88, 121, 128, 142
pheromones, 8, 26
physics, xv, 101
Phytopharm, 82
placebo, 29, 30, 49, 63, 65, 68, 85, 90, 102, 105, 111, 113, 123, 125, 129, 130, 135, 142, 143, 145, 146
Plantago psyllium, 89
plastic, 11, 133
Police, viii, 25
portion size, 12, 135
positive energy balance, 118
positivism, xiv, xv, 6, 7
Press, 35, 36, 139, 142, 152
Prevention, 135
protein, xx, 48, 52, 62, 146
Prozac, 70
psychodynamic, xiii, xiv, xv, 107
psychologists, viii, xiv, xvi, 9, 89, 102, 107, 115, 130
psychology, xiv, xv, xvi, 12, 107, 109, 122, 124, 129, 130, 149
psychopathology, vii, xiv, 110, 130
psychopharmacologists, xvii, 73
psychopharmacology, xii, xiii, xvi, xvii, xviii, 39, 124, 128, 133, 139, 141
Pyruvate, 89

Q

Qnexa, 57, 77
qualitative, xiv, 15, 107, 131
quality of life, 57, 59, 121
Quantitative psychology, xiv

R

receptor sub-types, xviii
receptors, xviii, xix, 48, 52, 54, 56, 59, 65, 66, 71, 72, 73, 77, 78, 143
registered medicinal product, xii
Regulation, xxiv
regulatory bodies, 23, 57, 63, 70, 98, 123, 128, 133
restrained eaters, 12, 18, 19
Rimonabant, 57, 72, 73, 87, 121

S

scaremongering, 16, 90
scientific journals, vii, xxiii, 35, 39, 41, 44
scientists, x, xvi, xvii, xxii, xxiii, 24, 27, 39, 63, 65, 68, 72, 79, 83, 84, 89, 91, 92, 96, 98, 122, 125, 134

search engines, 35, 37, 42, 94
selective serotonin reuptake inhibitors (SSRIs), 56, 70
selectivity, xxii
self-esteem, 6, 9, 15, 19, 110
serotonin, 55, 56, 65, 66, 69, 70, 71, 72, 78, 100, 139, 142
serotonin syndrome, 72
Sibutramine, 56, 59, 65, 70, 73, 77, 80, 121
side-effect, 93
side-effects, xxi, xxii, 22, 38, 44, 47, 54, 56, 57, 59, 61, 63, 70, 72, 73, 78, 80, 82, 83, 87, 90, 91, 92, 94, 97, 98, 103, 119, 120, 121, 122, 123, 128, 133
Sigmund Freud, xiv
slaphead diet, 29
sleep apnoea, 22
social comparison, 9, 11, 12, 13, 14, 15, 18, 19, 20, 127
Social comparison, 6, 9, 13
social policy, 134
Specificity, xxii
SSRI, 70
SSRIs, 59, 70
stomach, xi, xxi, 4, 53, 60, 62, 80, 101, 116, 117, 118
substance, x, xii, 21, 22, 27, 28, 29, 30, 33, 35, 36, 42, 43, 45, 48, 57, 58, 68, 76, 77, 79, 84, 85, 90, 94, 100, 101, 102, 104, 105, 106, 121, 128, 135, 136, 138
supplements, xii, 28, 38, 44, 54, 71, 79, 81, 82, 83, 86, 87, 90, 92, 93, 98, 123, 131, 144, 145, 146
surgery, 11, 115, 116, 117, 127, 130, 133, 149
surgical, viii, 47, 116, 117, 118, 119, 120, 133
surgical treatments, viii
synapse, 52, 56, 66, 69, 70
Synephrine, 90, 91

T

television, 1, 34, 92, 117
thermogenesis, 84, 85, 86, 93, 94, 145
thin ideal, 4, 7, 9, 10, 13, 15
thyroid, 93
Tonic signals, 54
Topiramate, 56, 77, 121, 143
toxins, 87, 95
Trade Descriptions Act (1968), 28, 29, 40
trading standards agency, 5
traditional herbal remedies, 23, 25, 86

U

UK, vii, 5, 21, 22, 23, 26, 34, 40, 42, 43, 44, 58, 67, 68, 69, 77, 81, 93, 94, 106, 122, 123, 128
Unilever, 82
US, 40, 79, 83, 99, 123, 144, 149

V

vendors, vii, viii, x, xxiii, xxiv, 3, 4, 5, 14, 15, 20, 22, 23, 25, 26, 28, 29, 30, 31, 33, 34, 35, 36, 37, 38, 40, 41, 42, 49, 50, 57, 67, 68, 69, 72, 73, 76, 80, 81, 87, 90, 92, 93, 95, 97, 99, 100, 110, 127, 132, 136
Ventromedial nucleus, 53
Venus of Willendorf, 9, 11
virtual, xxiii, xxiv, 6, 22, 25, 33, 68, 132
virtual environments, xxiii
VLCD, 115

W

website, xxiv, 5, 35, 37, 38, 39, 40, 41, 43, 57, 76, 95, 100, 104, 108
websites, 8, 36, 37, 38, 39, 40, 42, 44, 49, 76, 81, 83, 85, 90, 92, 96, 131
weight gain, xi, xiii, xix, 17, 18, 68, 70, 78, 119, 133, 135, 139, 142
weight regain, 55, 118, 119
weight status, xv, 1, 2, 3, 9, 10, 12, 15, 16, 18, 65, 77, 84, 99, 105, 117
weight-maintenance, 87, 118, 120
Weights & Measures Act (1985), 28
Western World, 67
wild cat, 106, 107
women, 3, 4, 6, 7, 8, 9, 10, 12, 13, 14, 15, 17, 18, 127, 137, 139, 140, 144, 145, 147, 152

α

α1-adrenoreceptors, 77, 78
α2-adrenoreceptors, 77, 78
αMSH, 55